AF593795

ARTISTS OF THE NORTH AMERICAN WILDERNESS

GEORGE & BELMORE BROWNE

ARTISTS OF THE NORTH AMERICAN WILDERNESS

GEORGE & BELMORE BROWNE

John T. Ordeman and Michael M. Schreiber

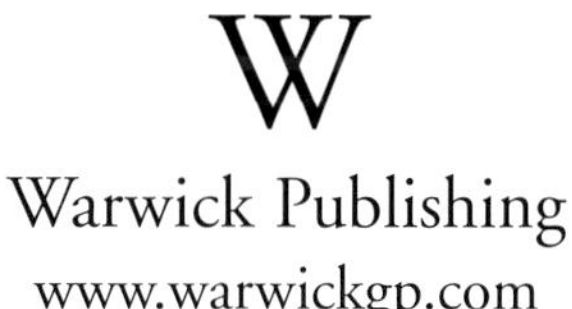

Warwick Publishing
www.warwickgp.com

We acknowledge the financial support of the Government of Canada through the Book Publishing Industry Development Program for our publishing activities.

The authors acknowledge with gratitude the financial support of Thomas Nygard, of the Thomas Nygard Gallery, and Michael Frost, of the J. N. Bartfield Galleries, principal dealers in George Browne's paintings, without whose contributions this book could not have been published.

ISBN: 1-894622-42-1

Two thousand copies of this book have been printed in this first edition. Of these, fifteen Collector's copies and sixty-five Deluxe copies have been signed and numbered by the authors. The Collector's copies contain an original drawing by George Browne; the Deluxe copies contain one of the cutouts George Browne used in composing his paintings.

Published by Warwick Publishing Inc.
161 Frederick Street, Toronto, Ontario M5A 4P3 Canada
www.warwickgp.com

Designer: Kimberley Young
Editor: Melinda Tate

Front Cover: *Startled Mallards* by George Browne, 1949

Printed and bound in Canada

Contents

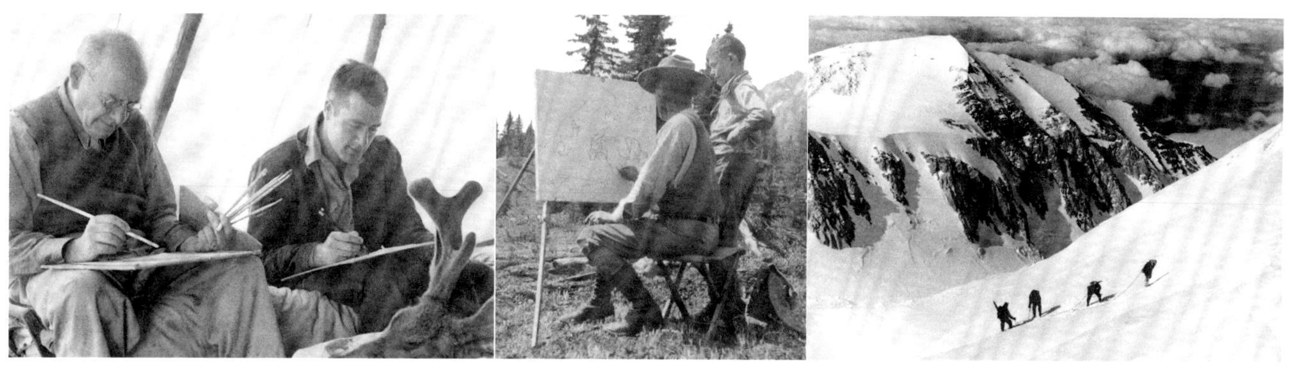

Acknowledgements

THIS BOOK HAS BEEN A collaborative endeavor: John Ordeman wrote the text, and Michael Schreiber located the Brownes' paintings and secured the permission of their owners—museums, dealers and collectors—to use them as illustrations. Dr. Schreiber also worked on the layout of the book, and he provided useful information as well as helpful suggestions for the text.

The authors express their appreciation to all those who, in giving freely of their help, advice and encouragement, have made invaluable contributions to this tribute to Belmore and George Browne. In particular, we are grateful to South Carolina sporting art dealer Bob Fraser, who generously lent material he had accumulated with the thought that he might one day produce a book on George Browne. We are also indebted to the authors of two publications: Tom Davis, who wrote the article "George Browne: the greatest wildlife artist that most people have never heard of," published in the November/December 1993 issue of *Sporting Classics;* and Robert H. Bates, author of *Mountain Man: The Story of Belmore Browne,* published by The Amwell Press in 1988. We also thank Philip N. Cronenwett, who oversees the Belmore Browne Collection at the Dartmouth College Libraries and was most helpful in providing research assistance as well as copies of requested materials.

We are grateful for the information and suggestions we have received from the staffs of the Corcoran Gallery, the Smithsonian Institution, the Boston Museum of Science, the Santa Barbara Museum of Natural History, the James Ford Bell Museum, the Glenbow Museum, the Leigh Yawkey Woodson Art Museum, the Ward Museum of Waterfowl Art, the National Museum of Wildlife Art and the American Museum of Natural History.

We also thank Stanleigh Arnold for his recollections of the Brownes; Bob Fraser, Bill Kerr, Steve O'Brien and Bill Webster, for their comments on the Brownes' work; and the dealers, museum officers and collectors who have provided photographs of paintings for reproduction in this book: Len Braarud (Len Braarud Fine Art), John Cavanaugh, Bob Drummond (Drummond Gallery), Sam Dyke (curator, Ward Museum of Waterfowl Art), Bob Fraser (Robert Fraser Sporting and Southern Art), Michael Frost (J. N. Bartfield Galleries), Roy Farrington Jones, K. C. Kaplan, R. W. Kaplan, Fred King (Sportsman's Edge, Ltd.), Don Luce (curator, American Museum of Wildlife Art Collection at the James Ford Bell Museum of Natural History), Tom Nygard (Thomas Nygard Gallery), John Powles, Bill Webster (owner, Wild Wings, Inc.) and Byron Webster.

Our special appreciation goes to J. Keith Schreiber, who digitally reproduced the photographs of the figures and plates after correcting for imperfections.

Finally, and actually foremost, we thank Hugh and MacGregor Robinson, who gave us free access to George Browne's studio journals, production records and correspondence with his parents and his dealers as well as to family diaries, commentaries and photo albums, all the while providing the most gracious hospitality.

Chapter~One

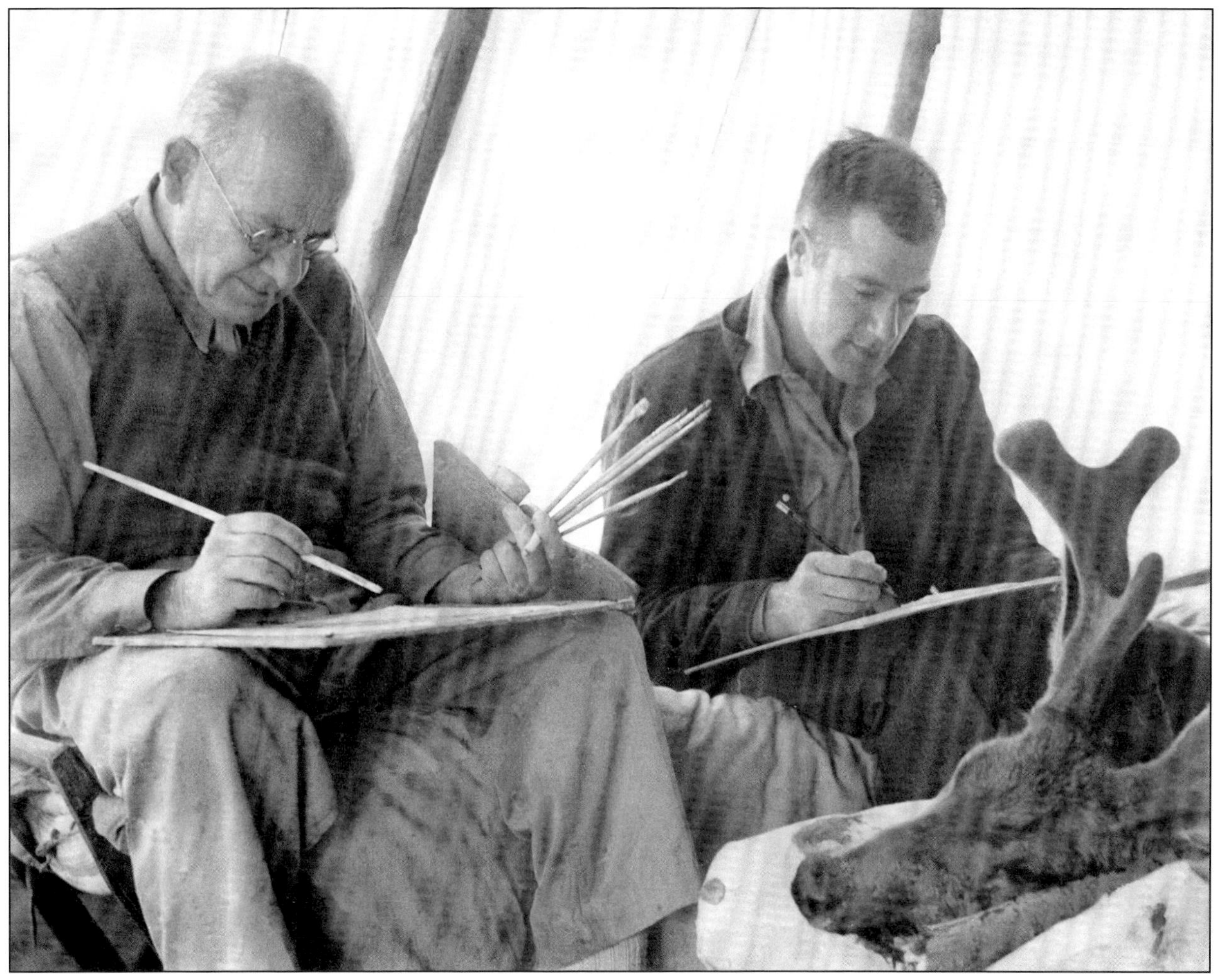

GEORGE BROWNE

"THE GREATEST WILDLIFE ARTIST MOST PEOPLE HAVE NEVER HEARD OF"

George Browne was recognized throughout the United States in the mid-1950s as a sporting artist of the first rank, the ascending star among American wildlife painters of his generation. His oils of waterfowl and upland game birds in flight were compared favorably to the works of Frank Benson and Roland Clark, and his paintings of big game animals, to those of Carl Rungius. Every painting he completed sold quickly, and his dealers were continually pleading for more of his pictures to satisfy the demands of their customers.

Belmore and George painting, circa 1950

Browne was talented and skilled and versatile; and as he was a sportsman who knew his subjects from lifelong experience, his pictures had authenticity. He was, furthermore, dedicated to his craft, a painter who worked constantly and conscientiously to improve his technique. Then, in the spring of 1958, at the age of forty, he was killed in a shooting accident, and a brilliant and promising career was abruptly ended.

Odd though it may seem, George Browne and his remarkable work were virtually forgotten in the years following his tragic death. As all of his paintings had been sold, dealers had nothing to offer; and the individuals who owned Browne's works held on to them and passed them on as family heirlooms. Only rarely did any of the 250 or so pictures George Browne had painted in the decade in which he worked as a professional artist come on the market. Consequently and ironically, because his paintings were so highly regarded by those who owned them, his name did not remain before the public.

For the first time in thirty-five years people had an opportunity to learn about George Browne and to see reproductions of his paintings when, in 1993, *Sporting Classics* published an informative and insightful article by Tom Davis, which served to reintroduce this remarkable painter and his work. Davis titled his essay "George Browne: The greatest wildlife artist that most people have never heard of."

"Those who *have* heard of Browne, and who know his luminous work," Davis wrote, "amount to a handful of astute dealers and collectors. To a person, they are in unanimous agreement that, had the fates granted Browne a normal lifespan . . . he would be regarded as one of the few legitimate masters of the wildlife genre."

Davis quotes Francis Lee Jaques, who was certainly a "legitimate master of the wildlife genre": "I fear I was a little jealous of George Browne's work, as I don't believe I was of any other artist. His work was a breakthrough. It was different—and better." That's what we lost when George Browne was killed in 1958.

Davis explained Browne's achievement—the "breakthrough," to use Jaques's term—in this manner:

> *While Browne's spiritual mentors—artists like Rungius, Kuhnert and his own father—had successfully merged animal portraiture with landscape painting, the depiction of birds still struggled to break free of the constraints imposed by the tradition of ornithological illustration that had begun with Audubon. The tradition dictated that the bird be portrayed with complete anatomical precision, and the background be nothing more than a suggestion of habitat. Without diminishing his animal paintings in the least, Browne's ability to integrate birds into a fully realized environment represented a quantum leap for the genre.*

Although this appraisal inexplicably overlooks the superb oils and watercolors of waterfowl in flight that Frank Benson produced even before George Browne's birth, it does make a useful distinction between Browne's paintings of waterfowl and upland birds—essentially landscapes in which birds in flight are featured—and the paintings of many of his contemporaries—detailed portraits of birds which convey no sense of motion.

Any study of the work of George Browne and commentary on his achievements must begin with some discussion of his father, the renowned landscape painter Belmore Browne. Rarely has a father had such a direct and profound influence upon a son as Belmore Browne had upon his son George. George not only loved and respected his father, but he chose his father as his mentor, both as an artist and as a sportsman, and modeled his life, to an extraordinary degree, upon his father's life.

Chapter~Two

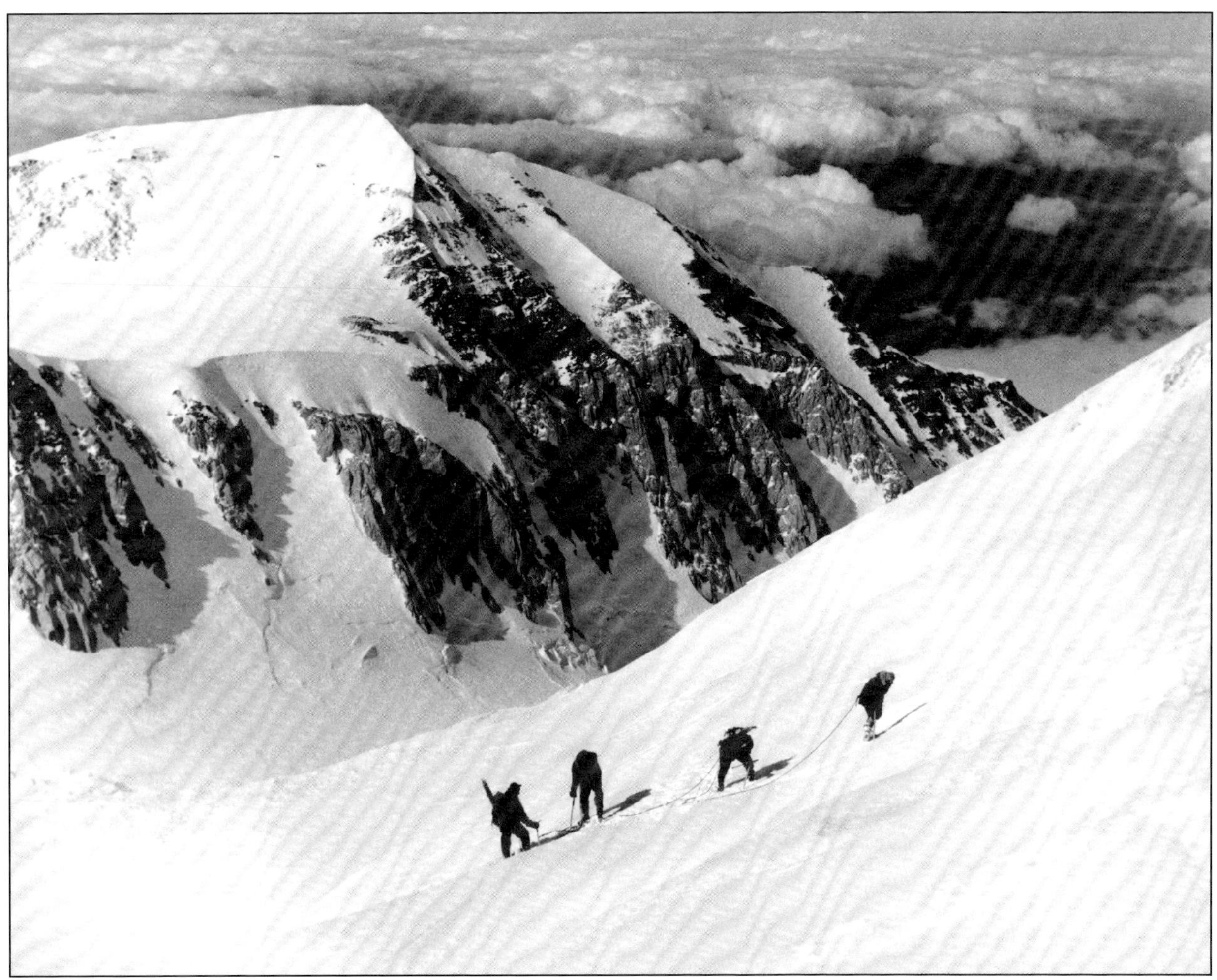

BELMORE BROWNE

EXPLORER, MOUNTAINEER, HUNTER, WRITER, PAINTER

Belmore Browne was thirty-seven years old when his son George was born on January 10, 1918. He had already achieved renown as an explorer, a mountaineer, an author and a hunter of big game. In his early twenties Belmore had participated in several expeditions that ventured into previously unexplored areas of the Alaskan wilderness, collecting animal specimens for the American Museum of Natural History.

Belmore party on Mt. McKinley—19,800 feet

He had been a member of three parties that had made assaults on the summit of Mount McKinley and had written the mountaineering classic, *The Conquest of Mount McKinley*, which focused on the successful 1912 ascent, which he led. Belmore was also the author of *Guns and Gunning*, a how-to book on wilderness traveling, camping and hunting, and of numerous autobiographical stories of outdoors adventures and authoritative pieces on hunting and on survival in the wilderness, which had been published in such magazines as *Harper's*, *Scribner's*, *Recreation* and *Outing*. He had written two popular boys' adventure books based on his experiences in the Arctic. He had played a key role in persuading Congress to designate the Mount McKinley region a national park. He had served as a captain in the Army Signal Corps in World War I. He was, furthermore, and most significantly for the rest of his life, a first rate painter of mountain landscapes and big game animals.

George Browne's father was a man of many accomplishments, a man who had earned the admiration and respect of all those whom he admired and respected, a man whose integrity and character were on the same high level as his talents and skills. This was the man George was given as his father and chose as his mentor and friend.

Belmore Browne had also been fortunate in the circumstances of his birth, and his childhood experiences were truly extraordinary. Belmore's grandfather, the descendent of a line of New England ship captains and owners and Revolutionary War soldiers, moved as a young man from Salem to New York City, where he entered the world of business and finance. His son George, Belmore's father, a Civil War veteran of numerous battles, acquired a seat on the Stock Exchange and established himself as a broker and importer. Having amassed a considerable fortune, he turned his financial affairs over to others in 1883 and took his family—his wife Nellie and his three sons: George, Jack and Belmore, the youngest—to Europe, where he devoted himself to the study of painting and architecture.

Belmore, born on June 9, 1880, was only three years old when he arrived in France. The Brownes lived in Paris, Venice and Florence and spent each summer in the Swiss Alps or the Italian Lake District, enjoying a lifestyle that might best have been chronicled by Henry James. A particular friend of the Brownes in Venice was the noted American artist Frank Duveneck, who painted a portrait of Belmore.

When the Brownes returned to America in 1888, Belmore was eight. The family traveled in the Pacific Northwest and eventually settled in the frontier town of Tacoma, Washington, where George Browne invested his resources to found the St. Paul and Tacoma Lumber Company. In order that they might retain a measure of the polish and graces they had acquired in Europe, the three boys were sent each fall to New England boarding schools—the Fay School and St. Mark's in Massachusetts, and, eventually for Belmore, Pomfret in Connecticut.

Summer vacations were spent back home—riding, camping, hunting and fishing in the undeveloped country surrounding Tacoma and sailing in Puget Sound. Belmore pursued his outdoors interests even when he was at school—hunting, fishing, maintaining a muskrat trapline and building a log cabin in the woods near Pomfret. Belmore was destined to follow his brothers to Harvard and passed the entrance examination; however, severe financial problems in the lumbering industry imposed constraints upon the Brownes. When his Pomfret classmates were enrolling in their Ivy League universities in the fall of 1897, Belmore was working as a laborer in a Washington lumber camp.

From an early age, Belmore had displayed a marked talent and interest in drawing, an activity that delighted his parents, both of whom painted as an avocation. His letters from school were filled with sketches, as were his journals of travels. At the age of eighteen, he decided to take up the ambition his father had abandoned, to make a career as an artist. After he had spent a year as a lumberjack, arrangements were made for Belmore to go east to live with a family friend, the artist Henry Clements, and attend classes at the New York School of Art. Among his instructors was William Merritt Chase, who, along with his friend Frank Benson, had been a founding member of the group of influential impressionist painters known as The Ten. Having completed two years of formal training, Belmore returned to the Northwest in 1900. Much of his time was then spent painting, enjoying various outdoors activities and working at a ranch near Toppenish, Washington.

Eight years after leaving the New York art school, Belmore decided that additional formal study would be to his advantage. Having received a substantial fee for a writing commission, he was able to fulfill the ambition of most young American artists to study in Europe. He sailed for France in 1908 to spend six months of intense work at the Académie Julian in Paris, the *école* that had been most favored by American art students since the 1880's.

Paris in 1908 was the vibrant center of the innovative twentieth century art movements. Picasso, who was a year younger than Belmore, was already a major figure. Having moved through his blue and rose periods, he was collaborating with Braque to develop the aesthetics of the cubist style. Led by Matisse, the Fauves—Derain, Vlaminck and Dufy among them—were laying the foundations of expressionism. As an art student in one of the principal academies, Belmore would have been aware of what these men were doing, but none of it was of interest to him. He was a traditional realist who painted what he saw. He was, in point of fact, offended by the paintings of the modernists. When he went to the Armory Show in New York in 1913, he found such works as the cubist Duchamp's "Nude Descending a Staircase" to be unartistic trash.

As a painter, Belmore Browne had the advantage of having received first rate instruction from men capable of teaching technique and composition, but it was his study of nature that was the foundation of his work.

BELOW: *A letter from Belmore to his mother, ca. 1893*

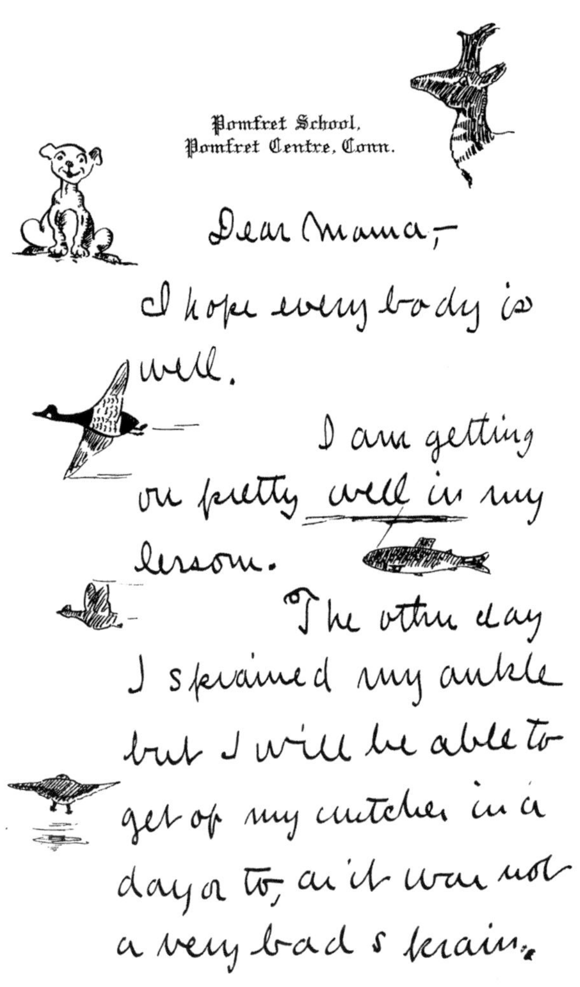

Pomfret School,
Pomfret Centre, Conn.

Dear Mama,—
I hope every body is well.
I am getting on pretty well in my lesson.
The other day I sprained my ankle but I will be able to get of my crutches in a day or to, as it was not a very bad sprain.

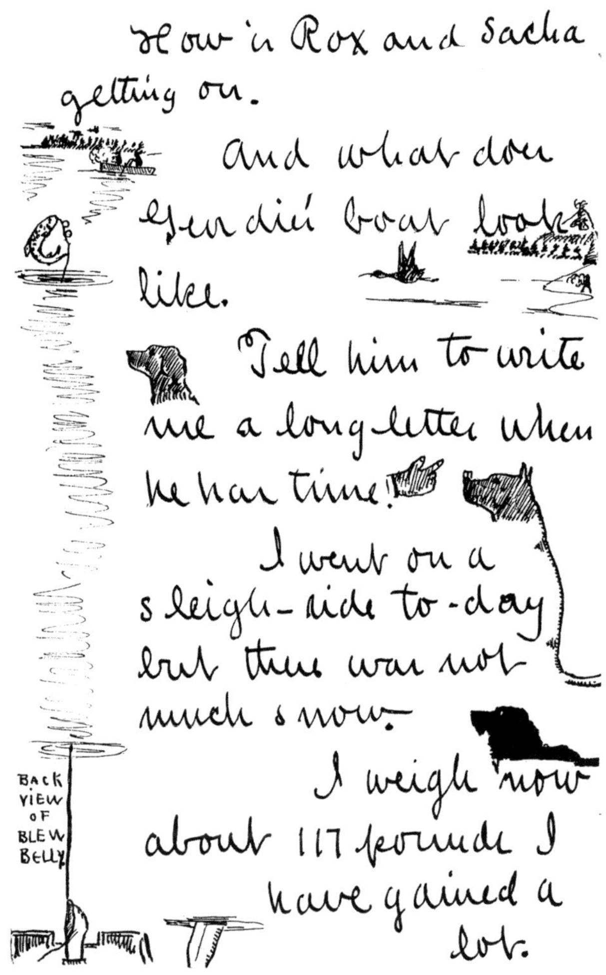

How is Rox and Sacha getting on.
And what does Gen did boat look like.
Tell him to write me a long letter when he has time!
I went on a sleigh-ride to-day but there was not much snow.
I weigh now about 117 pounds I have gained a lot.

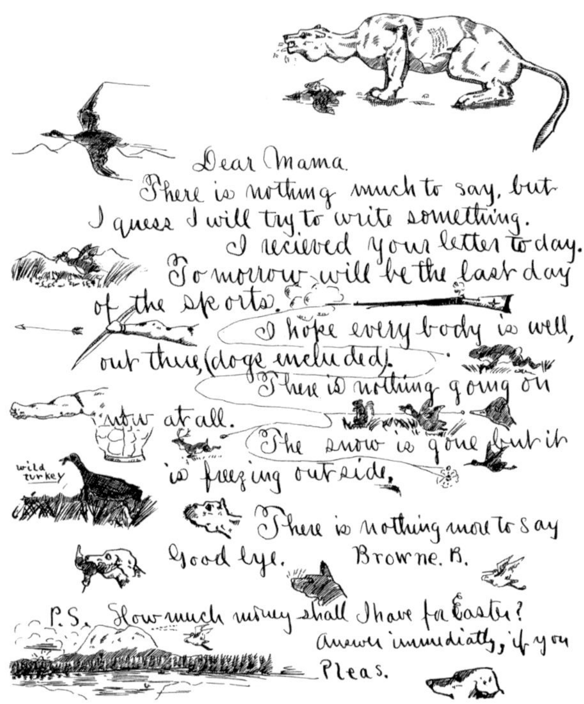

Dear Mama.
There is nothing much to say, but I guess I will try to write something.
I recieved your letter to day.
To morrow will be the last day of the sports.
I hope every body is well, out there (dogs included).
There is nothing going on now at all.
The snow is gone but it is freezing outside.
There is nothing more to say
Good bye. Browne. B.
P.S. How much money shall I have for Easter? Answer immediatly, if you Pleas.

I have not anything more to say so good bye.
From your loving son
P.S. Love to all. Belmore.

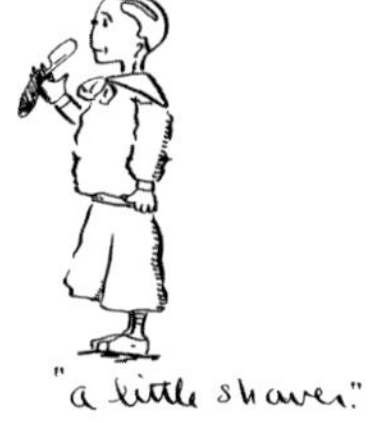

"a little shaver"

ABOVE: *A letter from Belmore to his mother sent while he was at Pomfret School, and an excerpt from another.*

Charles M. Russell, the noted Western artist, said, "Nature has been my teacher. I'll leave it to you whether she has been a good one or not." Belmore would have agreed with Russell about nature being the teacher; however, he would more likely have said, "I'll leave it to you whether I've been a good student."

In 1902 Belmore Browne was invited by the veteran wilderness explorer Andrew J. Stone to join an expedition sponsored by the American Museum of Natural History to collect mammal specimens in Canada and Alaska. Belmore proved to be a valuable member of the party, for he was not only a talented stalker and a crack shot but also a draughtsman who could make accurate anatomical drawings. The work accomplished by the Stone party was difficult, and it was often performed under trying circumstances. Belmore, however, was in his element. As a record of one day's activities, Belmore wrote in his diary:

> *Aug. 26th, 1902 I have been drawing all day. They went into the canyon and killed a bear (black). We will get it tomorrow. We have now killed eleven large game animals since we left Telegraph Creek. We salted them and cleaned all the skins today, cold work, as we had to wash them in ice water during a snowstorm. Had moose ribs for supper. Best grub I ever tasted.*

Belmore, now twenty-two years old, gained what would prove to be invaluable experience traveling and stalking in the wilderness on this expedition. He also became familiar with the Tlingit Indians and spent much of his time sketching them and their camps. He was honored when Chief Shakes of the Tlingits gave him the opportunity to make a voyage down the Stikine River to the sea in his *keahtyant*, a colorful war canoe. This trip and the sketches he made at the time were the basis for Belmore's best-known painting, "The Chief's Canoe," which won a national competition in 1926 and was purchased for permanent exhibition by the Smithsonian Institution.

For the next ten years, Belmore spent virtually every summer in the mountain ranges of the Yukon exploring, mapping, hunting and climbing. In 1903, he participated in explorations of the Aleutian Islands, where Alaskan brown bear specimens were collected, and also the Kenai Peninsula, where they found mountain sheep. Belmore devoted himself to perfecting his painting technique and to exploring and hunting in the northern wilderness. He

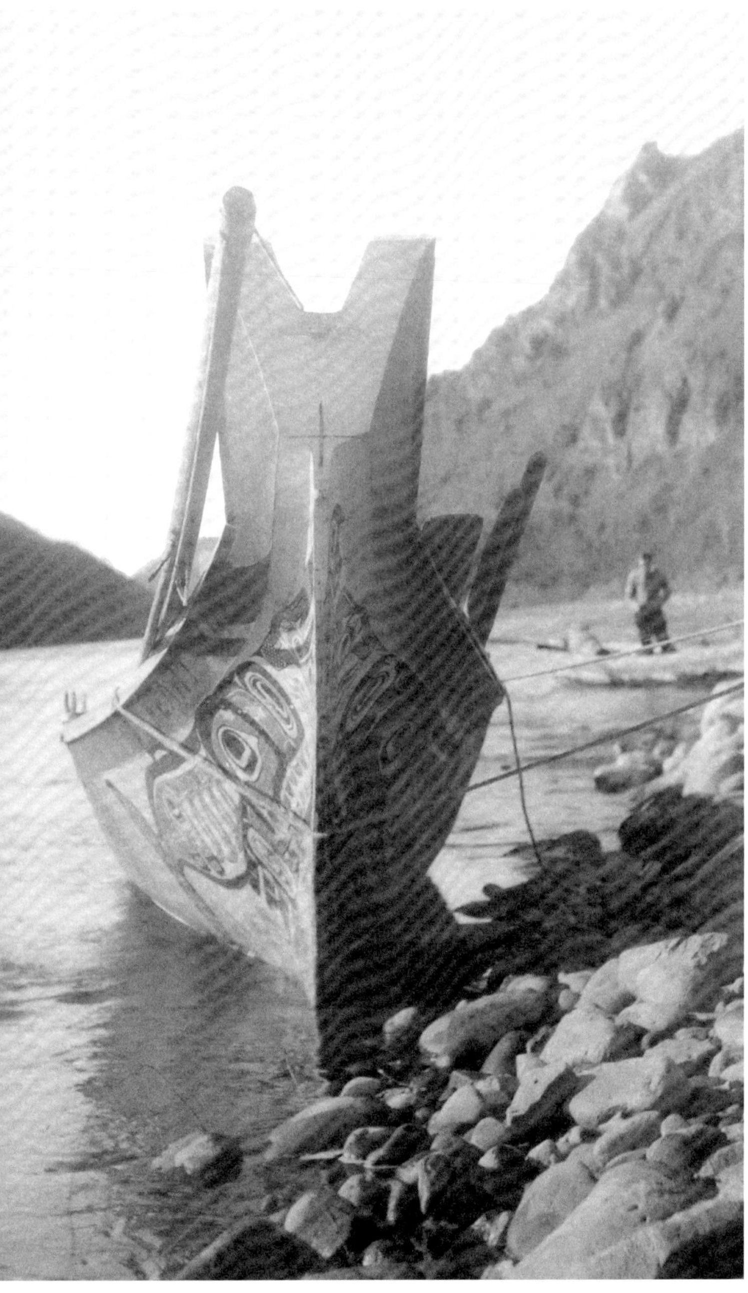

LEFT: *Chief's canoe, Belmore in background. Stikine River, 1902.*

also began to write and illustrate articles for various outdoor magazines, an activity that supplemented his income from painting sales and helped to establish his name with the public.

Most significant among his accomplishments in this decade were the first ascent of Mount Olympus, the highest peak of the Olympia Peninsula, in 1907, and his three attempts—in 1906, 1910 and 1912—to climb the highest peak in North America, Mount McKinley.

The events of the three McKinley expeditions are recounted in *The Conquest of Mount McKinley*, first published in 1913. The 1906 attempt, led by Dr. Frederick A. Cook and Prof. Herschel Parker, was thwarted when, after several weeks of exhausting travel through unmapped territory from the coast to the base of the mountain, with strength diminished and rations short, the party came to an unclimbable ice wall and was forced to withdraw.

When the men returned to the coast, Dr. Cook sent Belmore and several others off on various assignments to collect animal specimens. Cook and one other man retraced the trail to Mount McKinley and, upon their return, claimed that they had reached the mountain's summit—in only thirteen days. Belmore and the other members of the party were positive that this claim was false. "I knew Cook had not climbed McKinley," he wrote, "in the same way that any New Yorker would know that no man could walk from the Brooklyn Bridge to Grant's Tomb in ten minutes." He and his friend Herschel Parker publicly refuted Cook's claim, and having vowed to do whatever would be necessary to disprove it, they mounted the 1910 expedition.

Belmore led the climbing party halfway up the mountain to an altitude of 10,300 feet before they were forced to turn back by falling ice and the threat of avalanches. They did not, however, consider the expedition a failure, for they had obtained incontrovertible photographic evidence that Cook had not come close to the summit of McKinley in 1906.

The 1912 attempt, again led by Belmore and Herschel Parker, was very nearly a total success. Having reached a point only 300 yards of gently sloping ground from the actual summit, however, the climbers were twice forced to retreat in the face of freak snowstorms with fierce, chilling winds. It was simply physically impossible for Belmore, who was in the lead, to move forward. The men could have claimed that they had reached the summit, and no one would have questioned that assertion. According to the code of the mountaineer, however, there is, in Belmore's own words, "a distinction between a mountain top and *the* top of a mountain—we had not stood on *the top*."

Their accomplishment was, nevertheless, extraordinary; and it is universally recognized as one of the great

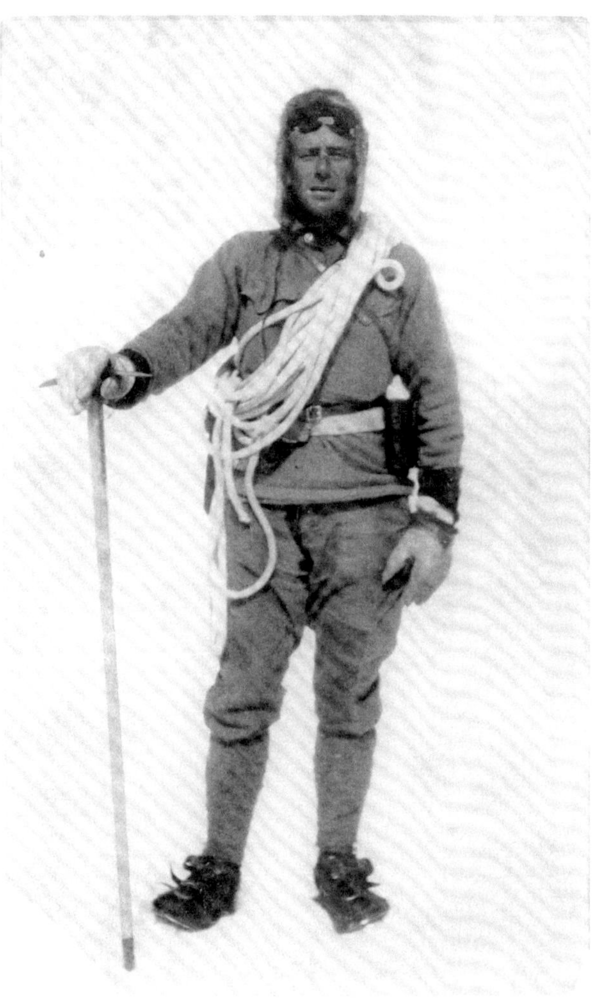

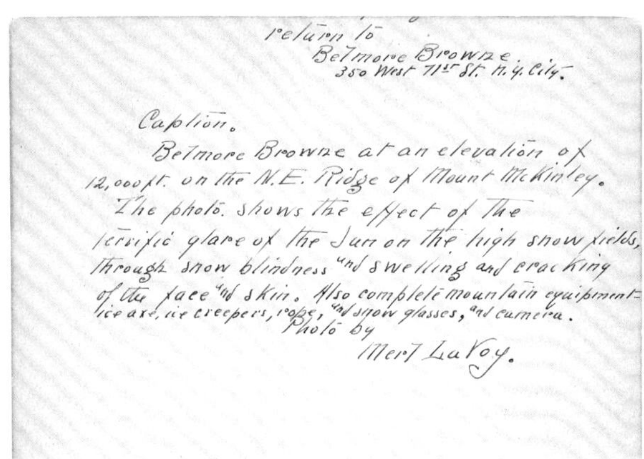

return to
Belmore Browne.
350 West 71st St. N.Y. City.

Caption.
Belmore Browne at an elevation of 12,000 ft. on the N.E. Ridge of Mount McKinley.
The photo. shows the effect of the terrific glare of the sun on the high snow fields, through snow blindness and swelling and cracking of the face and skin. Also complete mountain equipment — ice axe, ice creepers, rope, and snow glasses, and camera.
Photo by
Merl LaVoy.

ABOVE: *Belmore on Mt. McKinley, 1912, and the back of the same photo.*

achievements in the history of mountaineering. However, for Belmore and the other members of his climbing party that day in late June 1912, when they failed to reach the goal for which they had planned for several years and toiled for many weeks would always be "as cruel and heart-breaking a day as I trust we will ever experience."

Belmore gave his readers remarkable insight into the motivations and objectives that underlay his commitment to mountain exploring in his "Author's Note" to *The Conquest of Mount McKinley*:

> *To those of my readers who have never felt the lure of the mountains, I will give a few reasons for our undertaking so strange a task. The primal force at the base of all exploration is the call of the wild. Without this deep-seated love of adventure men would never be willing to meet the hardship that is waiting for them in the wilderness. But in addition to this there are many different sides of exploration, any one of which taken by itself is of sufficient interest to draw a man from civilization. I know of no task more absorbing than the mapping of an unknown territory; there is nothing more stimulating to the imagination than watching the growth of rivers and mountain chains on a topographer's plane-table. Equally absorbing is the geological interest of "new country," which runs through the whole gamut of human emotions from the frenzy of the gold-mad prospector to the unselfish enthusiasm of the geologist.*
>
> *Then come the daily study and companionship of the wildlife, from the smallest bird that dares a flight of thousands of miles to rear its young during the short arctic summer, to the big game herds that roam the storm-swept mountainsides.*
>
> *But always dominating man's endeavors is the struggle against the forces of nature—this is* Life*—and when all is said, this is the world-old magnet that draws alike scientist, explorer, prospector, mountaineer, and hunter. This was the force that brought men who joined our ventures, and they came from every walk of life.*

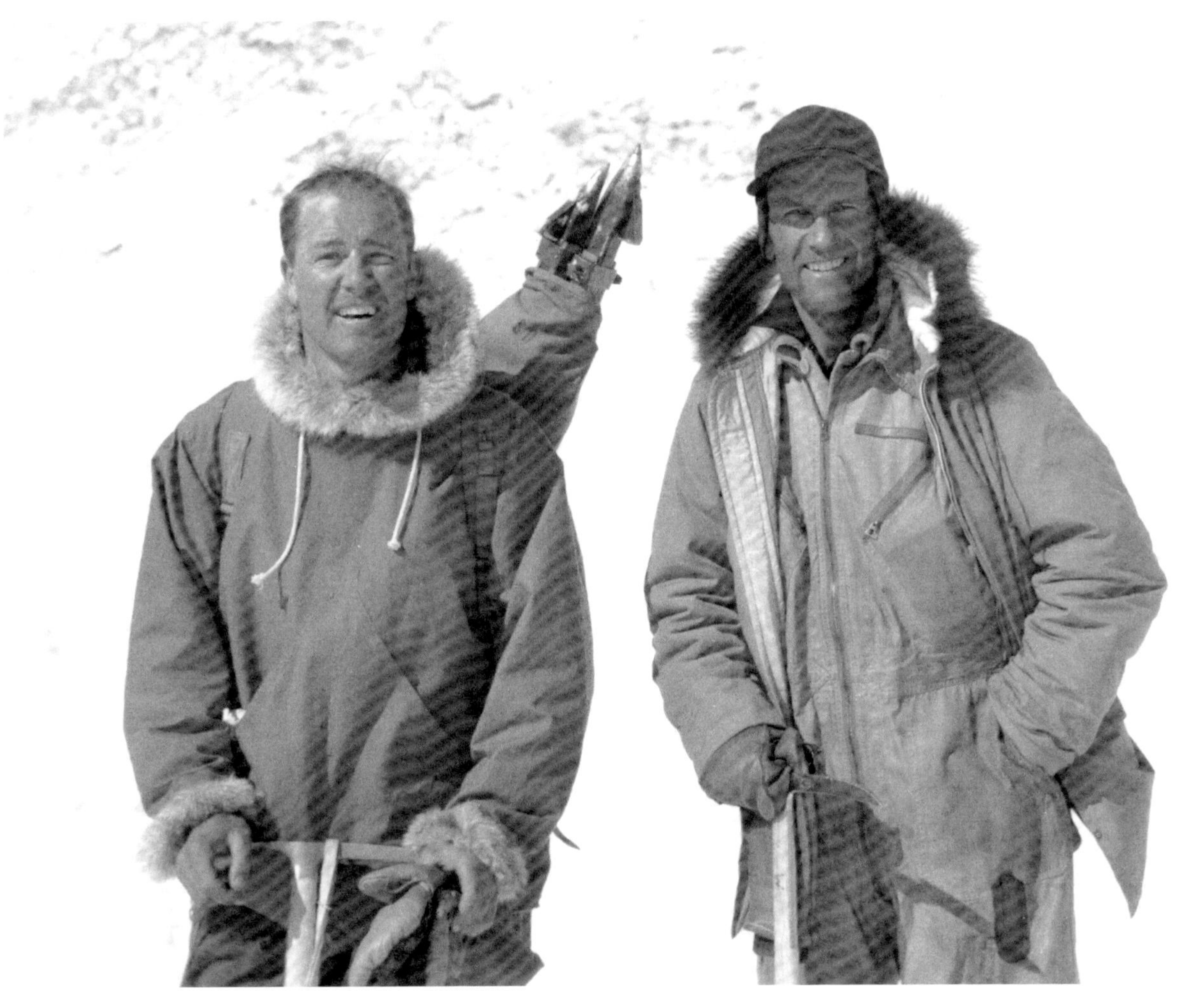

George Browne and Bradford Washburn on Mount McKinley, 1947.

> *Without the love for the unknown they would never have undergone the hardships they bore so cheerfully, and the material reward they received was not sufficient to repay them for even one day of the weeks of toil and danger they endured. Without men of this kind nothing would be possible, and in looking back on those wild, free days in the open I realize that my happiest memories are of the sun-tanned faces of my old companions.*

Belmore, reflecting further on motivation, wrote: "While Mount McKinley was a splendid mountaineering prize, our attempt to climb it had been in the nature of a sporting proposition."

Bradford Washburn, who led a successful climb of Mount McKinley in 1947 in which Belmore's son George participated, speaking as a mountaineer of the modern era—those who can fly in to the base of a mountain, have the benefit of efficient communications and are equipped with down jackets, nylon rope, freeze-dried food and light-weight gear—expressed astonishment and respect for the men "who first breached the dramatic barriers of the great peaks of Alaska and the Canadian Yukon at the turn of the century." In a tribute written for *Mountain Man,* Robert Bates's biography of Belmore Browne, Washburn wrote of his longtime friend:

> *Belmore Browne epitomizes this magnificent breed of men—who, after all, were far more arctic explorers than they were alpinists. They would almost surely have frowned*

> *on pitons and jumars, even if they had been available to them. Getting to the top of something did, indeed, have an appeal to men like Belmore, but, above all, he just plain loved the wilderness in any form it chose to take. He was, too, an expedition man—not a loner. He loved to share beauty, both on the spot and through reminiscences—and his superb paintings, his books, and his articles about his many trips leave a marvelous and indelible record of the expeditions that opened up the great ranges of the northwest and the men who led these exciting forays into the unknown.*

Writing of Belmore's third attempt to reach the summit of Mount McKinley, Washburn observed:

> *The reason that mountaineers have so admired Belmore Browne and his gallant companions over the years has not been because they set a new altitude record for North America, nor for their well-nigh incredible guts in climbing McKinley on their own feet up and back, all the way from Seward on the sea coast—but for the very quality of their undertaking, their daring spirit and their amazing determination. In their tragic defeat, they displayed a quality of fairness and nobility that is still applauded by climbers and outdoorsmen throughout the world, nearly three quarters of a century later.*

When an effort was mounted in 1916 to have 3,300 square miles of the Mount McKinley region designated a national park and game refuge, Belmore was a logical choice for spokesman. He testified effectively before the Congressional Committee on Public Lands and submitted his persuasive "Plea for a Mount McKinley National Park." He deserved and received much of the credit when Congress approved the plan and the park was established.

In 1958, shortly after George's death, Bradford Washburn urged the National Park Service to build a cabin for the comfort of climbers on the northeastern approach to Mount McKinley as a memorial to both Belmore and George. Although the proposal had the unanimous approval of the Boone and Crockett Club executive committee and the support of many admirers of the Brownes, who considered the project to be an appropriate tribute, it was rejected by the federal agency. Belmore had, however, already received an even greater honor, for a prominent spur of Mount McKinley at the 18,000 feet altitude had been named Browne Tower.

Belmore Browne's great friend Dan Beard is best known today as the founder of the Boy Scouts of America, but a century ago he was recognized as the country's leading authority on wilderness travel, hunting, fishing and camping, a reputation that derived from his prolific writings on these subjects. He was, therefore, the obvious choice when the J. Stevens Arms and Tool Co. wanted someone to write a guidebook covering the various skills required to travel and camp in the wilderness. Beard, however, passed the assignment on to "the talented young artist and arctic explorer" Belmore Browne. In his preface to this book, published in 1908 as *Guns and Gunning*, Beard wrote that the publishers could not have found "a more agreeable gentleman, a more accomplished real wilderness hunter or a more practical outdoor man for the work."

Belmore not only wrote the text, which covers virtually every conceivable aspect of living in the wilderness, with an emphasis on hunting (Stevens was, after all, a firearms manufacturer), but he illustrated the book profusely with ink drawings in the page margins in the manner of Frederic Remington and Ernest Thompson Seton.

Guns and Gunning is essentially a "how to" book, but it is enriched by Belmore's vivid descriptions of natural scenes and by his sage advice and wisdom. He tells the reader not only how to get along in the wilderness but also how to appreciate all that Nature offers to those who are receptive to her lessons and to her charms.

John H. Batten's foreword to *Mountain Man* reprints some of Belmore's articles that tell of his memorable wilderness excursions and his hunts for North American big game. Batten wrote, "Belmore Browne's gifts as a writer were such that one lives breathlessly through the events—achingly through his superlative descriptions—without awareness of reading the written word."

"Neither a scientist—though most of his far northern hunting was for scientific specimens—nor a trophy seeker," Batten continued, "Browne's joy in hunting, as opposed to Nature observation, lay primarily in the stalk. He rejoiced in pitting his growing knowledge and experience against the intelligence and wariness of his quarry."

A reading of several of Belmore's hunting stories will convince the reader that, as Batten observed, it was the challenge of maneuvering into range without spooking the animal and of making a clean killing shot that were Belmore's pride. He might take and mount the trophy, but the head of a dead animal meant less to him than the memory of a hunt that was well planned, properly executed and successfully concluded. In *Guns and Gunning*, Belmore wrote:

> *When the hunting days are over, and the old gun is resting above the fireplace, our ideas of hunting change. The successful kill becomes merely an incident of the hunt, not a lasting pleasure. The living memories are of the long, wild days in the open, the glare of the Northern sun on ice-coated mountains, and the sound of rushing water. The killing of game is not the most important feature of hunting. In reviewing the pleasure of bygone hunts, we find that the exercise, sunlight and open air all have a place in the sport.*

An entire issue of *The Monitor*, that of December 1914, was devoted to a lengthy essay entitled "Alaska," by Belmore Browne, who was identified as "Explorer and Artist." The article began:

> *It has been the writer's good fortune to travel some of the long trails that criss-cross our great northern possession. My first glimpse of Alaska was secured on one of the regulation tourist trips through Southeastern Alaska to Sitka and return. On my next visit I joined an expedition sent out by the American Museum of Natural History, and our explorations in search of big game animals led us across the Alaska Coast Range and northward toward the Yukon headwaters. In the following year we completed our collection among the mountains of the Alaskan Peninsula, the southern coast of the Bering Sea, and the rugged ranges of the Kenai Peninsula. There followed a second expedition into the coast range.*

He went on to describe his three attempts to climb Mount McKinley between 1906 and 1912, and then wrote, "In the off years I busied myself in prospecting for minerals, and in painting the wildlife and mountains of Alaska." He concluded his introduction by stating, "In my wandering I lived the life of the Alaskans, red and white, and the statements that follow are based, therefore, on what I saw with my own eyes during my life in the open." Having established himself as an authority on Alaska, Belmore devoted the body of his essay to an in-depth discussion of the topography of the area and its inhabitants.

Of particular interest is a letter Belmore wrote to the editor of *The Monitor,* which was printed as a postscript to his article:

> *While I look with pride on the growth of the land, it stirs me too with a feeling of sadness, for since the day when the foot of the first discoverer felt American soil, the wilderness has always been there to challenge American courage and stimulate our nation's imagination; but when Alaska is civilized, we will have to turn the last page in the winning of our great country, and the first chapter of the book of our national destiny will be finished.*
>
> *For this reason I wish that America might always have an untamed Alaska, so that down through the coming ages we might have a frontier on which to strengthen the sinews and cleanse the blood of our young men.*

Belmore Browne was a man of many parts; not least among his accomplishments was his success as an author of boys' adventure stories. He wrote three books: *The Quest of the Golden Valley* (1914), *The White Blanket* (1917) and *The Frozen Barrier* (1921). All were published by G. P. Putnam's Sons in New York and London, and all contained several full-page reproductions of paintings by the author illustrating dramatic episodes in the narratives. One of the books was dedicated to Dan Beard; the last one to "my son George."

The novels form a trilogy with George Draper, an orphaned youth of exceptional character, fortitude and self-reliance, as the protagonist. *The Quest of the Golden Valley* opens with George engaged in thrashing the detested bully of a rural prep school in Connecticut. Rather than accept the punishment for fighting, which he knew to be undeserved, George decides to take up a standing invitation to live with his Uncle Dan in British Columbia. His cross-country train trip—the account no doubt based on Belmore's annual rail journeys between

Tacoma and his New England boarding schools—is an eye-opening and maturing experience for the unsophisticated country boy. It is at Dan Draper's ranch and subsequently in the Alaskan wilderness, however, that George undergoes the gradual transformation from Eastern tenderfoot, a "chechawker," to a "sourdough," a competent outdoorsman of the Northwest.

George Draper, together with Fred Morgan, a local boy a couple of years his senior, becomes virtually a son to Dan, and the boys learn to rely on each other as loyal and dependable friends. Their talents are complementary, for where Fred has the more developed skills in woodcraft and pathfinding, George's mental acuity makes him the prime problem solver and decision maker. "In three things only were they alike: in their affection for each other, in their love of the great outdoors and in their adoration of Dan Draper, their foster father."

Following the narration of one of George's adventures in *The Quest of the Golden Valley*, Belmore wrote, "It was these trips where he was forced to exert his strength and resources more and more, that caused a great change to come over him. He was beginning to find himself, and under Dan's and Fred's tutelage he was rapidly perfecting himself in the many different kinds of knowledge that a man must master before he can look out for himself and be of help to others in the rough life of the western frontier."

Belmore's books were clearly intended to serve as guidebooks as well as adventure stories, for as George is instructed, the reader learns. In *Guns and Gunning* Belmore wrote, "An eighty-pound pack will hold you to the bottom [of a swift-moving river] when without it you would be swept away . . . [and] rocks or gravel will help if your pack is too light to hold you down." When Fred and George are preparing to ford the Kachiltua River in *The Quest of the Golden Valley*, Dan Draper says, "Now in fording, the principal danger is that the current may sweep you into deep water . . . . Increase [your pack] with rocks from the river bank, for an eighty-pound pack will hold you down."

Throughout the three books, the reader is taught many of the techniques Belmore covered in *Guns and Gunning*: making snowshoes, stalking game, paddling a kayak, tanning a hide, tracking an animal, baking biscuits, constructing a shelter—a myriad of the skills required to live in comfort and, indeed, to survive in the arctic wilderness. In *The White Blanket*, before taking a shot at a caribou, George "opened the breach of his rifle and blew through it, lest in his stalk it had become choked with snow, and a broken barrel might result." The author, who had lost the sight in his right eye when an ice-plugged barrel burst in his face, was teaching his readers a lesson he had learned through painful experience.

Belmore also found opportunities to put forth tenets of the philosophy that was at the core of his very existence. The wise old trapper in *The White Blanket*, for example, tells the boys, "Money kin only buy you grub, clothes and shelter—it can't buy strength, or self-respect, or health, or friends, or anythin' that is worth while—like bein' contented."

These three novels have, perhaps, suffered unfairly from being classified as "boys' adventure books," for they are superior in plot, character development, depth of theme, authenticity of dialogue and general quality of writing to the shallow potboilers that are the standard of that genre. In the tradition of boys' adventure books, the trilogy does present numerous suspenseful accounts of circumstances in which the boys' courage, strength and ingenuity are tested to the limit; and they often perform extraordinary feats of derring-do. These narratives, however, possess the richness of good novels, and the reader finds much to enjoy beyond the vicarious thrill of dealing with life-threatening forces of nature, wild animals and evil men. Of special interest are the vivid descriptions of geologic features and meteorological events, descriptions that evince the author's intimate personal knowledge of the settings of his books. The George Draper trilogy has much more in common with the adventures of Huck Finn and Tom Sawyer than with those of the Hardy Boys.

Soon after the third McKinley venture, in the year that *The Conquest of Mount McKinley* was published, Belmore married Agnes Evelyn Sibley, whom he had met six years before when she was visiting a cousin in Tacoma. Together with their two children—Evelyn, born in 1916, and George, born in 1918—Belmore and Agnes lived for several years in New York City, for Belmore wanted to be at the center of the American art world. His energies were concentrated on his painting, but he had opportunities to lecture and to write on his exploring and mountaineering adventures. He also took an active part in the ongoing controversy over Dr.

Cook's claims to have reached the summit of Mount McKinley, a claim that was ultimately discredited.

Belmore, however, yearned to live in the regions in which he had spent the most interesting years of his life, preferably in a cabin in the Alaskan wilderness. If he was to make a career as a painter of the great mountains and the big game animals of the Pacific Northwest, he needed to live where he could study and be inspired by them. Out of concern for the welfare of her two young children, Agnes had reservations about living too far from civilization; therefore, Belmore settled on Banff, in Alberta, which was then a small frontier village. They bought a one-room log cabin located at the conjunction of the Bow and Kananaskis Rivers. Belmore added a living room, a second bedroom and a studio; and he named their house "Illahee," which is a Chinook word meaning "home."

The move to Canada proved to have been a wise one, for in the early 1920's Belmore began to gain recognition in the Eastern art world. Several of his paintings were included in exhibitions at the Corcoran Gallery, in Washington, and in 1923 his landscape "Spring, Canadian Rockies" was selected for an international exhibition in Venice.

Significant as Belmore's achievements as an explorer and a mountaineer had been, it was as a writer and as a painter that he could earn a living and support his wife and children. Pay for articles was meager considering the time required to produce them; painting, therefore, was his best option. It was not until 1923, however, that he was given the opportunity of a one-man show—an exhibit of twenty-three oils—which was held at the Macbeth Gallery in New York. The catalogue, by way of introducing Belmore to the Eastern art world, stated:

> *Belmore Browne needs no introduction to lovers of the great outdoors. As the conqueror of Mount McKinley and for his explorations in other wilds, he is known throughout the length and breadth of the country. That he is able to record his impressions through the medium of paint, however, is known to but comparatively few. Still fewer know that he is one of the very best painters of rugged mountains.*

The initial exhibition was obviously a success, for the Macbeth Gallery gave the artist a second one-man show in 1924 and a third in 1928 and sold a significant number of his paintings over the years.

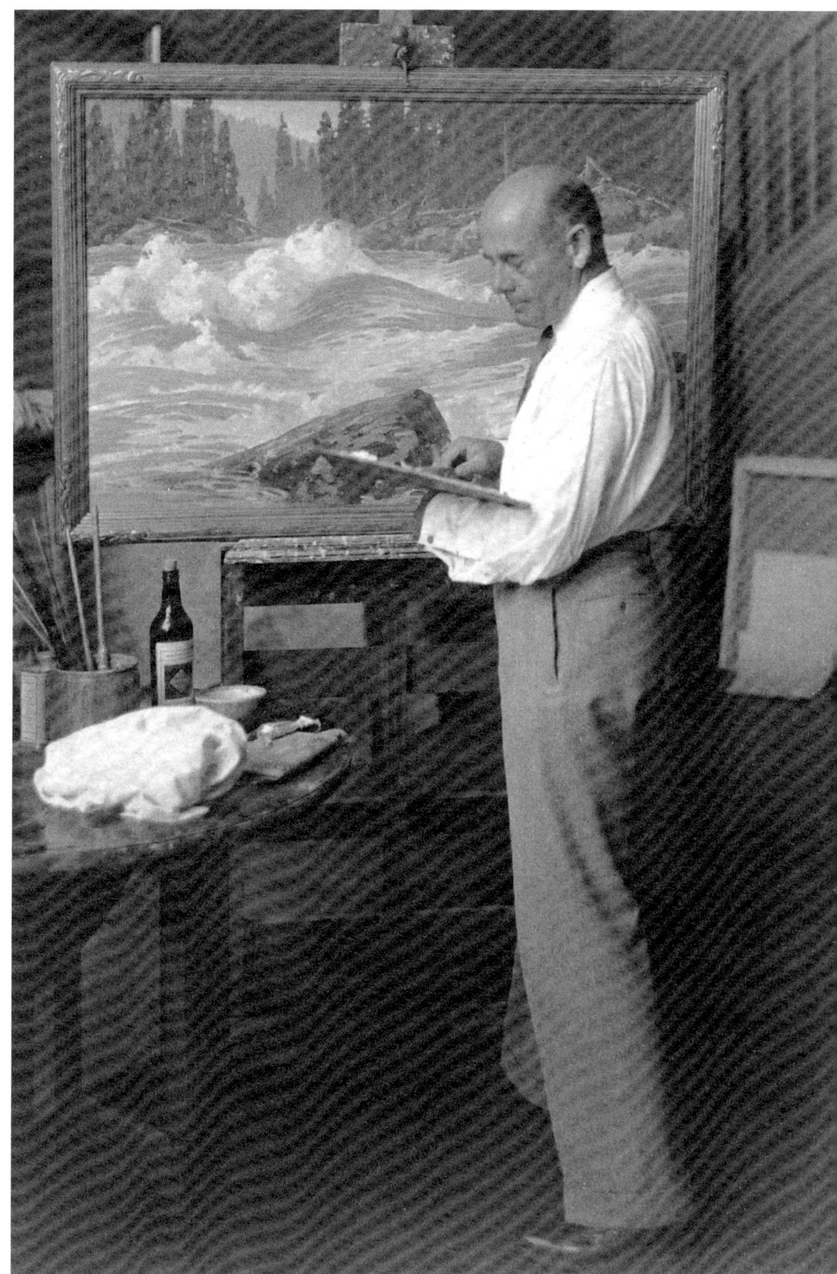

Belmore in his studio

By the mid-1920's, Belmore was a regular exhibitor at prestigious national invitational shows including exhibitions at the Pennsylvania Academy of Fine Arts, the O'Brien Galleries in Chicago, the National Academy of Design, to which he was elected an associate member, and the Corcoran Gallery. It was at a 1926 exhibition in Washington that "The Chief's Canoe" took first place and was purchased by the Smithsonian. A critic for the *Washington Star* wrote of this painting, "It is a scene in the Canadian Rockies, a lake in the lap of the great hills, partially snow covered and cloud capped. A painted canoe with high prow . . . moves from the shadow of the great cliff, making scarcely a ripple in the mirror-like surface of the water." In 1954, an officer of the Smithsonian wrote Agnes Browne, "We are very proud of our possession of 'The Chief's Canoe,' which has long adorned the outer office of the Secretary of the Smithsonian. It hangs opposite the entrance, where many distinguished visitors admire it as they pause before seeing the head of our Institution."

A reviewer of one of the national exhibitions singled Belmore's paintings out for praise. He compared Belmore favorably to Frederic Edwin Church, Albert Bierstadt and Thomas Moran, "who likewise searched out monumental American subjects to picture with a desire to produce work typical of this country." The three predecessors, however, were described by the writer as "essentially realists, copyists of nature"; whereas Belmore was one of those who "are striving to render not mere fact, but emotion, to interpret truly the impression of grandeur and bigness that they find in the awe-inspiring presence of these great manifestations of nature untouched by man."

Another critic wrote that Belmore's landscapes were "steeped with the air of solitude" and that they stood out with "a kind of glistening richness of painted surface, with veracity and sureness of brushstroke." The *New York Times* critic commented favorably on his work and referred to him as "a stout-hearted naturalist."

The move to Banff began what Agnes described as "the most productive period of Belmore's life as an artist."

"He loved working outdoors in the winter," she wrote, "and would often wear three pairs of socks on his hands, with the brushes pulled through so that he could move his fingers easily within the socks. This system permitted his painting in temperatures of even thirty degrees below zero, but at lower temperatures he couldn't work because the paint froze. Summers were spent in the mountains, where Belmore collected materials for the coming winter."

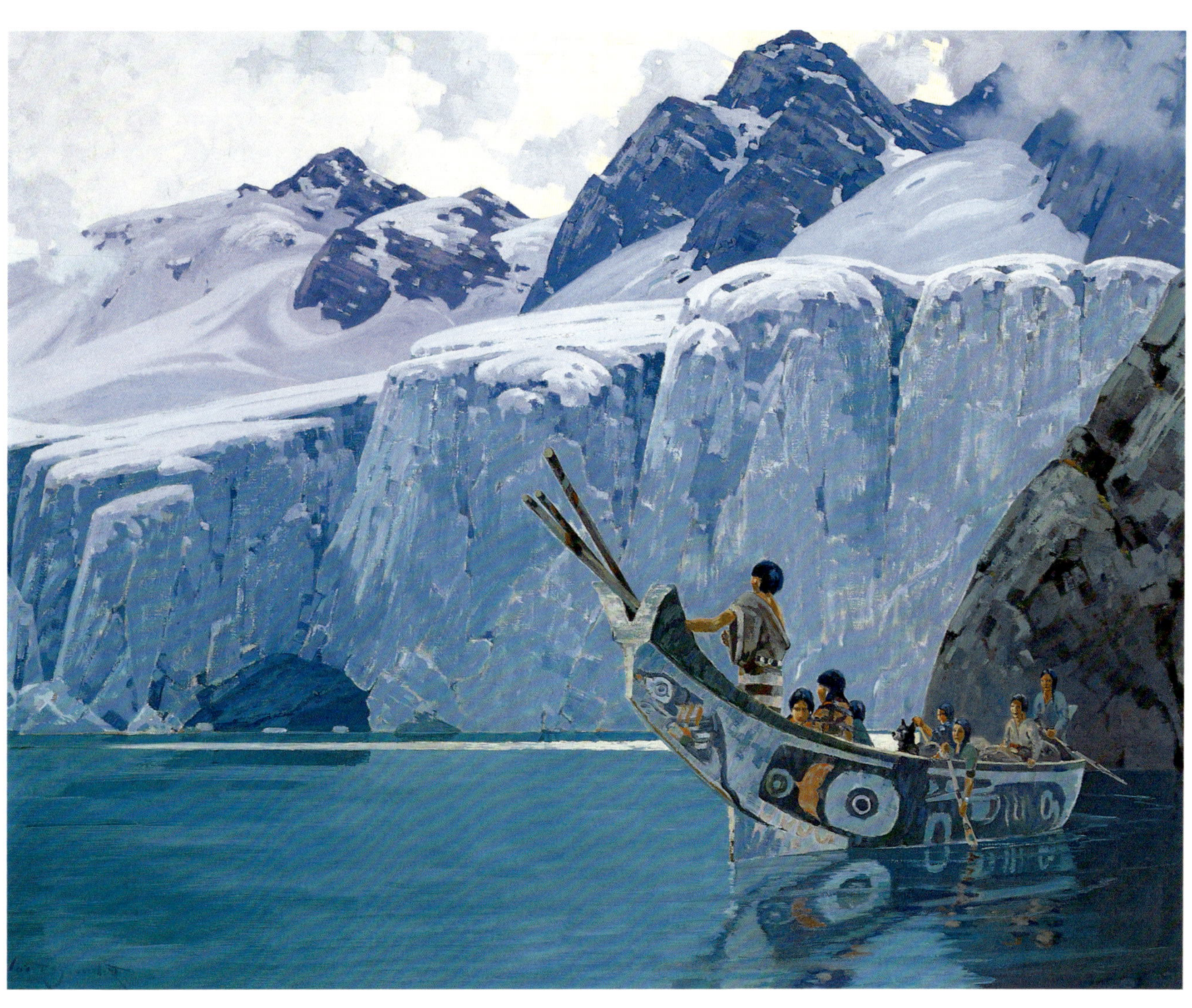

PLATE 1
Belmore Browne
The Chief's Canoe, 1926
oil on canvas, laid on board 36 x 48 in.
Smithsonian American Art Museum
Bequest of Henry Ward Ranger through the National Academy of Design

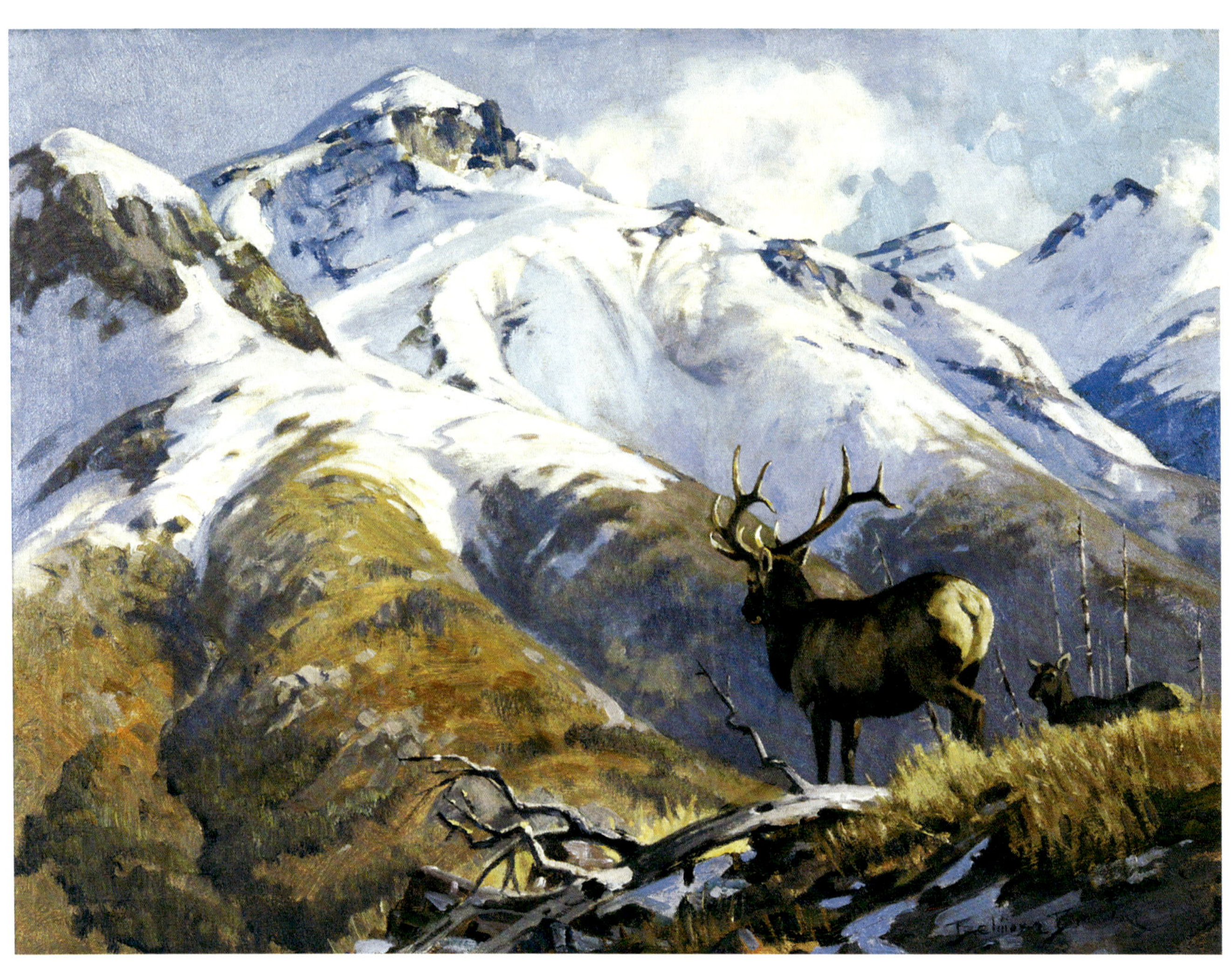

PLATE 2
Belmore Browne
Bull Elk study, 1947
oil on canvas, 18 x 24 in.
Drummond Gallery

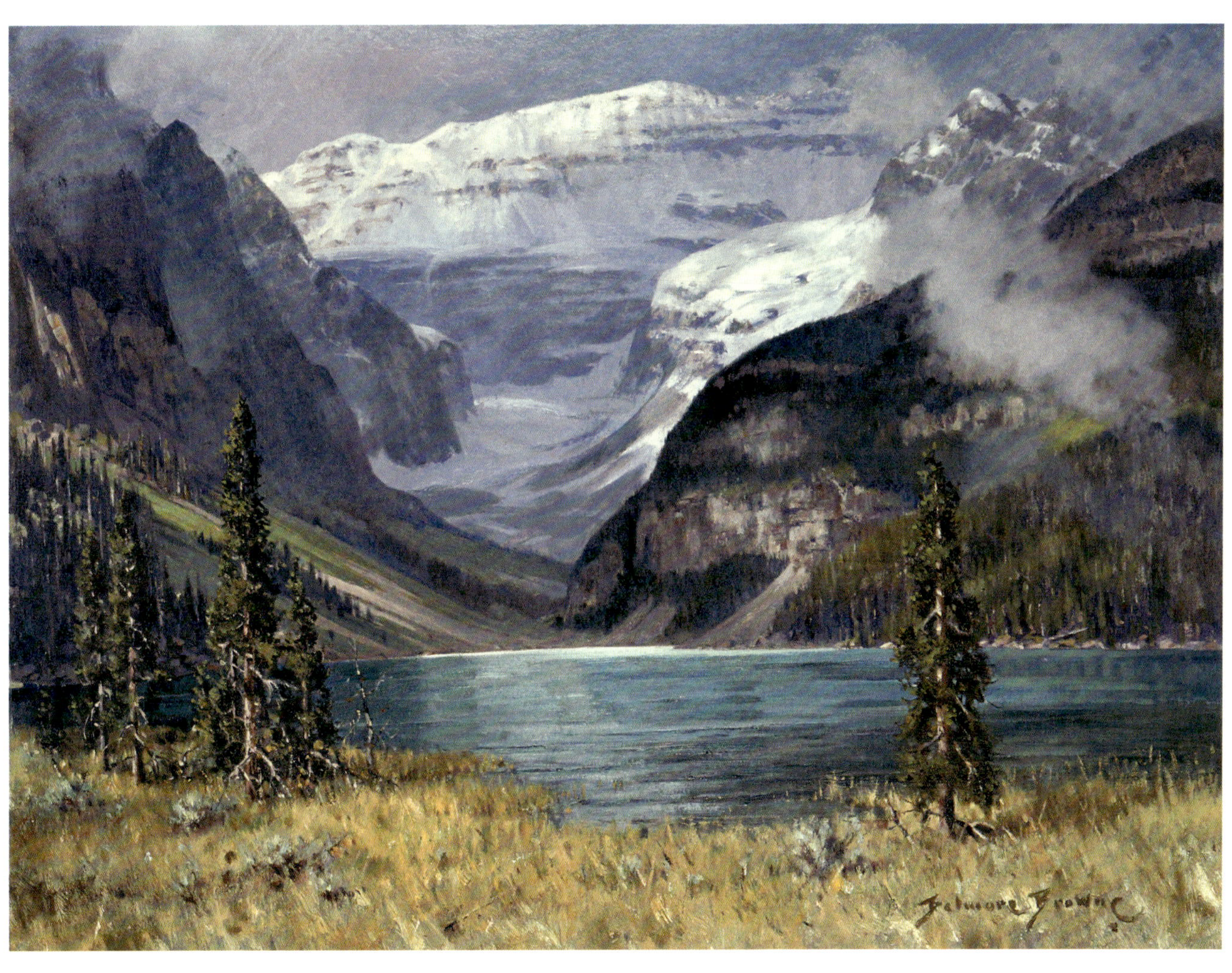

PLATE 3
Belmore Browne
Lake Louise, Early Spring 1948
oil on canvas, 30 x 40 in.
Len Braarud Fine Art

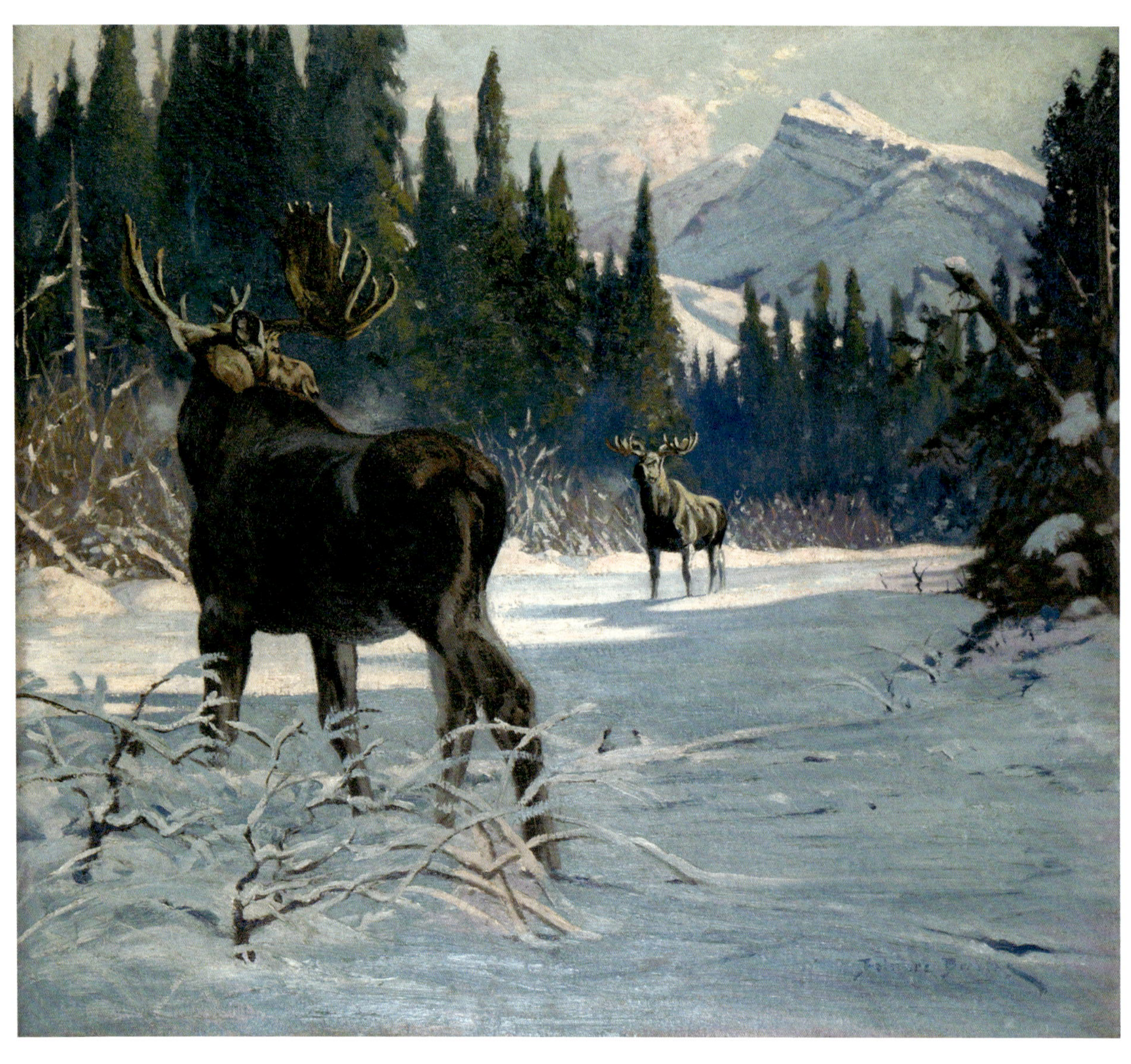

PLATE 4
Belmore Browne
The Challenge 1945
oil on canvas, 36 x 40 in.
Len Braarud Fine Art

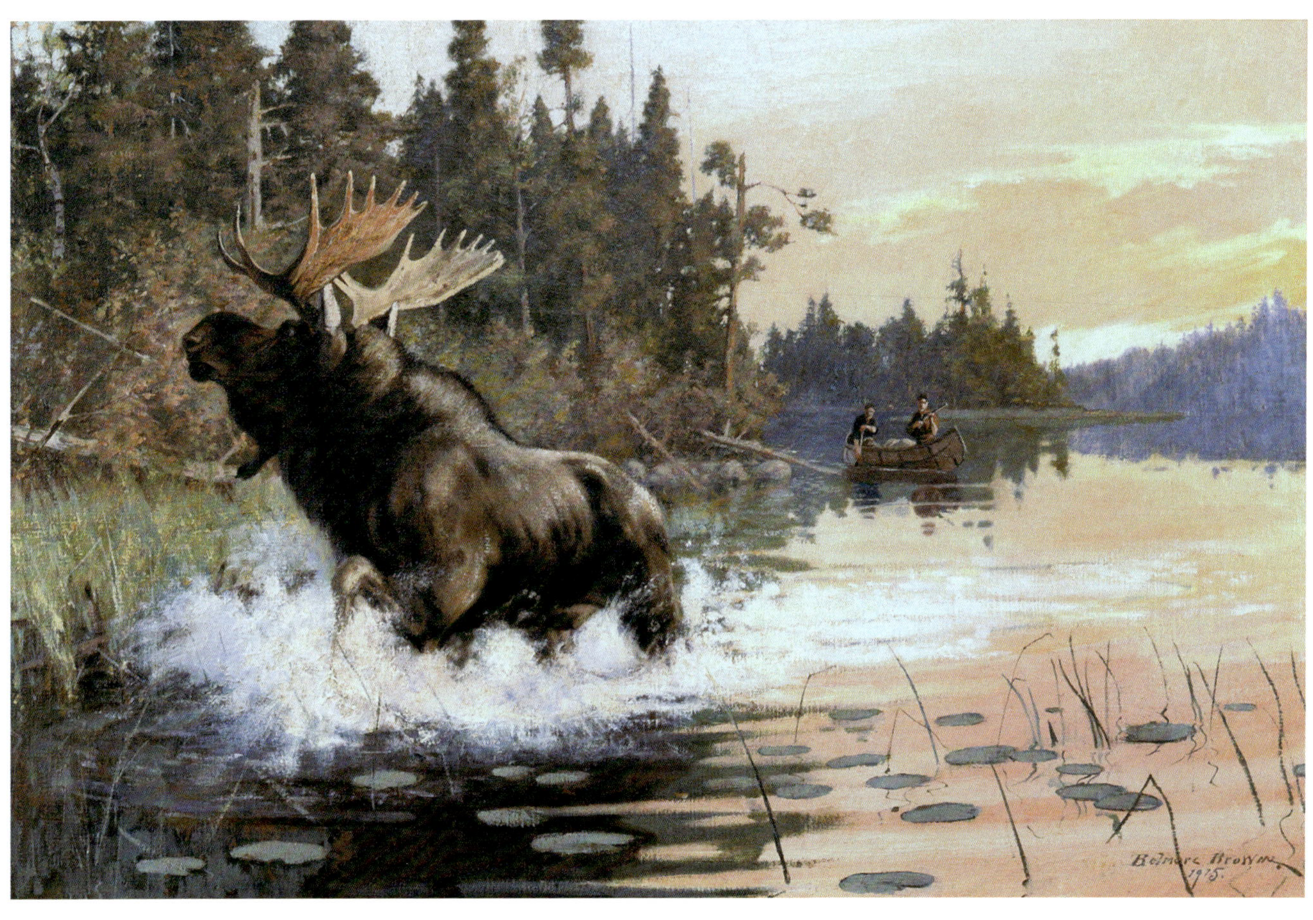

PLATE 5
Belmore Browne
Surprised 1915
oil on canvas, 20 x 30 in.
Len Braarud Fine Art

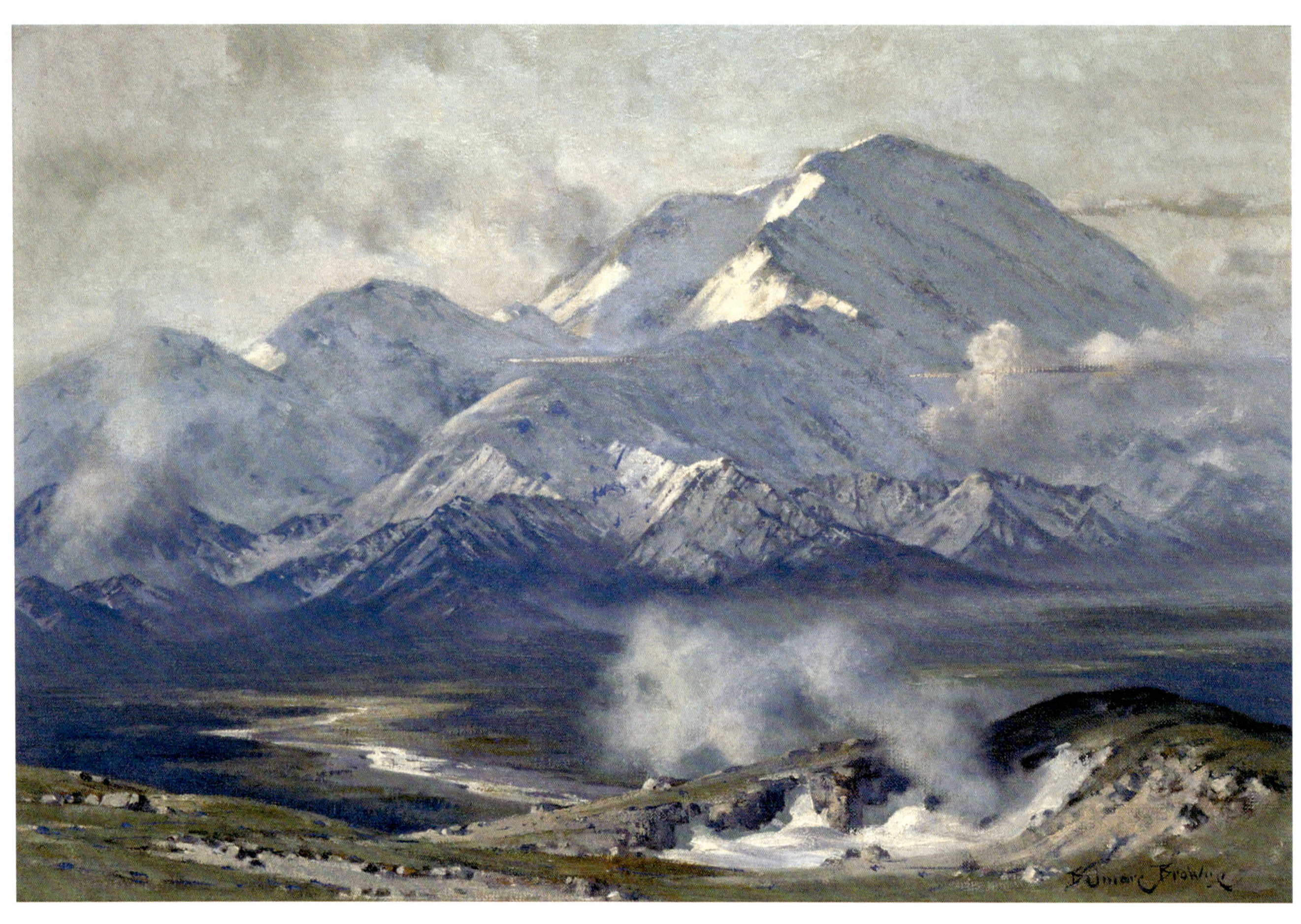

Plate 6
Belmore Browne
Mt. McKinley 1951
oil on canvas, 20 x 30 in.
Len Braarud Fine Art

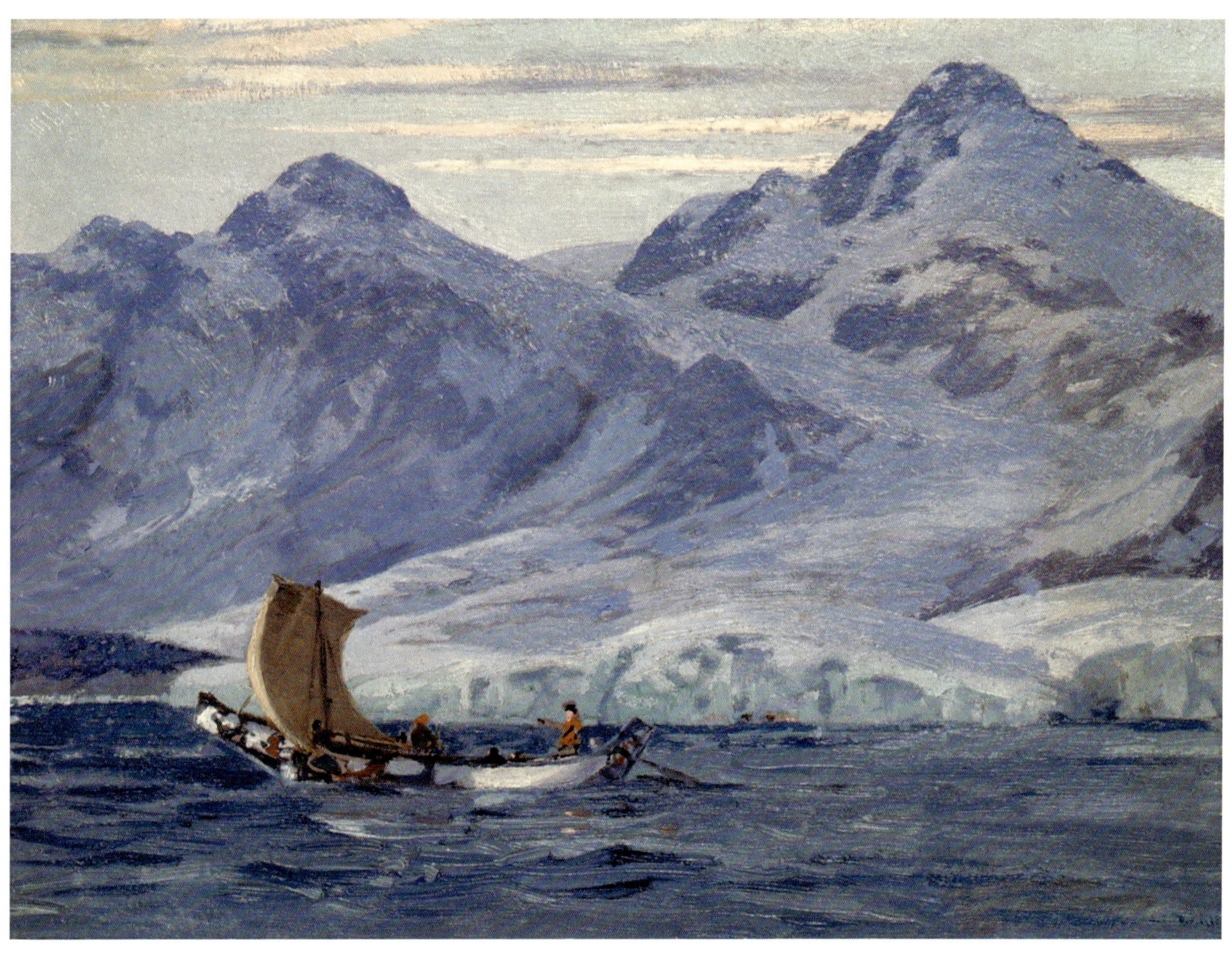

Plate 7
Belmore Browne
Squaring Away For Wrangell 1956
oil on masonite, 11½ x 15 in.
Len Braarud Fine Art

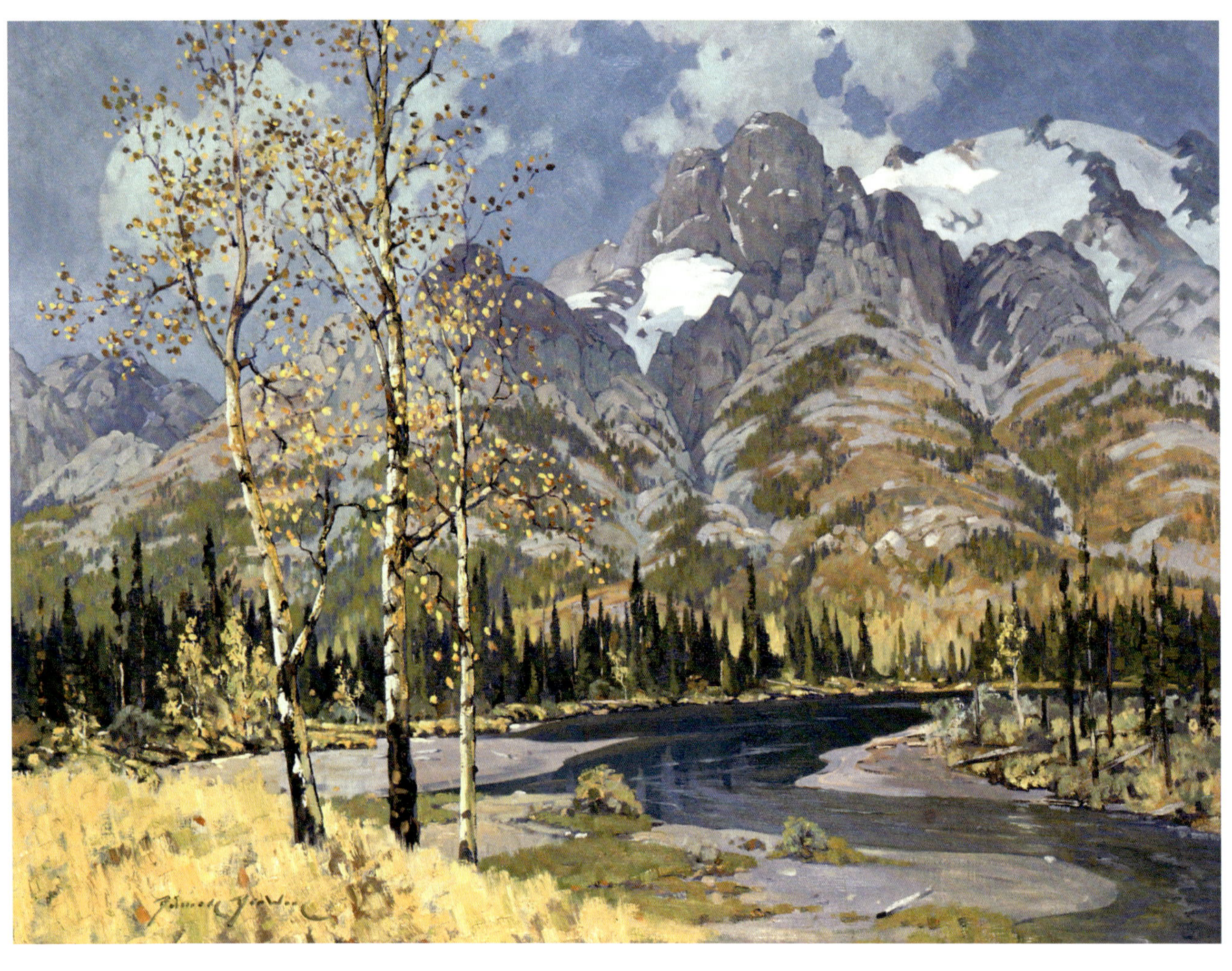

PLATE 8
Belmore Browne
Indian Summer, Rockies 1939
oil on canvas, 30 x 40 in.
Len Braarud Fine Art

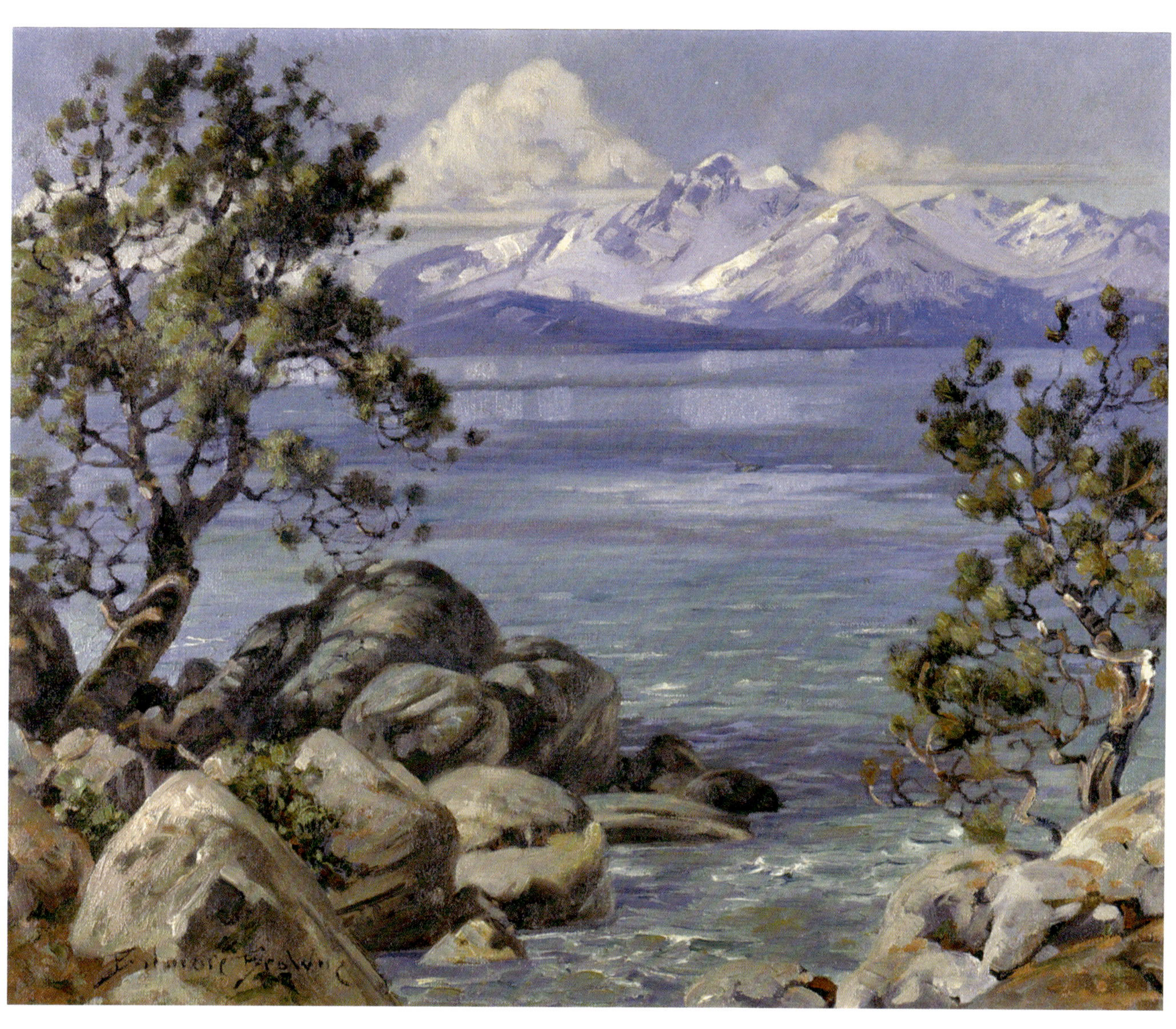

PLATE 9
Belmore Browne
Lake Taho From Glenbrook 1938
oil on canvas, 16 x 20 in.
Roy Farrington Jones Collection

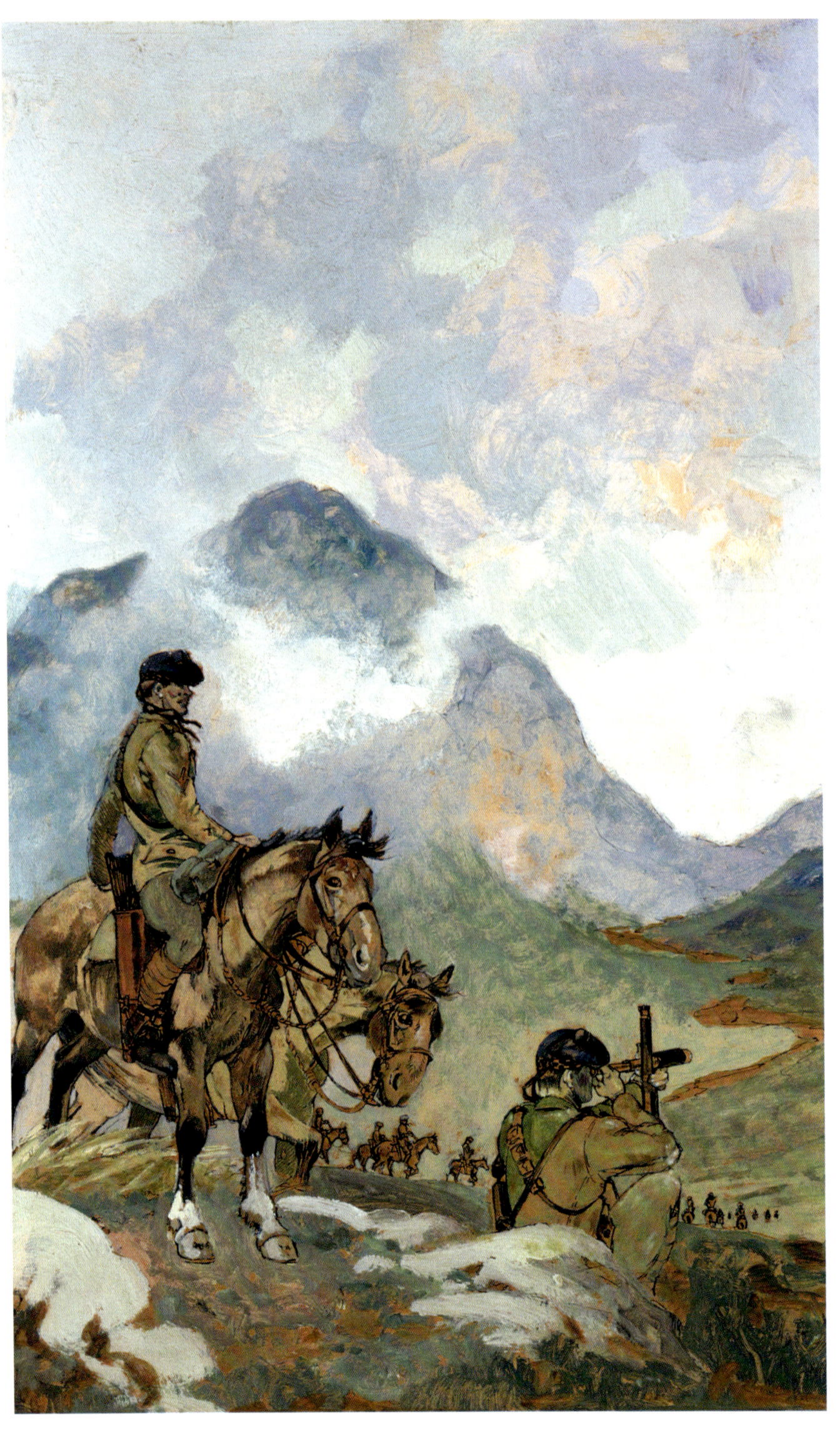

Plate 10
Belmore Browne
Scouts Lovat ca. 1943
oil on canvas, 21 x 13 in.
Collection of Hugh Robinson

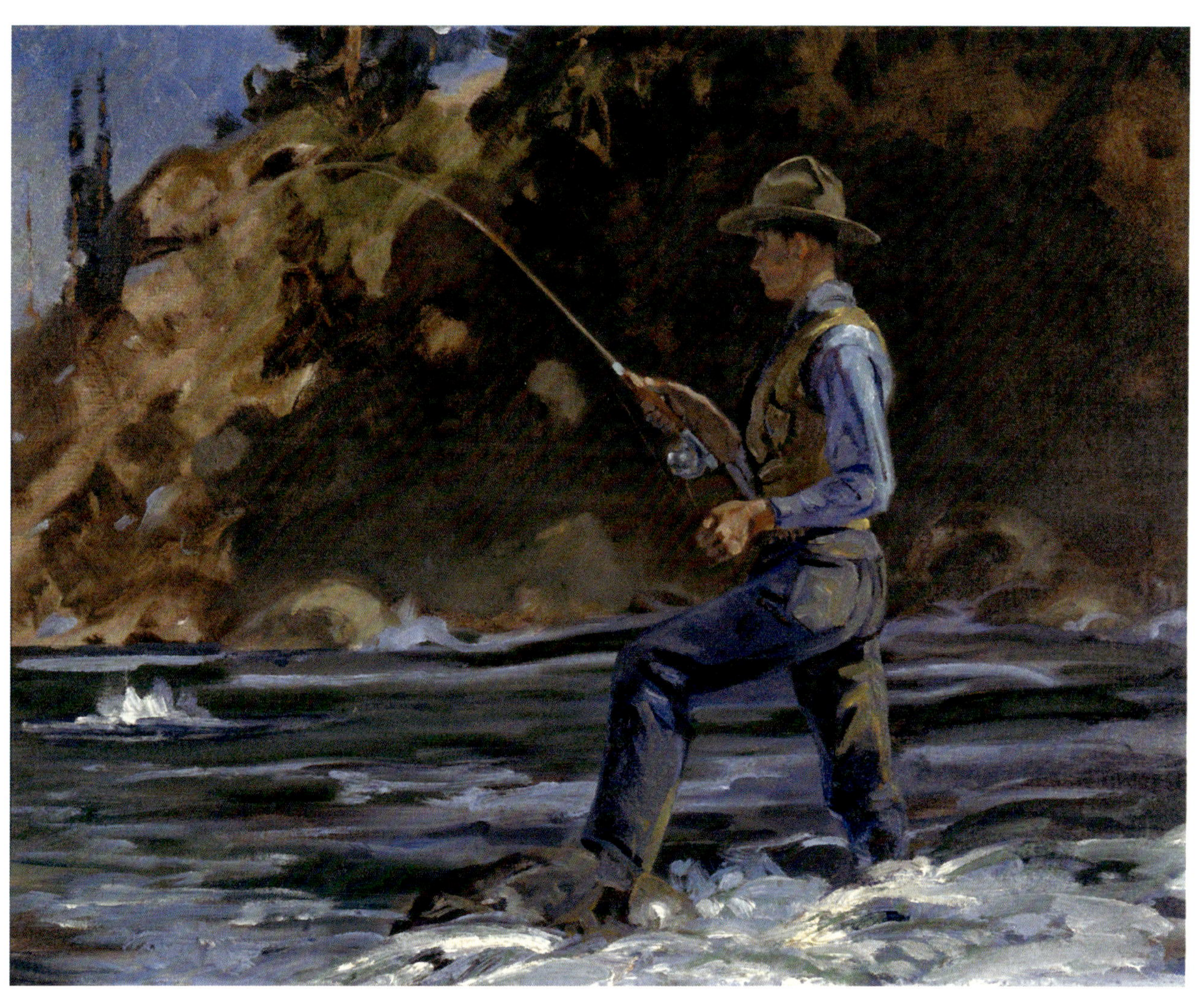

Plate 11
Belmore Browne
George Flyfishing 1934
oil on canvas, 16 x 20 in.
A wedding gift to Tibby and George
Collection of Hugh Robinson

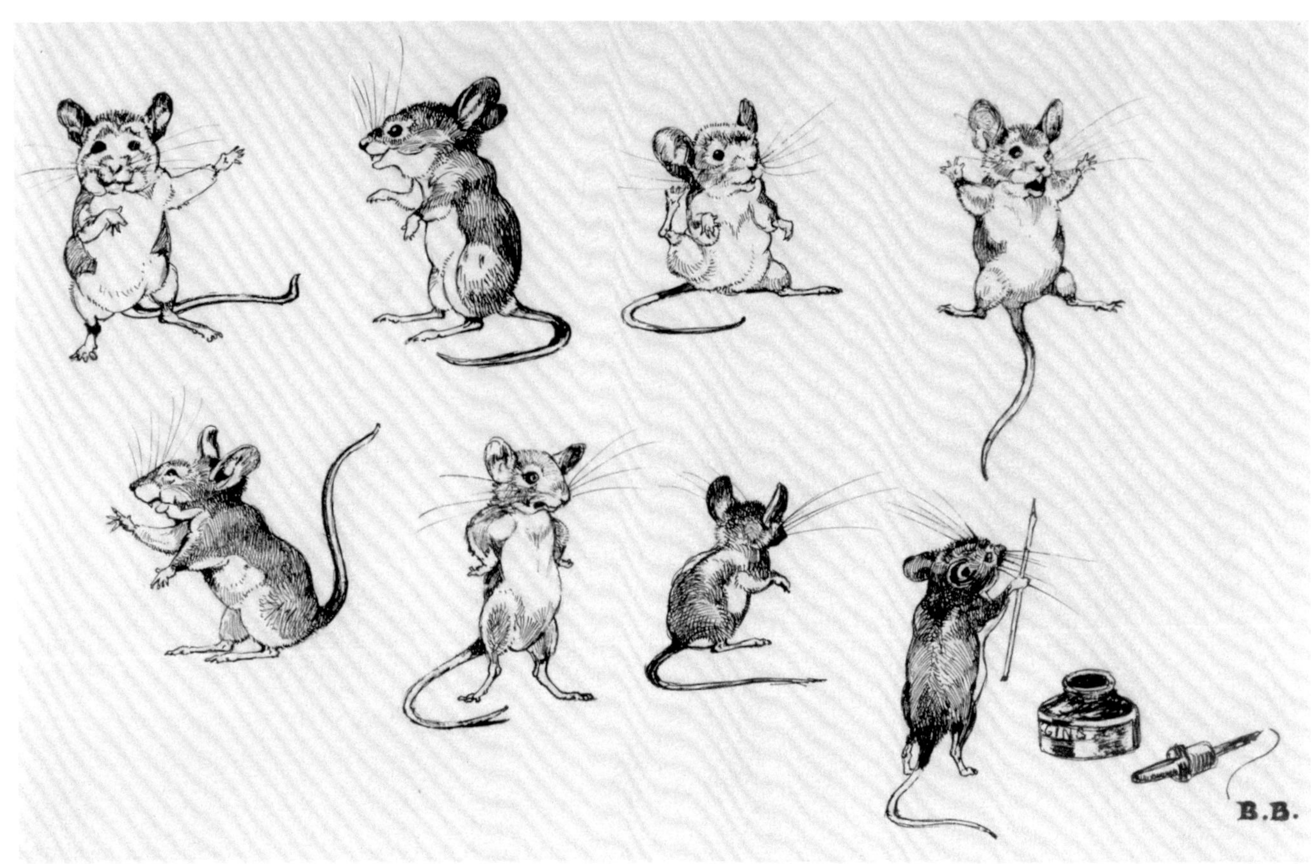

PLATE 12
Belmore Browne
Mice sketches 1957
pen and ink, 8½ x 11 in.
Gift to granddaughter, Isabel
Collection of Hugh Robinson

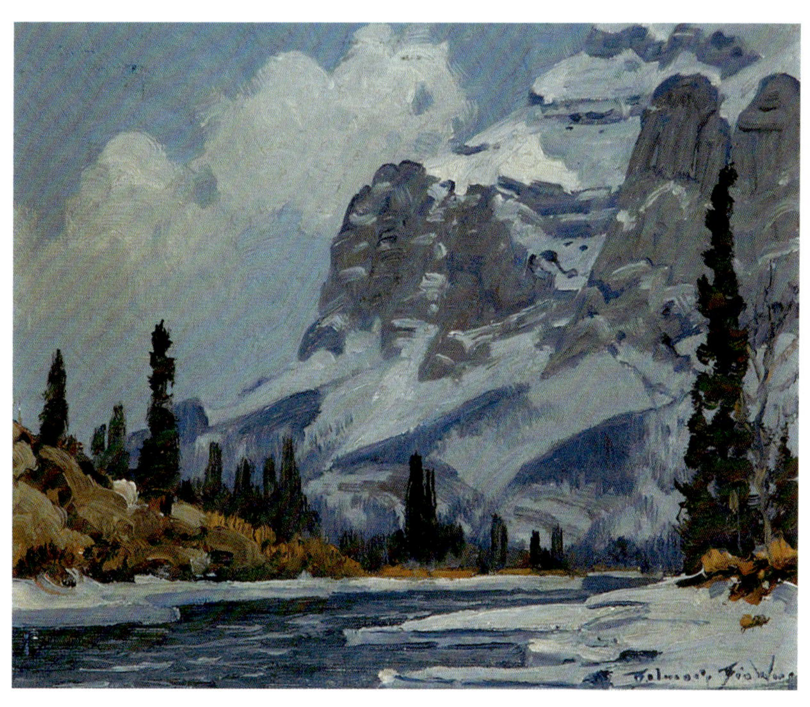

Plate 13
Belmore Browne
Snow Covered Cliffs 1928
Oil on canvas laid on board, 9 x 11 in.
Private Collection

Chapter ~ Three

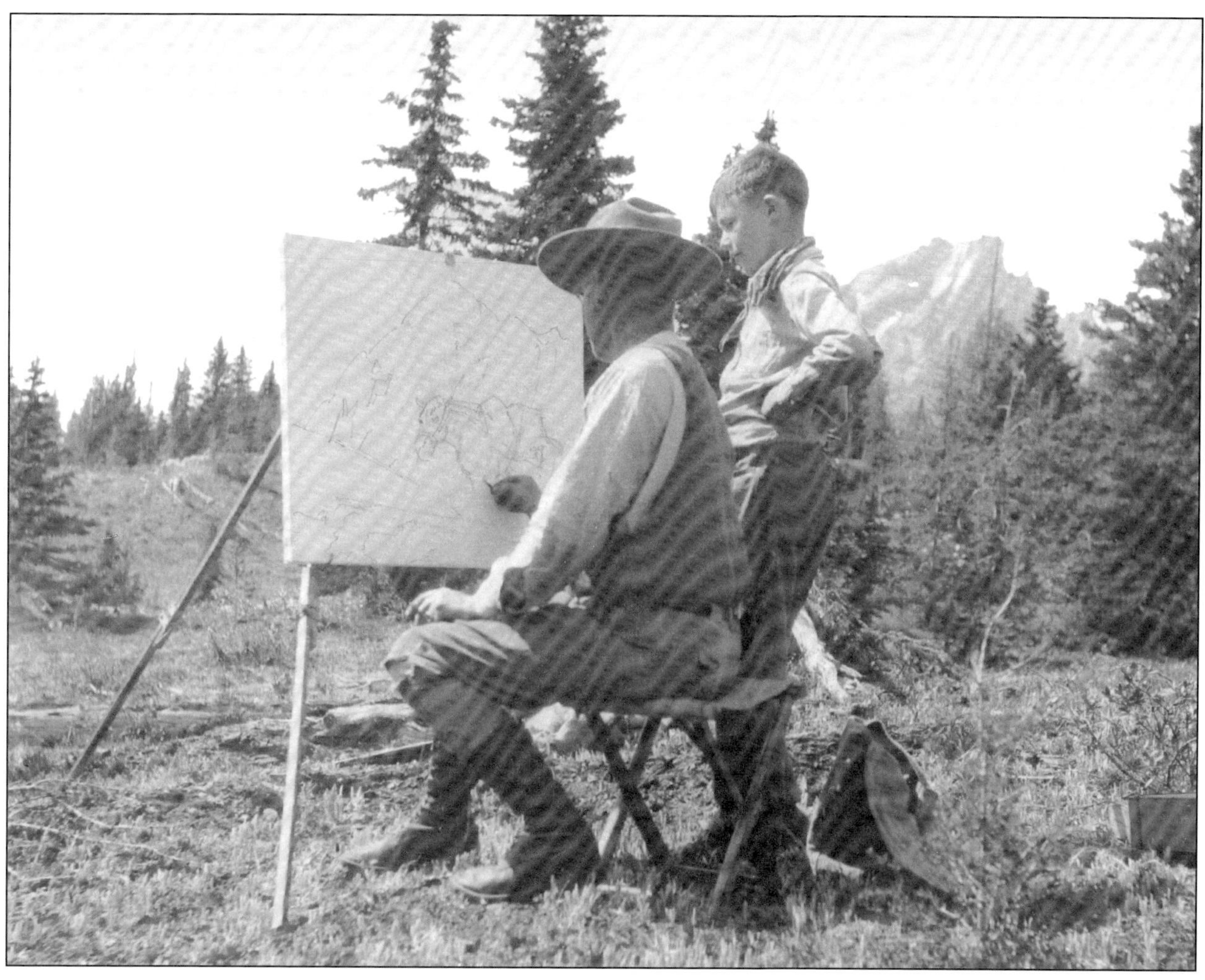

GEORGE BROWNE

THE YEARS OF APPRENTICESHIP

Agnes Browne saw the move to Canada as the beginning of "an idyllic existence" for the children. Each summer for the next decade, the Browne family would make several trips on horseback with pack mules into the wilderness, where they would camp, explore, hunt and fish. Belmore spent much of his time drawing, acquiring sketches for paintings he would work on in the winters back in Banff. In a few years, George was joining his father on sketching forays, and drawing became a consuming interest for the lad.

George and Belmore sketching

RIGHT: *George on horse, Evelyn behind*

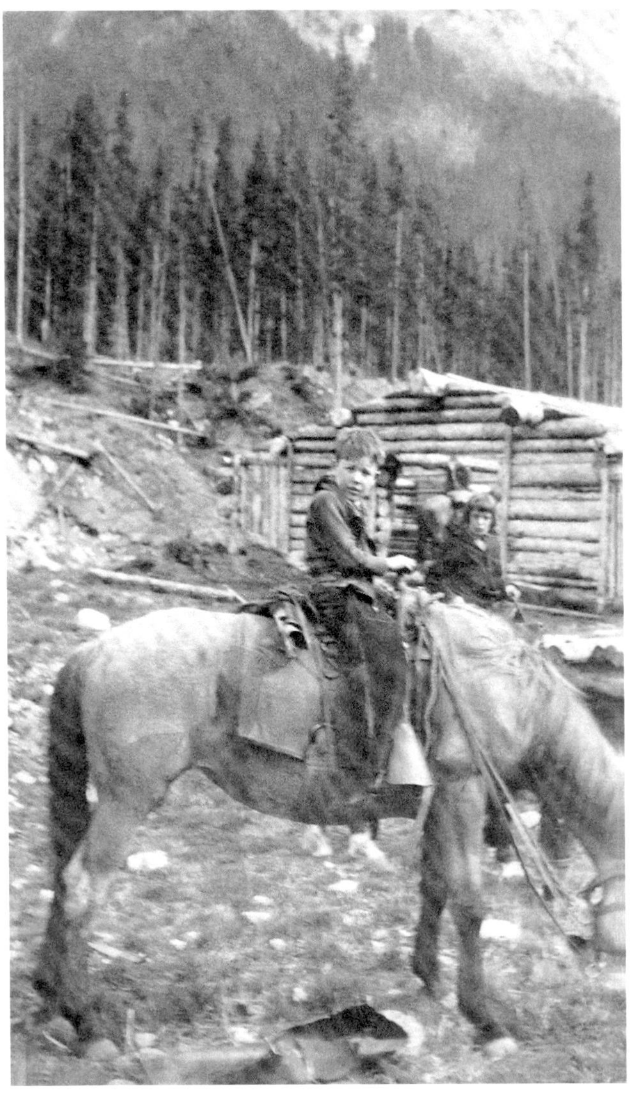

Agnes's diary account of one particularly memorable day, August 24, 1921, shows how Belmore undertook to give his daughter and son instruction and experience he believed would be of interest and value to them. Agnes wrote:

> *About four thirty, Belmore stopped his painting and took us all over the hills back of our camp to try and see some game. We went very slowly and never spoke above a whisper—the children's eyes getting big and round at the thought of really stalking game. Fresh trails everywhere—bear and deer—and as we came out into an open glade we'd sit down quietly and just watch. Belmore telling the children real hunting stories and making them familiar with all sorts of phases of wild life. What an experience for the little mites.*

Apparently Agnes Browne considered the development of character and self-reliance to be the principal benefits the children derived from these annual camping trips: "I have a feeling of thankfulness for Belmore and two such splendid children that are more than paying us for all we gave of ourselves to them, and I only hope they in their turn will carry on some of the ideals we are striving for—only do it far better for the physical life we are able to give them."

At the end of a 1922 expedition she wrote, "One could hardly estimate the success and value of a trip such as we have had." Speaking of the children—Evelyn was then six, and George was four—she observed:

> *I'm very proud of them, I must say. They've seen magnificent country and have learned to love it and appreciate it. Because they walked, they've learned the deer, bear, goat and sheep tracks and many of the wild flowers. They've learned the discipline of keeping up and bearing fatigue, hunger and even cold from the rain. They've learned to be good sports, to cast a fly, and no one can ever take from George an interest in fishing that has been awakened on this trip. He has been a constant source of amazement to Belmore and me. This ability to travel—the way the trip has developed him and roused him and with it all his sweetness to all of us.*

George also occasionally wrote accounts of the family's activities on their camping trips. An entry from the summer of 1930, when he was twelve, reflects not only his interests but his severe dyslexia:

> *We saw a big bull moos wading in the lake got are sent and rain a crous the lake and a way.*
>
> *I went fishing in the streem I cought one little one but the beaver had scard them all a way When I got to the lake I went from end of the lake to the other and only saw tow fish jump, then I went back to the outlet and landed to big cut throut trout a boat a*

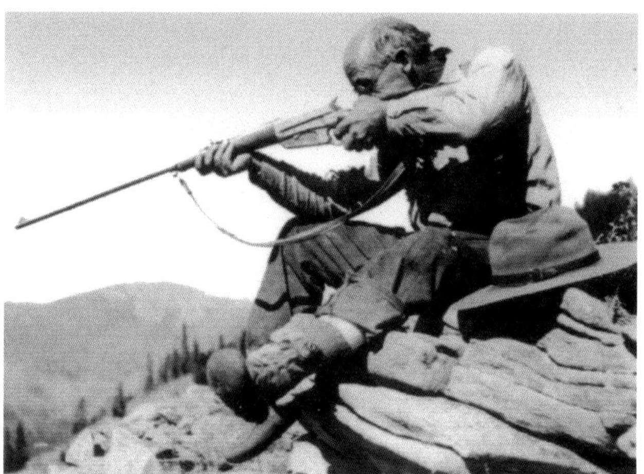

LEFT: *Belmore shooting*

BELOW: *Sketch in Belmore's sketchbook*

pound a peace I cought them on a browne hecles I went back and cleaned them and then we went back up the lake to look for pictures to paint we saw a Beaver come out of his house then he hit the water with his tile then we saw a nother one but we hode to go home for supper.

Another entry of the same year reads:

> *We went up in a vally and saw a Greezaly digging then Ba* [his name for his father] *panted a picture then we went over the pass and throw some snow we saw 2 ciotes 22 Elk and a band of 15 sheep.*

Referring to these years and their summer excursions in the wilderness, Agnes wrote, "What Belmore wanted more than anything in the world was to get right out in the mountains and paint pictures. What George wanted more than anything was to go camping way off from everybody and just fish the little streams for trout and watch the big animals way up high, and he made up his

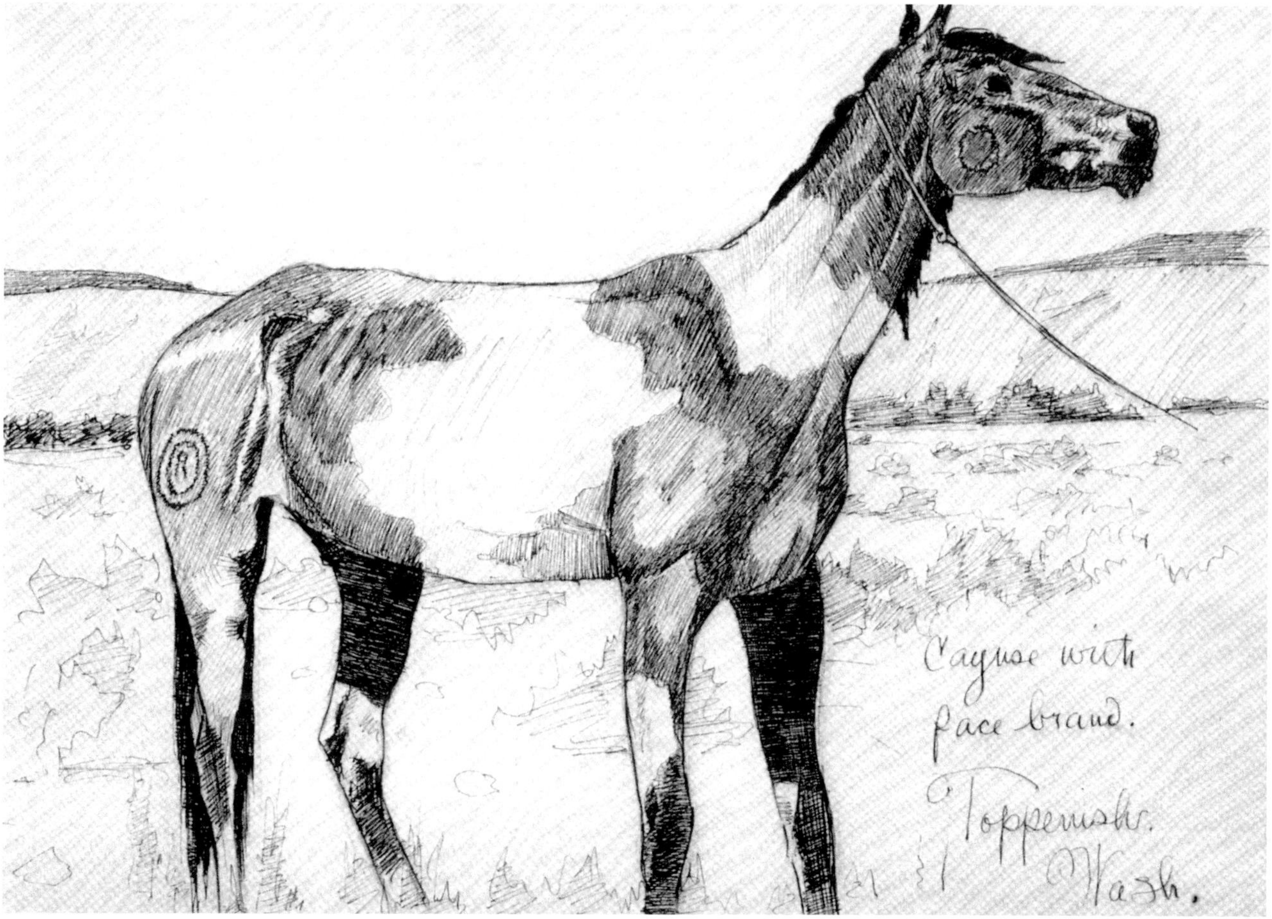

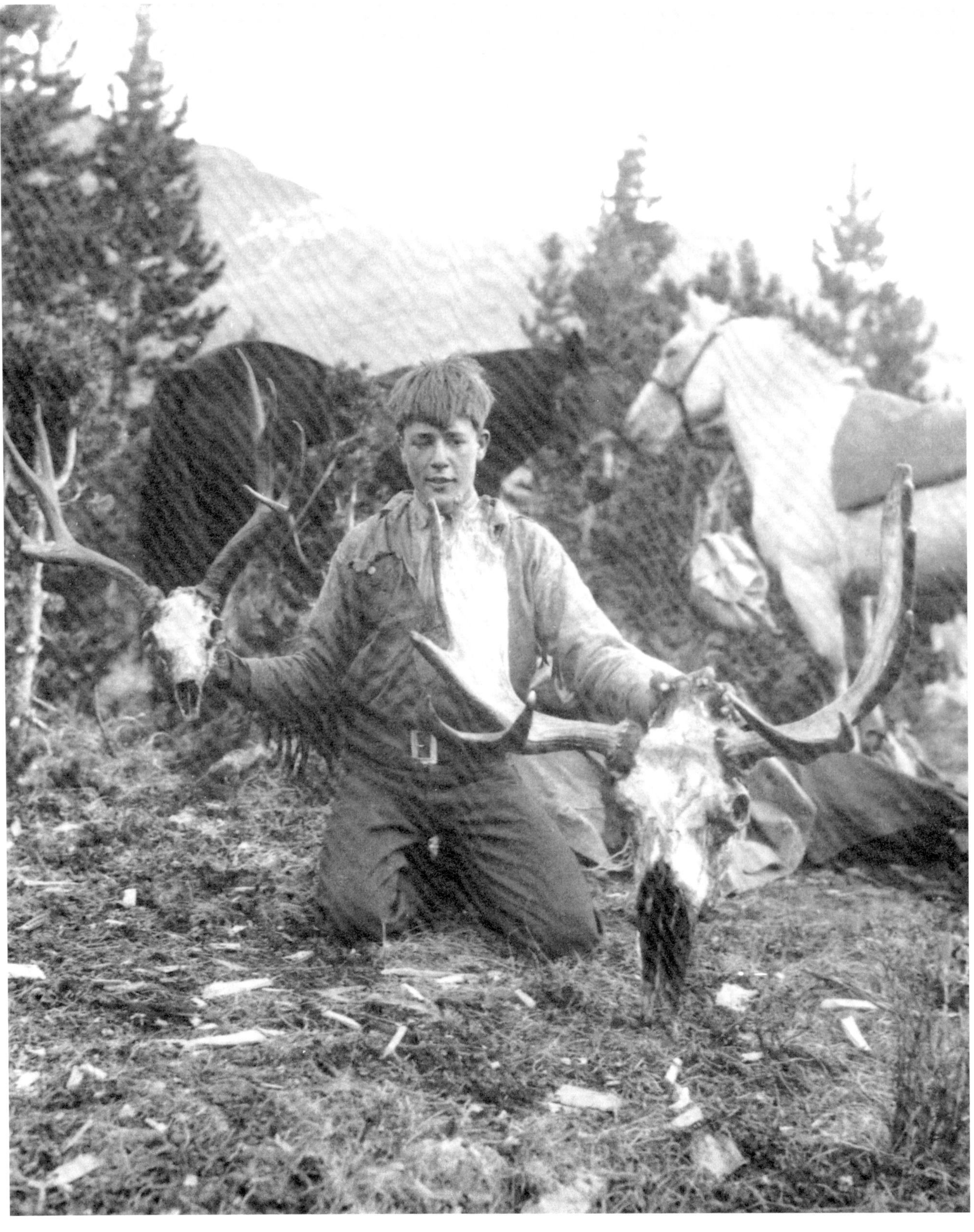

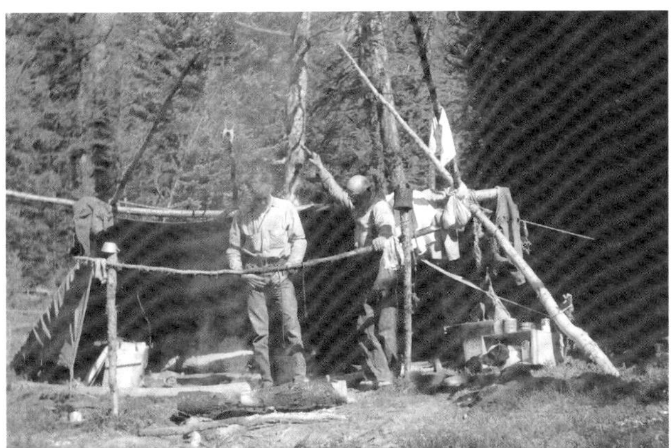

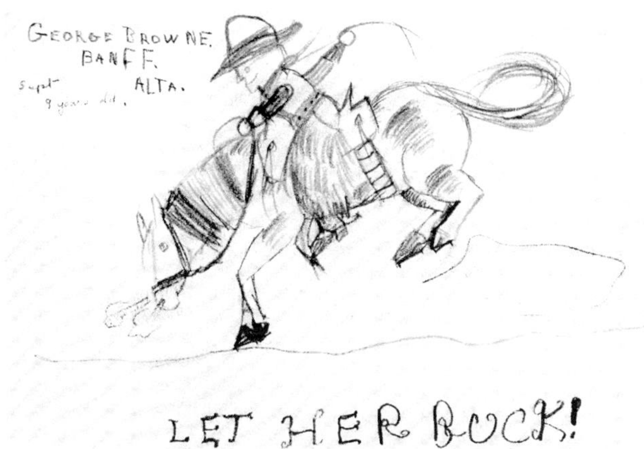

OPPOSITE: *George: "My first deer age 13"*

LEFT: *George and Belmore camping*

BELOW LEFT: *First known painting of George's, age 9*

mind that when he was big enough he wanted to paint too and hunt the Rocky Mountain big horn sheep like Ba."

In a July 1932, diary entry, Agnes noted, "George painted a sketch in oils today—the first he ever handled in oil. He did not get much, but he learnt a lot & is very keen."

With regard to George's early artistic work with his father, his sister Evelyn wrote, "I can never remember our childhood together when George was not drawing something, whether we were in 'civilization' [winters in Santa Barbara] or in the wilderness where father would take us on long pack trips into the heart of the Canadian Rockies in the summer."

"Even on the trail," she continued, "when George wasn't fishing or hunting, he was drawing with father. Father was a gentle and patient teacher."

Because of his dyslexia, George had struggled with academic work. He was, furthermore, in his sister's words, "always a live wire and a mischief maker in school." When he was a little boy in the school in Banff, the headmistress reported, "He is often 'not there' unless kept up to scratch, but I find that he seldom wastes his time. His mind goes on private exploring expeditions." One of George's teachers at his school in Santa Barbara some years later wrote, "George resisted formal education with greater ferocity than any student I have ever had."

When he was fifteen and in the eighth grade, George expressed a desire to quit school in order to devote his full time to the study of drawing and painting. Incredible as it may seem, his parents granted this request, and George began a rigorous apprenticeship at home with his father as the master. "If you want to paint, then paint you shall," Belmore is quoted as saying at the time, and he set George to work eight hours a day, six days a week. Evelyn Browne, several decades later, wrote, "I always remember George's telling me one night in Seebe, 'Ev, I'll never forget father when he told me he was taking me out of school and sending me to art school. He looked at me and said, "Now this is your big chance, George, so make the best of it."' George added, 'You better believe I got the message.'"

The Brownes had by this time moved from their wilderness cabin in Alberta to the San Francisco Bay area for the winter months, returning to Canada each summer. George was enrolled in the California School of Fine Arts, where he received formal instruction for the next five years.

Recalling her brother's student days, Evelyn wrote, "He entered life class at a very early age and used to bring home spectacular drawings of voluptuous female models which shocked my mother and which father and George would sit and analyze as if his sensuous drawing was as interesting scientifically as a hairy rhino on the ceiling of the Lascaux caves." George was getting the benefit not only of the traditional training provided at his school but of the daily critiques of his work by his father, the teacher whose opinions he valued above all others.

George, to use his mother's term, "chaffed" at the confinement and the rigid demands of art school, and he protested that his father's teaching was far more valuable. His father, however, insisted that the boy submit

 RIGHT AND OPPOSITE: *Belmore painting background of Alaskan brown bear exhibit, American Museum of Natural History, 1938*

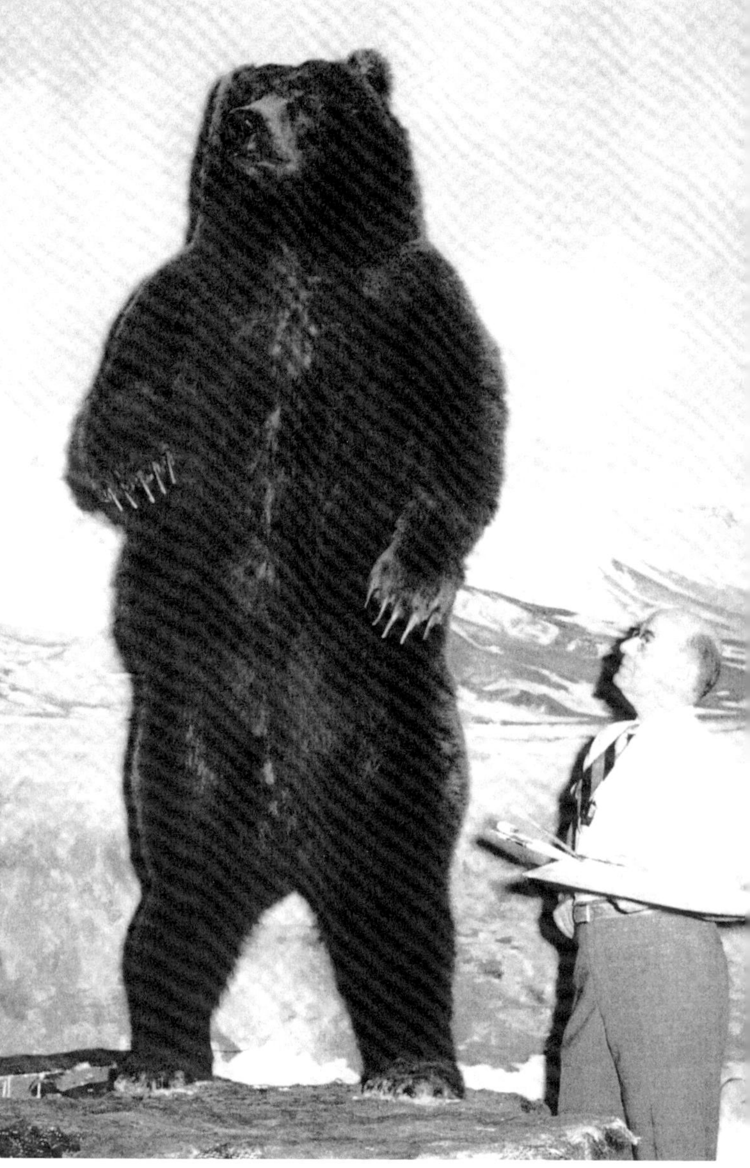

himself to the same discipline of formal instruction that he had received in New York and Paris.

Reflecting on a decision that had made her very anxious, but one in which she typically deferred to her husband, Agnes wrote:

> *I am frank to say that it was with many misgivings that George stopped school when he did. I believe now that Belmore had the longer view and certainly George owes everything to the vision and faith as well as the assured belief that the decision he made for George was justified in what he sees of his possibilities as an artist.*

In 1933, while serving as director of the Santa Barbara School of Art, Belmore was offered an assignment for which he was uniquely qualified, the commission to paint the diorama backgrounds for the display of pronghorn antelope and grizzly bear at the Santa Barbara Museum of Natural History. Other artists would have had to rely on photographs or brief visits to the animals' habitat to be able to paint the appropriate scenes, but Belmore had spent years exploring and hunting in the regions he was to paint, and he had been a painter of wilderness landscapes for three decades. Knowing the big game animals as only an experienced hunter could, he would be sure to fashion an appropriate background for each specimen. He painted the large Santa Barbara dioramas—approximately thirteen by twenty-two feet—on closely woven canvas that was attached to a curved wall of plaster held by mesh to a wood frame. Each diorama took about three months to complete. His choice of materials has proven to be appropriate, for a recent conservator's survey of these paintings found them to be in perfect condition.

Belmore's most famous dioramas are those in the North American Mammals Hall of the American Museum of Natural History in New York, which he started to work on in the early 1940's. In addition to two paintings of extinct pre-historic mammals that flank the entrance to the hall, Belmore painted the backgrounds for the displays of bighorn sheep, Grant's caribou, Dall sheep, Alaskan brown bear, Osborn caribou and mountain goat.

Although the museum's records list George Browne along with his father as the painter of only one of the dioramas—the Osborn caribou—he actually served as Belmore's apprentice on most, if not all, of the pre-war works. He also joined his father at the AMNH for several weeks in January 1943, when he was on leave from the army. George painted many of the small animals and birds in the dioramas, and he carved and painted the salmon in the foreground of the Alaskan brown bear display.

These collaborative projects were, in the opinion of George's wife, Tibby, a significant event in her husband's development as an artist. "George's tremendous interest

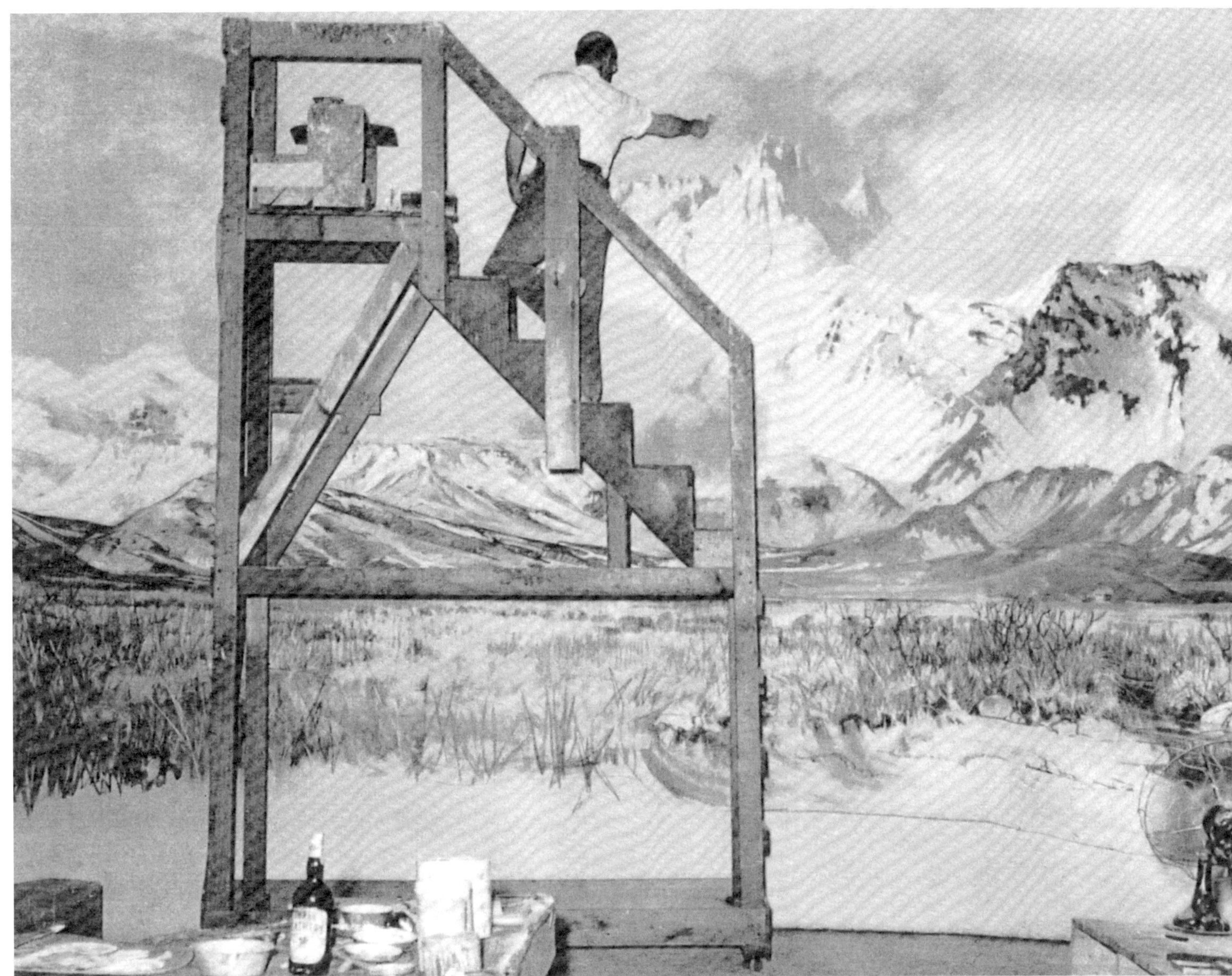

and self-taught knowledge of birds and wildlife contributed greatly to his fascination with this work," she wrote, "but the seeds were being sown for his eventual far more deep and abiding interest in painting pictures."

Of the first six months that George assisted his father with AMNH dioramas, the winter of 1941–42, his mother wrote:

> *George had a tremendously developing winter. He not only did a good job and was a real help to Belmore, but he met the fine types of men that were connected with the Museum, and it proved a real education for him. He had led a rather different life from the average American boy; perhaps he was none the worse for it either, but this was giving him a picture of the life in a big city and what it was all about. It taught him what was to be done to make a go of the life of naturalist painter, etc. and I saw a great development as the winter wore on. The work Belmore and George did speaks for itself. The big Alaskan brown bear with the Alaskan Range in the background is superb—and the caribou group, and finally*

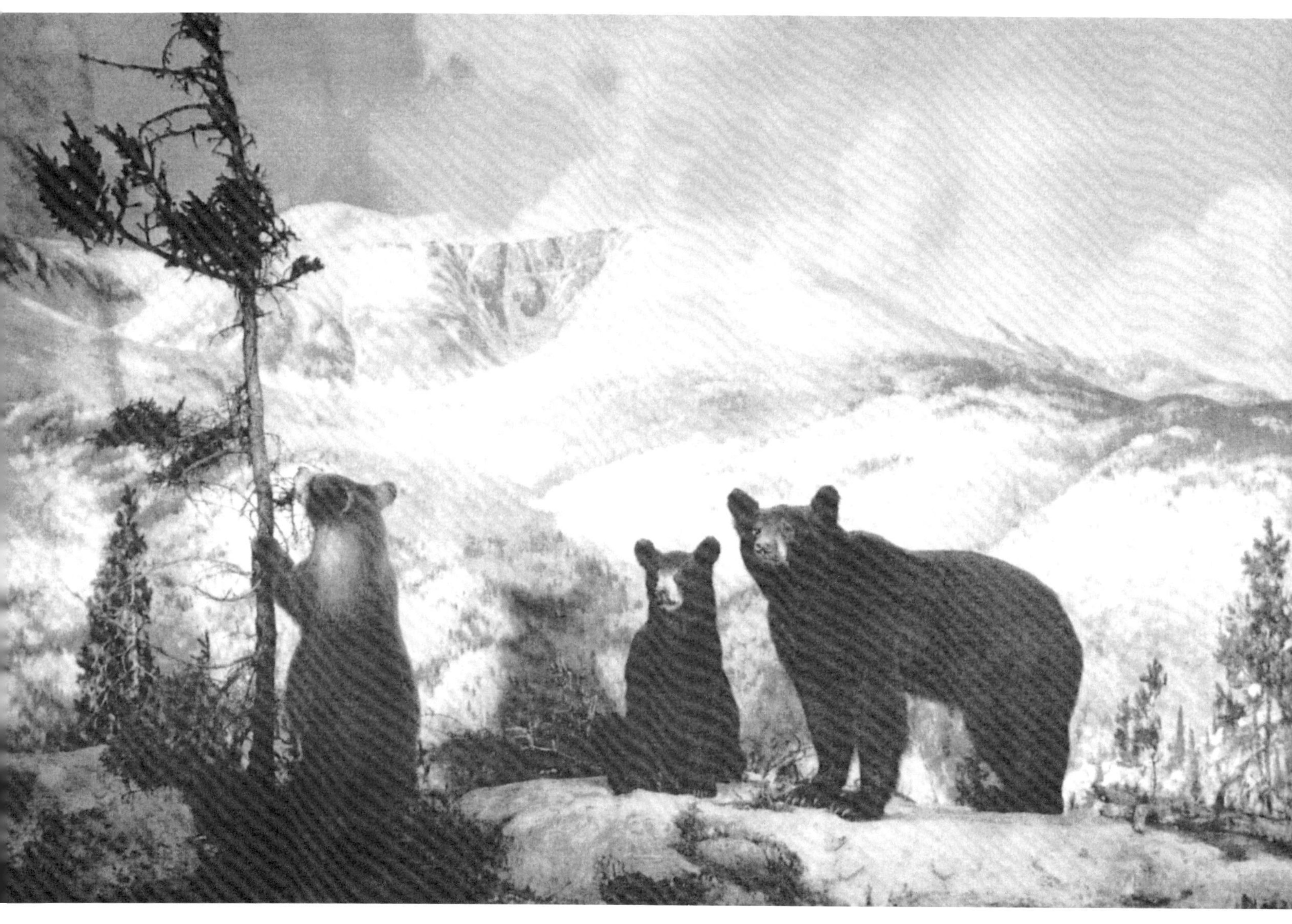

Belmore's background, black bear diorama, Boston Museum of Science

> *the white sheep of Alaska and Mount McKinley in the background. All can be proud of their winter work.*

The splendid work he had done at the American Museum of Natural History established Belmore as the foremost painter of dioramas, and in 1948 he was hired to paint the landscape background for a diorama featuring African water buffalo and lion for the California Academy of Sciences. In 1953, his friend Bradford Washburn, who was the director of the Boston Museum of Science, asked Belmore to paint a New England mountain background for the display of a family of black bear. In preparation for this work, Belmore spent several weeks sketching in the White Mountains. His painting shows Mount Washington capped with snow with the lower slopes in autumn foliage. Speaking of Belmore's work, Washburn said, "He had a wonderful capacity for painting brilliant, vibrant mountain landscapes—he had the feel of the wilderness—a marvelous sportsman, a terrific outdoor man—we're proud to have at the museum the last work he did, work done especially for us." When he had finished the diorama for

Washburn's museum, Belmore accepted the assignment to paint the landscape background for an Alaskan brown bear display at Yale. He had just begun this project when he died on May 2, 1954.

When the first stage of the work on the dioramas at the American Museum of Natural History was completed in 1942, the Brownes returned to California; and George, for the time being, took up again the daily work routine that he had followed for the past several years. As America had entered World War II, however, Belmore and George both looked for ways in which they could serve. Belmore, because of his vast experience as a wilderness explorer, became a civilian consultant for the army—testing equipment, writing and illustrating training manuals and teaching survival techniques. He also worked in Canada with the Lovat Scouts, a Scottish regiment that subsequently distinguished themselves in combat in Europe.

George tried to enlist in the Royal Canadian Air Force and in the American services; however, the fact that he had limited vision in his left eye—the consequence of the accident when was ten*—caused him to be rejected on each try. Ironically, he was then drafted into the army, and he served until the end of the war in the Army Air Corps.

George was assigned to a unit that tested survival equipment for aircrews forced to bail out of crippled planes. He was the first person to survive a parachute jump from over 40,000 feet after several others had frozen to death in the attempt. He volunteered for the experiment and succeeded by employing a technique that he himself had conceived—delaying the opening of the chute and free falling through the freezing upper atmosphere.

"I get a lot of fun and personal satisfaction out of jumping, a really great thrill and a privilege," he wrote his parents, "truly the best fun I've had in the Army." In another test George survived three weeks without food or water adrift in a small inflated life raft in the Gulf of Mexico.

In July 1945, Tech. Sgt. George Browne served as technical advisor for a training film on the airborne life raft he had tested. He so impressed some MGM professionals that he was offered a job as a technical director on a movie based on a Nordoff and Hall adventure novel. It must have been an intriguing offer; however, "nothing," he wrote his parents, "will prevent me from the life of a mountain painter."

George did not have much free time to devote to painting during his army years, but he made good use of his free Sundays, concentrating on improving his technique in painting skies and water. His letters home are filled with references to his painting.

"I can no longer continue life without a paint brush in my hand," he wrote shortly after his induction, "and when I get paid . . . I will go into town and purchase a small oil paint kit. Then when Sunday rolls around, I will rise at dark and go out and get some duck skies for future reference and to keep in practice. I will also get some sketches of water with both lakes and streams with reflections of trees, grass and mud banks."

"The dead grass and autumn trees," he continued, "will provide me with valuable sketches for bird pictures, and after the war I will be as good and probably better as a painter than if I just let it go. I always was weak on skies and landscape."

George often sent paintings home for his father to critique. "I am sending you these pictures with the idea that Ba will give me a criticism on them. Ba has been much too easy on me all these years, and for my own good, I want him to criticize these sketches as one artist to another."

"I know the criticism will be severe," he concluded, "but that is the way I want it."

In a subsequent letter, he wrote, "I am really getting back in line now, and in most respects my landscapes are better than they ever were . . . I am learning a lot from my Sunday painting, and it means a lot to me." In another letter to his parents he wrote, "Painting is my biggest form of recreation and takes all my days off. For the first time I am beginning to know a little about water and reflections. I have been painting a lot along the river and the lake, and this practice is just as valuable to me as painting in the Rocky Mountains, but not so much fun."

"I feel I'm the luckiest person in the world," he wrote, "because . . . as long as I can scrape together a few paints and have two legs to get into the mountains, I can ask for nothing else."

The painting that George did during his first months in the army not only gave him pleasure but increased his

** There are two accounts of this accident. According to one, George was struck in the eye while climbing a tree by a pellet from the shotgun of a careless quail hunter. George is reported to have told a friend, however, that he was wounded by the ricochet of a shot he himself had fired.*

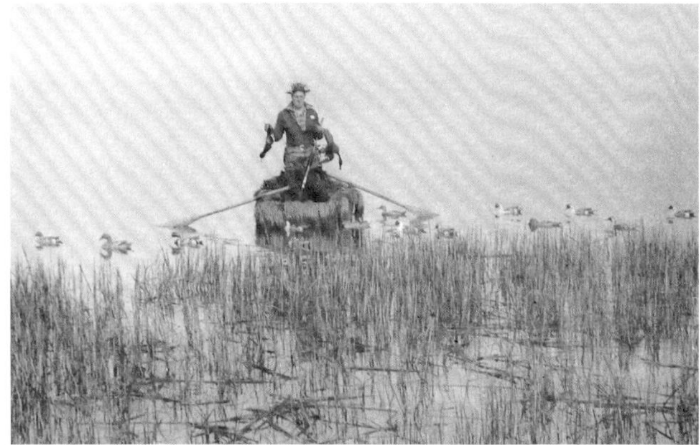

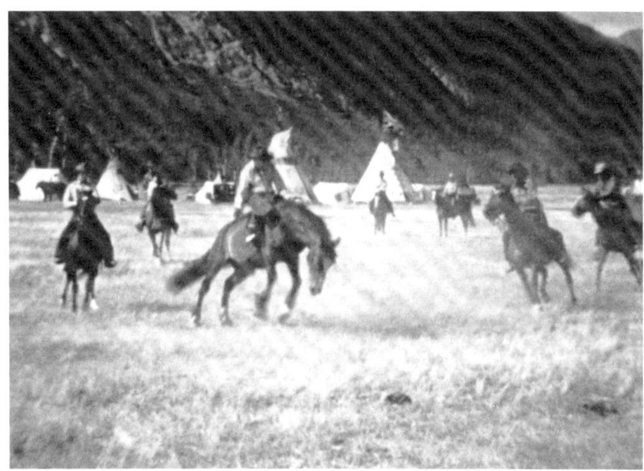

TOP: *George setting decoys*

ABOVE: *George riding a bronc*

commitment to his chosen profession. He wrote his mother:

> *The thing that makes me most happy is my growing desire and determination to paint. This has been greatly stimulated by my Sundays' painting. Although my work will never equal Ba's, I believe I will gain an individuality and originality found in the work of men who are inspired by their subject rather than by themselves.*

George was able to do some hunting during his military service. One anecdote he related to his parents gives an idea of just how bold, self-reliant and physically capable he was:

> *I will now tell you about the most wonderful experience that ever happened to me in the way of waterfowling. It was a calm morning, but very dark, and I was putting out my decoys, without even any star light. I was about a mile and a half off shore over about 15 feet of water. I had untied my gun and moved it to one side and was tossing out decoys; a half hitch got in the gun some way in the dark and over went my gun. At once I got my clothes off and remembering which decoy I had last thrown out, I dove in and guided myself down the decoy line, being careful not to raise the decoy anchor. I made seven dives and could not find it anywhere. Then I realized that it must be sunken in the mud. On the eighth dive I was digging in the mud, and about a foot in the mud I felt it and recovered it. What a relief it was! And what luck recovering it in the darkness.*

Clearly luck alone did not account for the recovery of the shotgun. Physical strength and toughness and stamina, courage and perseverance and daring—qualities that he had both inherited and developed—were all required. Few men would have attempted to recover the gun under such difficult circumstances; fewer still could have succeeded. George Browne was obviously an exceptional man.

A great friend of George Browne's, Stanleigh Arnold, has written of his ethical sense and sportsmanship:

> *He was, physically, a very tough man and one who loved to meet challenges. He was an excellent hunter and killed a lot of sub-arctic big game—elk, moose, bighorn sheep, mountain goats. He was brought up in the school that taught one never to leave a crippled animal to die alone, that one must do everything possible to hunt it down and give it as speedy a death as possible. Once, I know, he crippled a duck on the west shore of San Francisco Bay and chased it, rowing all the way across to the east shore, perhaps five miles, dispatched the bird and rowed all the way back. One way or the other, he had to be bucking the bay's swift tides.*

George was also an exceptional rider. A rancher for whom he had worked in Canada wrote this recommendation: "George Browne has for the past eight years spent each summer on my ranch breaking and gentling colts to the saddle. He is an exceptionally good man for the job and consistently turns out fine saddle horses." George also rode occasionally in rodeos, bronco riding being a sport that appealed to his risk-taking nature.

Although he found his work during World War II in developing survival equipment to be interesting and worthwhile, he was eager to get on with his career. "Boy, is the paint going to fly after the war is over," he wrote his parents, and as soon as George received his discharge, he immediately took up his palette and returned to his easel.

Commenting on the progress George was making with his painting after his discharge, as well as on the pleasure he and his father were deriving from water fowling, Agnes wrote:

> *About Nov. 1st [1947] saw them home once more and ready to tackle some duck shooting with the painting for George. They had a marvelous season's shooting. Almost every day they went out—they went out three mornings a week—they got their limit and then began George's intensive work on getting them on a canvas. He made many sketches and laid in 4 canvasses, his first real pictures in the sense they were composed and arranged. Belmore was hard at work writing in the evenings to finish ten chapters for the new Boy Scout manual on tents, camping and hunting. In the day time he was working on three big canvasses to take to the Grand Central Galleries—a pretty steady grind—but lovely pictures were being produced. George was developing fast—the grouse picture, a beauty—the groups of pintails on the marshes in the early morning. The blue bills around his decoys. And he often worked into the late hours by electric light.*

Remembering this period of George's life, Stanleigh Arnold wrote:

> *His father, Belmore, and he would go on long summer expeditions into northern Canada making detailed sketches with extensive color notes. In the winters, here in Marin County's town of Ross, they would set up their easels in the attic and create wildlife paintings using the sketches to form backdrops. Beside each painter's chair was a redwood block. When either tired of painting, he would work on his block, turning it into a decoy. The Browne decoys, of which I have a pair of canvasbacks, were—are—some of the finest working decoys ever carved. These decoys they used on the bay, along with duck boats which they used in what I believe to be a unique way, lying in the bow with a canvas sheet, laced with rushes, pulled up to the chin, like a blanket. A short length of broomstick was attached to the end of the canvas so that the hunter could flip the camouflage aside quickly.*

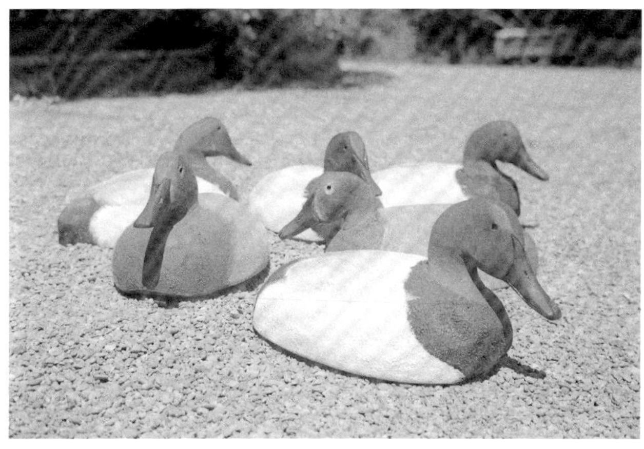

Decoys carved by George

George's painting did not always go well. Of one period of discouragement during a summer in the mid-1940's in Alberta his mother wrote:

> *George is having a tough time just at this point. He is attempting mountain landscapes to be used as backgrounds for his wildlife and big game pictures. His ducks have gone so easily and it is something of a challenge to attempt something entirely new in a way. He and Belmore sat up late last night talking and going over the whole thing. It takes a lot of character not to get discouraged at times, but today he went off to tackle a fish down by the river and he went with a look in his eye of, "I'll make it this time."*

At the invitation of Bradford Washburn, an accomplished mountaineer and a friend of Belmore's, George

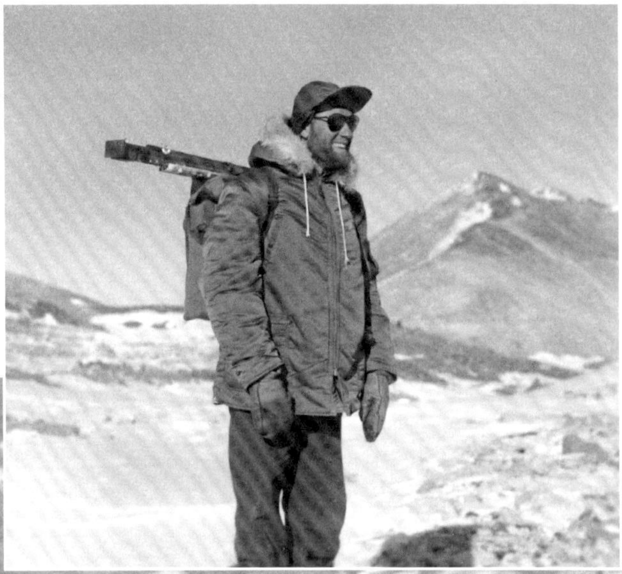

LEFT: *George climbing Mount McKinley—18,500 feet.*

BELOW: *George painting on Mount McKinley, 1947.*

spent the summer of 1947 as a member of a party Washburn led to the summit of Mount McKinley. In an article on the expedition, Washburn identified George as "a young veteran of a lifetime spent as a wilderness artist and outdoor man."

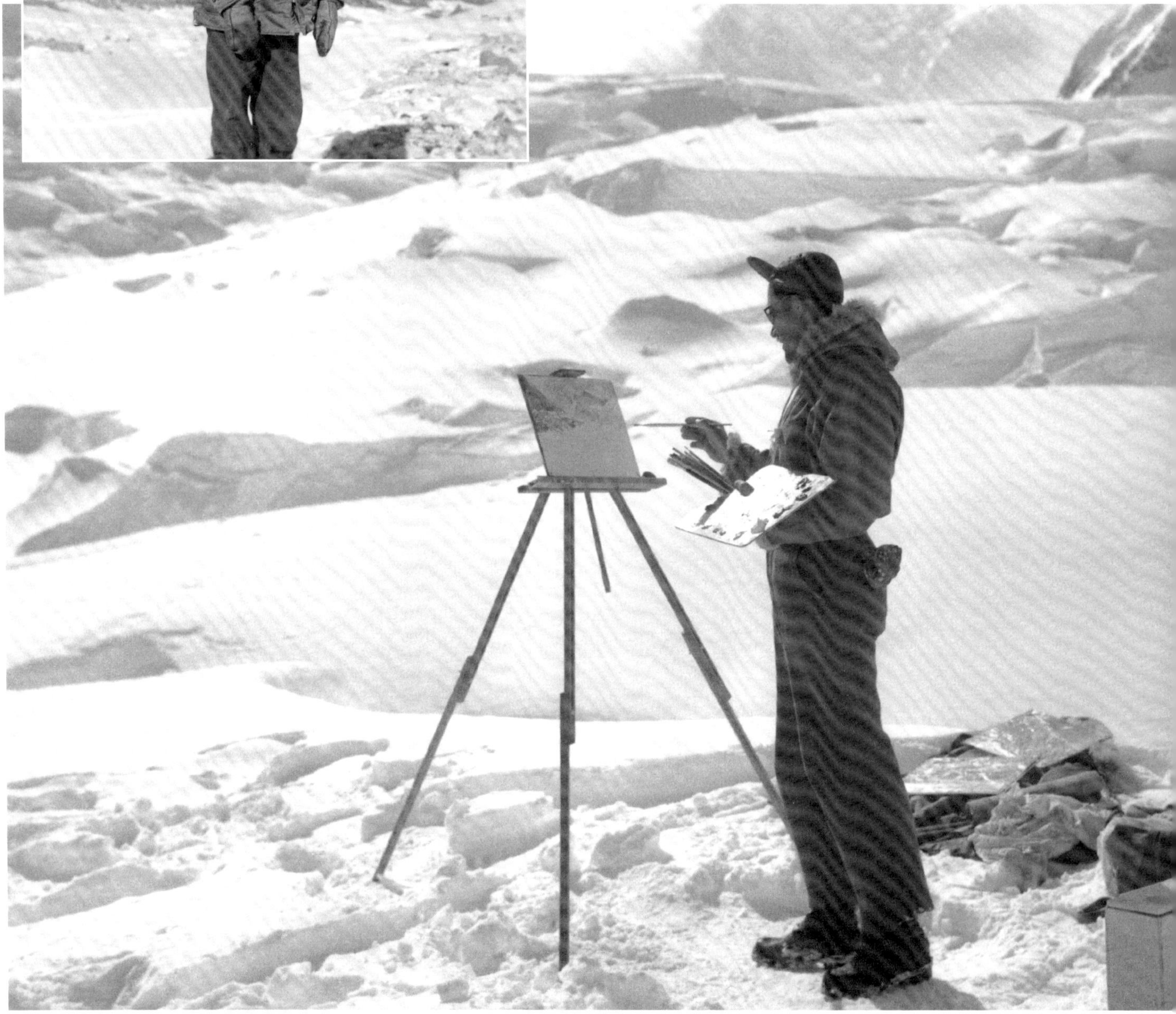

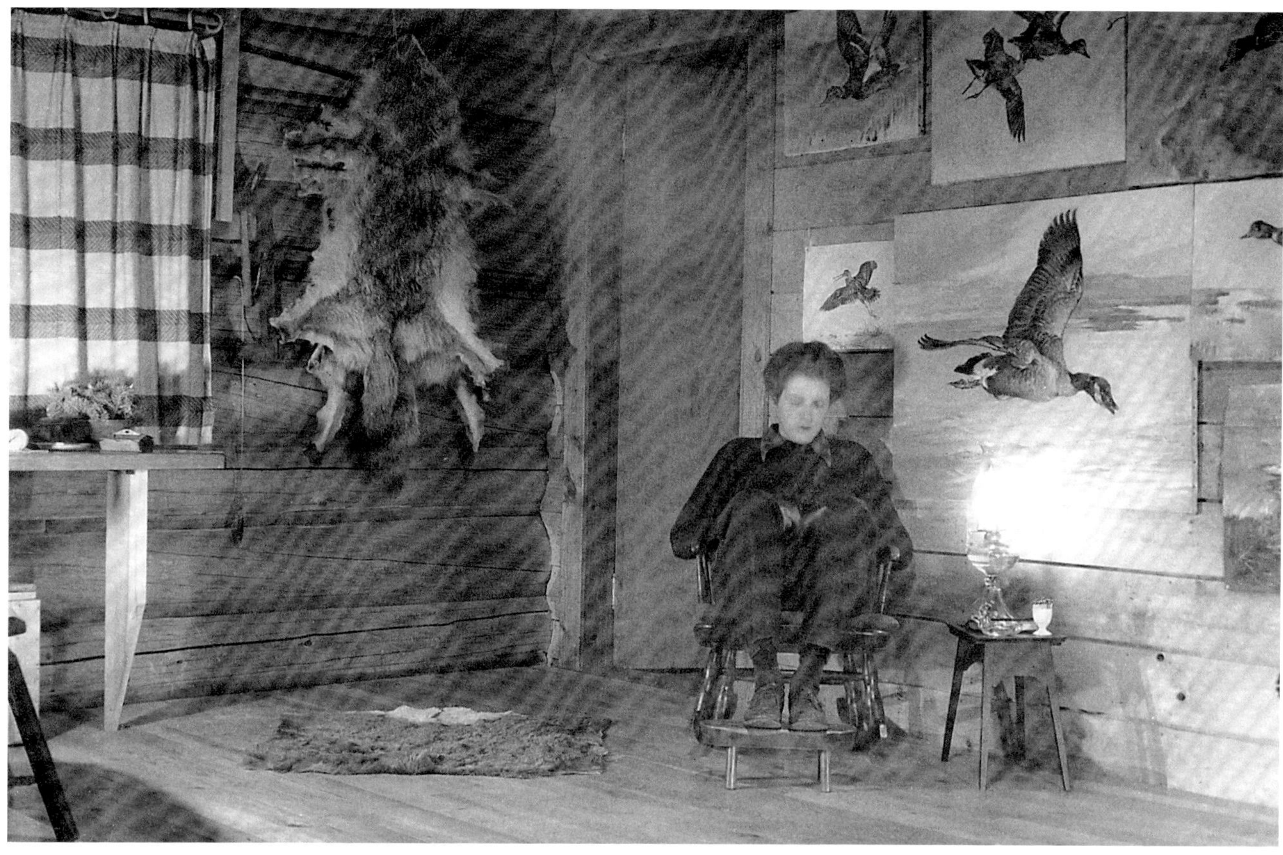

Tibby in George's studio at Seebe, Alberta, ca. 1948.

"You never needed to assign him a load or to check to see how much he was carrying—unless you had to make sure that he wasn't carrying too much to be safe."

George served as the expedition's artist, and he was able to sell several of the oils he painted on the slopes of the mountain. Among the pictures George painted on the McKinley expedition is a landscape featuring Browne Tower, the spur named in his father's honor. The fact that he had been able to reach the summit of his father's mountain was no doubt a source of great pride and satisfaction to both George and Belmore.

Shortly after his discharge from the army in early 1946, George met and fell in love with a beautiful young woman, Isabel MacGregor, known as Tibby, who, at the age of eighteen, was ten years his junior. It took two years for George to persuade Tibby to marry him; however, in April 1948, they wed and set up housekeeping in a cabin of three rooms that George's parents had built for them in Seebe, Alberta, between Calgary and Banff in the Canadian Rockies. Tibby, a most remarkable woman, was able to make the adjustment from a comfortable home with all the modern conveniences in a suburb of San Francisco to a wilderness cabin not only with ease but with joy. With her encouragement and support, George devoted himself with discipline and dedication to developing his talent; and at first gradually, and then with remarkable rapidity over the next decade, he managed to acquire a following and a reputation as one of America's foremost sporting artists.

Chapter~Four~

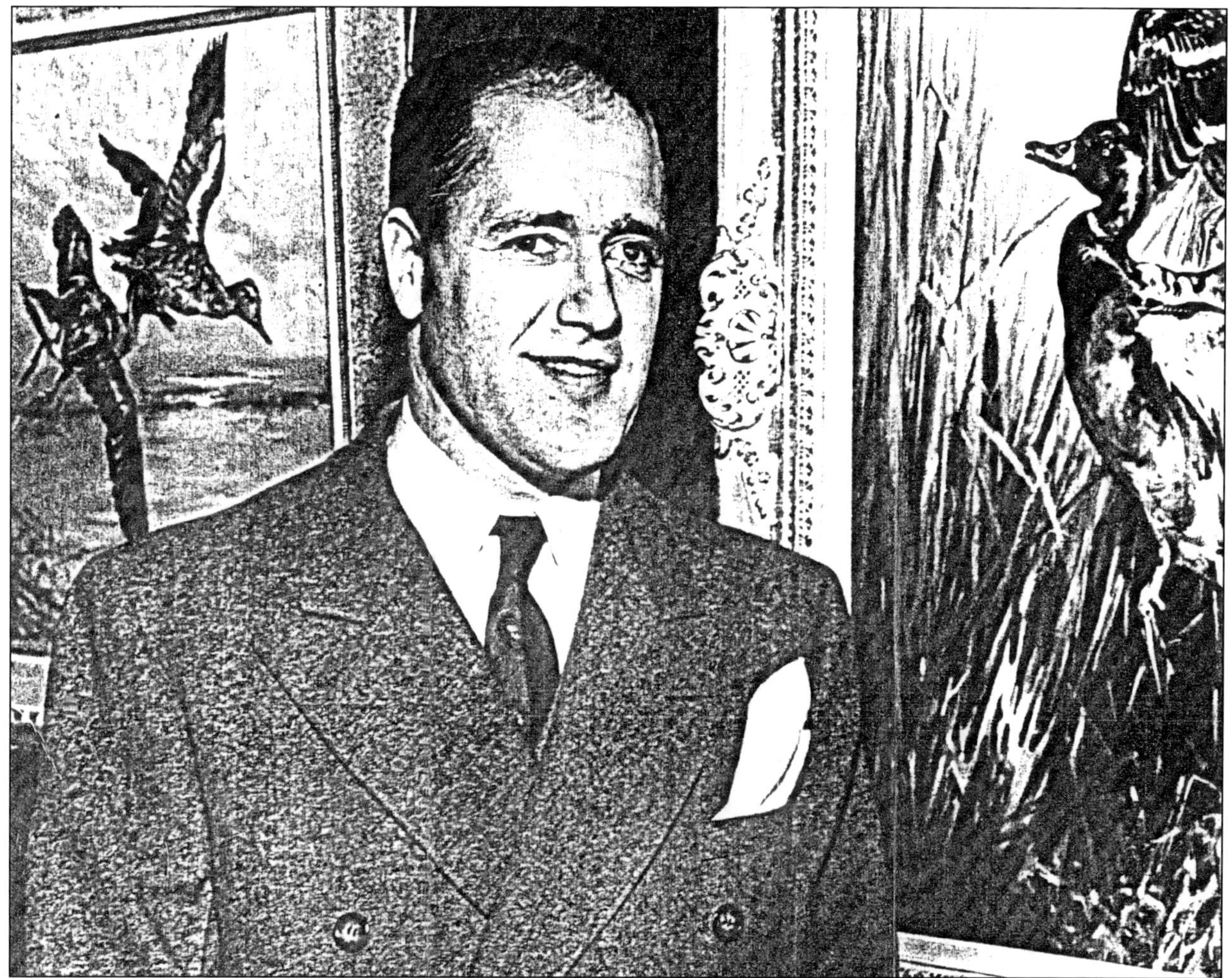

GEORGE BROWNE

THE ASCENDING STAR

The Brownes lived in Seebe, Alberta, for the next seven years, generally driving to California or Connecticut to spend three or four winter months with George's parents. Their daughter Isabel was born in Alberta in 1951, and their son Belmore in Connecticut in 1953. George's principal dealer and his eastern friends and patrons in time persuaded him that he should be living near New York, the center of the sporting art business. Furthermore, as the demand for his paintings was primarily for pictures of upland game birds and waterfowl,

George at Grand Central Galleries show, 1950

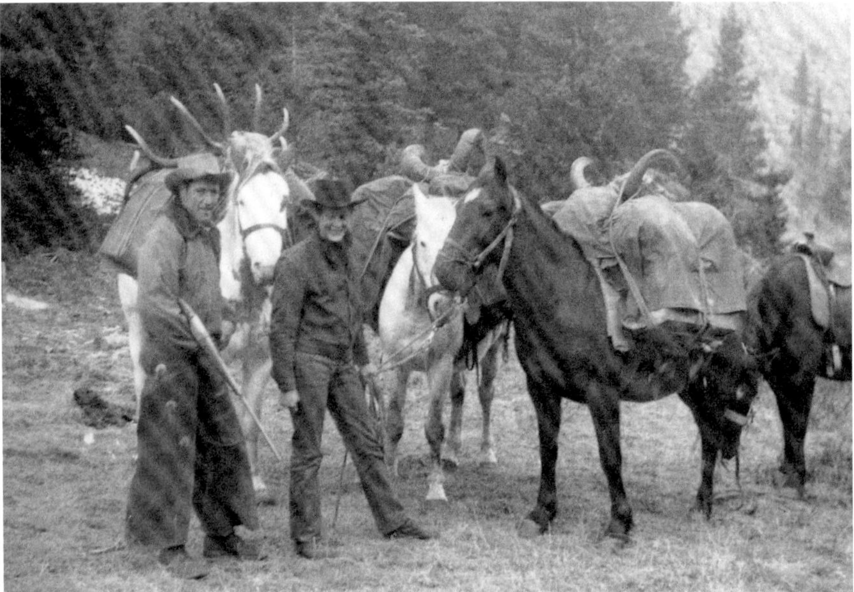

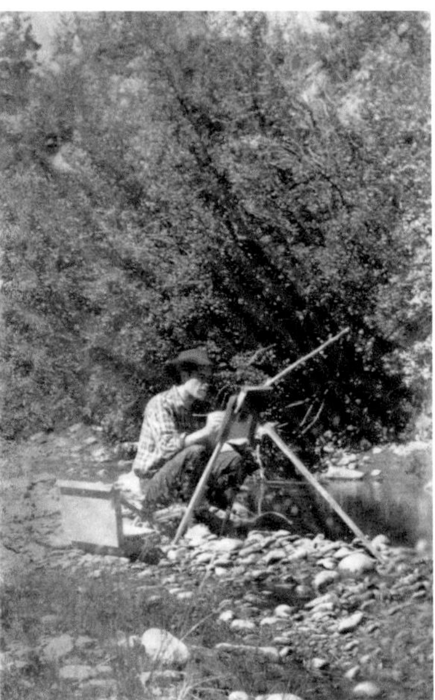

LEFT: *George and Tibby with pack horses*

RIGHT: *George painting*

it made sense for him to live in the East rather than in the mountains of Canada.

In 1955, George and Tibby decided to give up the house in Seebe. They accepted a friend's offer of the use of a house in Norfolk, in the northwest corner of Connecticut; and in 1956 they purchased land in Norfolk and began construction of a home of their own. They returned to Alberta to sell the Seebe house that summer, and the following spring they moved into their new home.

"Painting and hard work continued to be the order of the day," Tibby recalled of this period, "though with furnace, electric light, water and other civilized amenities, the physical labor of running a house eased tremendously."

"I can well remember the joy of not having to anticipate the commute across the Continent in the spring and fall," she wrote, "and our first year in Norfolk indicated from every standpoint the wisdom of George's determination to live in the East." Without what she referred to as "the pressure of the necessity of continual moves"—drives of several thousand miles twice a year with two infants—Tibby could enjoy the comfort of the "civilized amenities" and George had uninterrupted time to paint.

Tom Davis, in his *Sporting Classics* article, presented several interesting observations on the effects of the move east on George's work.

> *He was delighted to discover that the increased humidity—"atmosphere" to painters—of the East allowed far greater subtleties of mood and interpretation than the often harsh light of the Western plains and mountains. Almost daily his work grew stronger, richer, more poetic. Not only did he have the gift for breathing life into his birds and mammals, he knew how to arrange them in a composition for maximum dramatic effect. Few artists have been better at creating the illusion of space, of three dimensionality; perhaps it was because Browne's own lack of depth perception, a function of his monocular vision, forced him to pay extra attention to perspective.*

Davis described the effect of a George Browne oil painting as being "potent and evocative and moving. . . . You feel yourself being drawn into the painting's world."

George had been trained in art school to paint in watercolors as well as oils; however, he worked professionally exclusively in oil, the medium that better suited his meticulous style and enabled him to develop a picture over a period of days or even weeks. The advantage of oil is its adaptability. The artist can scrape out what he does not like and repaint or wipe the canvas clean and start again.

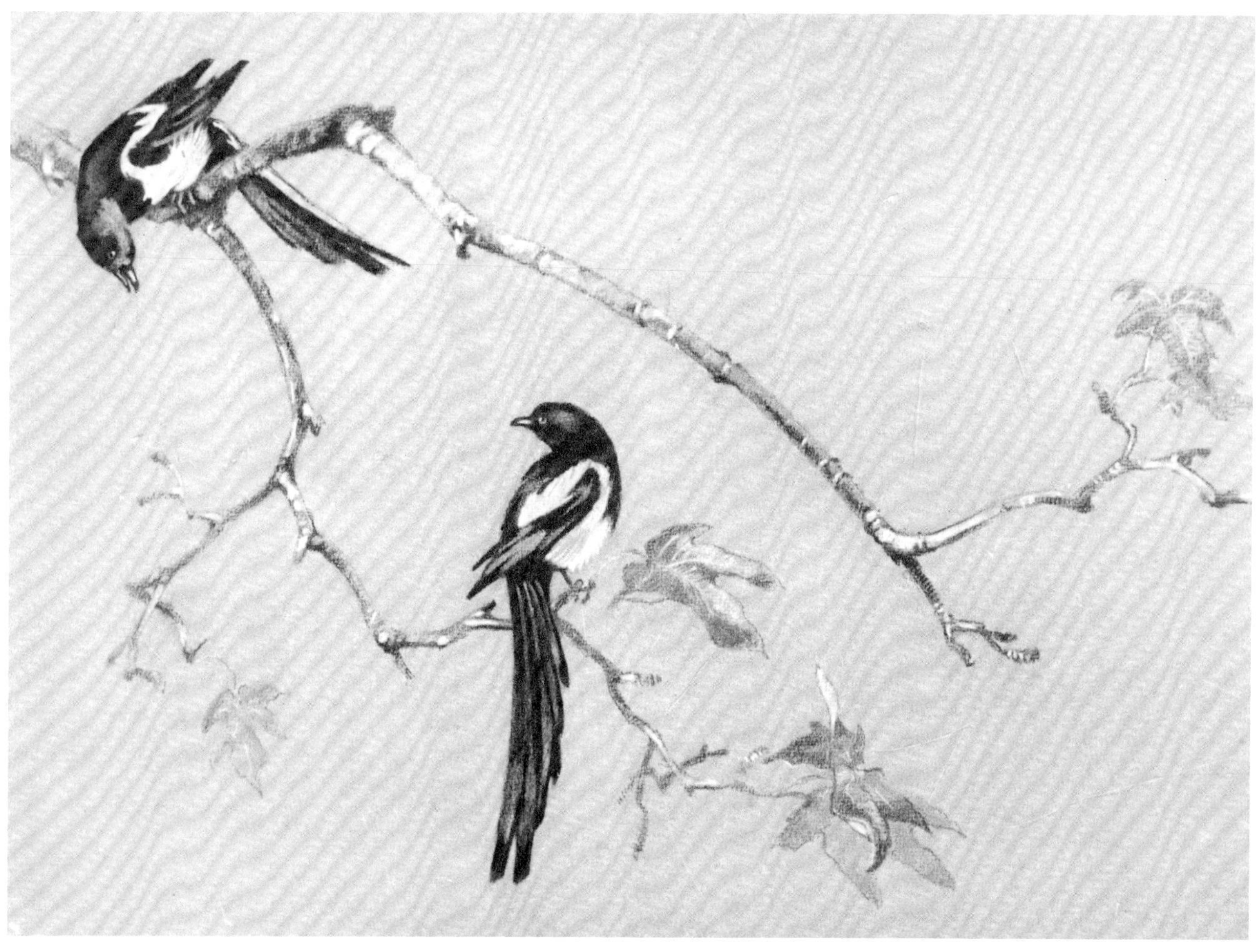

Magpies—original sketch for gold screen, ca. 1938, George's first commission

Although he had decided at a very young age that he would be a painter like his father, George's professional career spanned little more than a single decade, from 1947 until his death in 1958. He had sold a dozen or so paintings for $10 to $50 in the years prior to his military service, and he sold three pictures—two for $25 and one for $45—through a New York dealer during his army years. In the year and a half immediately after his return to civilian life, he sold only five paintings for a total of $235. In 1947, however, the Grand Central Art Galleries, a New York firm that had been handling his father's work, agreed to exhibit George's paintings. Grand Central sold two of his oils in 1947, one for $300 and one for $450. Four more were sold in the following year, the largest for $650; and in 1949 another four were sold, one of which brought $750.

George was committed to a career as an artist but very concerned about having sufficient income to provide for his young family. He wrote his father in early 1949, "1948 was a poor year for me. I only averaged $100 a month, but according to my figuring, which has been checked and rechecked and based on the most pessimistic factual data of past production and increase thereof, I should at least, everything being equal, double that figure of $100 a month to $200 in 1949."

George Browne was apparently considered to be a rising star, and the Grand Central Art Galleries demonstrated interest and support by giving him a one-man show of twenty-seven paintings in February 1950. The catalogue for George's exhibition made this statement: "It is the artist's belief that it is possible to reproduce on canvas an impression so vivid and artistic that the observer

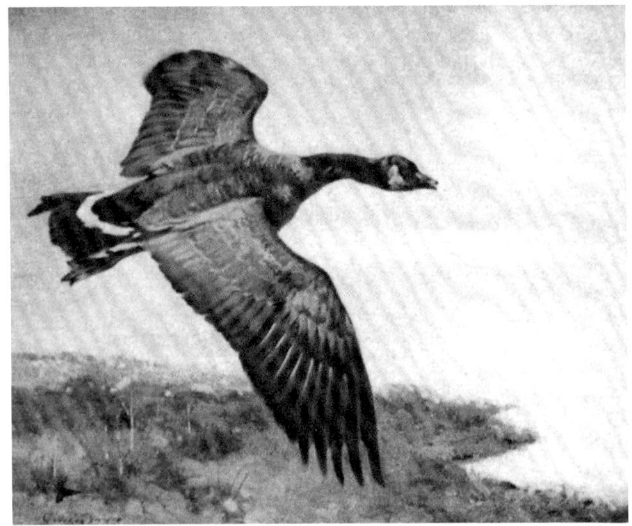

"GAME BIRDS"
Exhibition of Paintings by
GEORGE BROWNE

February 14—February 25, 1950

Grand Central Art Galleries, Inc.
15 Vanderbilt Avenue New York City

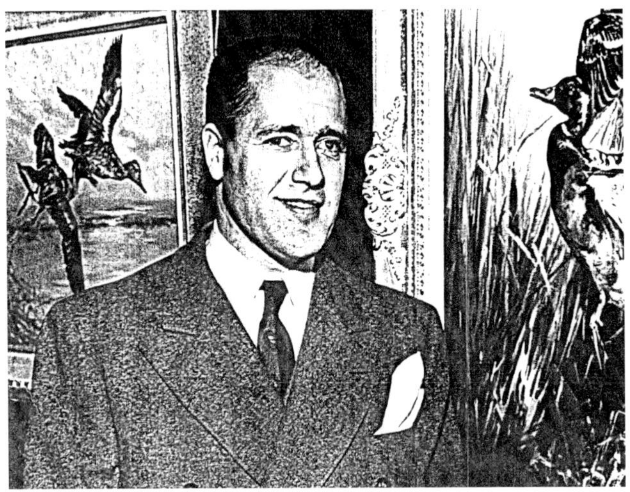

LEFT TOP: *Grand Central Galleries show catalogue 1950—front cover*

LEFT BOTTOM: *George at Grand Central Galleries show, 1950, in front of* Startled Mallards *(Plate 14)*

may feel himself a part of the scene." This exhibition was a significant event in his career, for it established George's reputation and a demand for his work. Grand Central sold sixteen Browne oils, including one for which the Texaco Company paid $800 for reproduction rights. In all, he sold twenty-two pictures with retail prices totaling $5,840 in 1950.

Although he was grateful to Edwin Barrie and George Nelson at the Grand Central Art Galleries for their efforts in promoting his work, George decided that he would benefit from having his works offered by a gallery that specialized in sporting art and had a national clientele. James Jeffery, the managing director of the Sporting Gallery and Bookshop, was interested in handling his paintings, but apparently Barrie at Grand Central objected to the artist's being represented by another New York gallery. Jeffery wrote George in April 1950: "I am, of course, very disappointed, and I cannot understand the attitude of Grand Central Art Galleries. I can only see that it is not quite fair to you, for a gallery such as ours gives a sporting artist a year round display and continually brings to the notice of sportsmen the work of sporting artists." He might also have mentioned the fact that the Sporting Gallery and Bookshop's catalogue would have brought George's work to the attention of many people interested in sporting art who lived outside the New York area.

Apparently Barrie had no objection to George's being represented by an out-of-town gallery, for when the Vose Galleries in Boston expressed an interest, George sent them several oils. Two small paintings were sold in 1950, and Vose agreed to give him an exhibition in the fall of 1951. This show, however, was not a success; none of the paintings were sold. The following year, having decided that his works were more likely to sell in New York, George asked Vose to return the unsold pictures. Morton Vose, the galleries' director, wrote: "Of course, your decision to use these paintings elsewhere is not unexpected, and entirely reasonable. You are good to speak so appreciatively of our efforts in your behalf, which, although they have been genuine, have had small results indeed. Naturally, that is a matter of real regret to me."

Without the benefit of an exhibition, George's sales dropped substantially in 1951, and his income was less than $4,000. The Grand Central Art Galleries sold only three of his pictures, although they held more than a dozen in inventory. When he realized that Grand Central could not sell enough of his paintings to provide him with the income he needed, George approached Ralph Terrill at the Crossroads of Sport early in 1952, sending him photographs of some of his paintings and asking whether Crossroads would handle his work. Terrill responded promptly and eagerly. He said that George had been recommended to him by Carl Rungius, the renowned painter of North American big game animals and a neighbor of the Brownes in Alberta, who was represented in New York by Terrill's gallery. "I should be very glad indeed," he wrote, "to have examples of your work here for exhibition and sale."

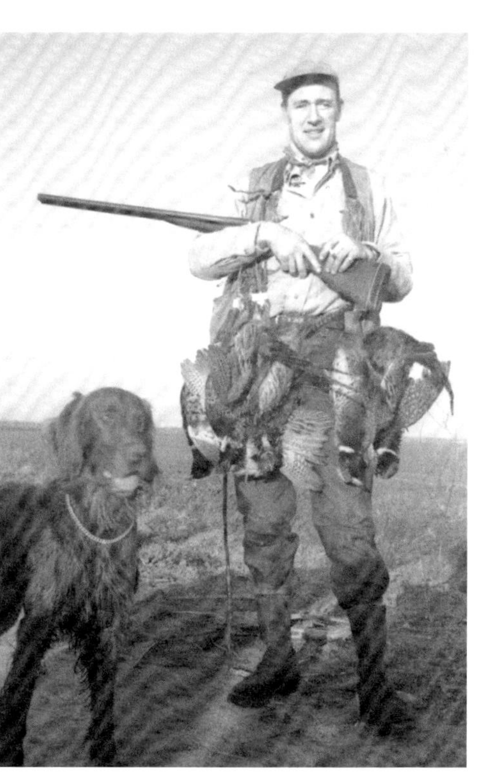

George with "Kelly"

Thus began an association that would prove to be vital to the making of George Browne's career, for from early 1952 until his death six years later, half of the paintings he produced were sold through the Crossroads of Sport.

Terrill, furthermore, took a personal interest in George's development as an artist, advising him about the sort of pictures that would sell most readily and introducing him to men who would invite him to visit parts of the country he did not know—Chesapeake Bay, Georgia and the Carolinas in particular. George was, therefore, able to paint pictures that appealed to a broader range of Terrill's clients.

In March 1952, Terrill wrote to George, who was then still living in Alberta:

> *Our chief calls in paintings here are for those which have more or less an eastern background around the bird subject matter. People seem to like to buy something which reminds them of their favorite shooting terrain, when they can, and I think it is very important, as you suggested in your letter, that when the shooting season opens next autumn, you make a trip east and avail yourself of some of the invitations for shooting which will come your way, simply to familiarize yourself with our eastern background. Don't worry about the quail, dove and turkey things. They will come in due time, and if possible I will try to arrange, while you are east, for you to get down to Georgia in the heart of quail, turkey and dove country, to do a little shooting and sketching, and I think this can be done.*

In another letter Terrill gave George additional practical advice: "Generally speaking, we find that mixed flocks of ducks don't sell . . . and the best sellers, as far as species go are: 1) mallards, 2) pintails, 3) greenwinged teal, 4) Canada geese, with redheads, broadbill and bluewinged teal running about neck and neck." He also stated, "In the upland birds, quail, grouse, woodcock, dove and turkey outsell pheasants, even though statistics tell us that there are far more pheasant hunters than the others combined. I should like to have, as soon as possible, examples of the quail, dove and turkey subject matter."

Terrill also noted that "paintings up to 24″ x 30″ will outsell larger areas . . . and landscape style pictures outsell uprights." He concluded with the promise that he would "comment very freely" on George's work, "for I think I know my market and what will sell. In no sense of the word," Terrill wrote, "do I want to dictate the type of painting you do. I have simply tried to point out what, from my experience, has proved to be the most saleable." George no doubt appreciated Terrill's pragmatic approach to the marketing of sporting art.

With reference to a trip to the South that he was trying to set up for George in the fall of 1952, Terrill wrote:

I want you to see a flock of doves over a 'benney' field. They are really quite a sight, and I am certain that a visit with a sketching board and color in a turkey swamp will ultimately prove profitable.

Quail will probably outsell dove or turkey, but those who want dove or turkey things really want them, and I will do my best to hook you up in either Thomasville or Albany, Georgia, for a chance to see these birds in their nature haunts, if I can.

Terrill explained that Crossroads followed the standard practice of taking a commission of a third of the retail price established by the artist. He went on to say: "The only thing we can promise you is that your work will be readily available to any interested person, at any time, and that as far as our limited facilities give wall space, there will be at least one or two of your paintings on the walls here where they are easily visible at all times." In point of fact, Terrill did much more for George, for Crossroads' annual catalogue featured his paintings each year from 1952 on, thereby introducing his work to virtually every collector of sporting art throughout America.

The 1952 catalogue contained reproductions of three George Browne oils, priced from $275 to $450. The accompanying statement read: "It is a pleasure to show for the first time in this catalogue, the paintings of George Browne, from the Pacific Coast. He paints with vigor and sure touch, and we believe his work will find ready favor with sportsmen. You'll enjoy seeing his studies of upland birds and waterfowl." Terrill's prediction of George's work finding favor with sportsmen proved accurate. The first paintings offered sold quickly, and from that time on Terrill was continually asking him for more paintings than he could produce to meet the demands of Crossroads' customers.

In particular Terrill wanted pictures of upland game birds. "We have the waterfowl paintings of Dick Bishop, Francis L. Jaques, J. D. Knap, Harry Adamson and Eric Sloane on exhibition and sale at all times, and up to the present, we have been very successful in selling their work. In the field of upland bird painting there is, in my humble opinion, far less competition. We have only the upland bird paintings of Bill Schaldach and Lynn Hunt plus the shooting and fishing scene paintings of Ogden Pleissner. Pleissner, of course, does no bird pictures, as such, and I have always felt that there was ample room in the upland bird field for the man who could do outstanding work on grouse, woodcock, quail, dove, wild turkey and pheasant." Obviously he intended that George should be that man.

The fact that Terrill was putting George in the company of many of America's most well-known sporting artists must have been most gratifying to the young man, who was a newcomer in the field. He now had the confidence and support of Ralph Terrill, who, first as the head of Abercrombie and Fitch's art department and then as the founder and director of the Crossroads of Sport, had acquired the reputation of being America's foremost dealer in sporting art.

At Terrill's suggestion, the prices established for George's pictures were in line with the prices that had been placed on his works at the Grand Central Art Galleries—$300 to $550. George had initially suggested higher prices, but Terrill explained: "I am just as interested in obtaining the maximum price for your paintings as you are for, naturally, there is more nourishment in it for us. On the other hand, too drastic a jump, at one fell swoop, has in my experience, reacted unfavorably on the sale of an artist's work." He noted that over the years the prices on Ogden Pleissner's paintings had been raised by $50 or $75 a year and that the standard price had been doubled over a period of years without any "sales resistance." George's pictures were, therefore, priced to sell, and sell they did. The prices were raised gradually, and they were generally in the $600 to $750 range five years later, and the price of a large oil was $1,100 in 1957.

Four of George's oils were illustrated in Crossroads' 1953 catalogue with the statement: "George Browne's paintings of duck marsh and upland cover are increasingly in demand. He paints both with equal beauty. You'll enjoy seeing our collection of his work." The 1954 catalogue again reproduced four paintings; the text read, "George Browne's oils of upland cover and duck marsh reflect his keen enthusiasm for upland shooting and waterfowl gunning. Backgrounds and game are painted with skill and quiet beauty."

The statement in the 1955 catalogue read, "George Browne's oils of ducks and upland birds are painted with skill." By now George's paintings were being priced above those of all the other artists handled by Crossroads with the exception of Pleissner and Rungius, and his pictures had been moved to a position in the annual catalogue immediately after the works of those two long-established artists.

In 1956, the catalogue text stated: "These are by all odds the finest group of upland bird and waterfowl paintings George Browne has yet done. They are worth seeing." The following year's catalogue, the last to carry George's paintings, drew Terrill's patrons' attention to a painting of a big horn sheep. "This is the first oil of North American Big Game by George Browne we have ever illustrated. His work in this field shows the same touch as his waterfowl and upland bird paintings." George had painted a picture of mule deer commissioned by a Crossroads client earlier in the year, and it had impressed a number of Terrill's regular customers. Although Terrill was hesitant to introduce paintings of big game animals by another artist for fear of offending the venerable Carl Rungius, he wrote George that he was reasonably sure that Rungius, who had, after all, recommended George to Terrill, would not object to Crossroads' carrying an occasional painting of large Western mammals by him, though the subject had been Rungius's exclusively in past years. Terrill, therefore, encouraged George to paint a few pictures of large animals, assuming, perhaps, that he would eventually succeed Rungius in this area.

After establishing his relationship with Crossroads in 1952, George had gradually withdrawn from the Grand Central Art Galleries. He sent them no new pictures in 1952, but he did give them seventeen pictures in the next three years, only nine of which they were able to sell. Erwin Barrie had written him in 1953, stating, "I can't tell you how surprised and hurt I am to realize you have been here [living in the East] so long and haven't even been in to say hello." He went on to say, "Two or three people have told me in the last few days that your work is on sale at the Crossroads of Sports [*sic*]. We would not object to this if you were sending us good paintings also." George's works had been on display at the Crossroads gallery, a dozen or so blocks from Grand Central, for over a year, and they had been featured in the catalogue Terrill had issued four months before Barrie wrote to George.

In 1954 Barrie wrote: "We are all a little disappointed in your lack of close cooperation with the Galleries. I don't believe you are getting the full benefit from the Galleries that you might receive if you worked with us a little more actively. We all like you and your work and could sell much more of it if we had a greater variety of sizes and subjects." Perhaps it was this plea as well as appreciation of Barrie's having been an early sponsor of his work that prompted George to send Grand Central five pictures in 1954 and three in 1955. However, sales through Grand Central were slow, and Ralph Terrill was constantly pleading for more pictures.

"Keep the brushes flying. We can use everything you can send on," he wrote in 1954. "As you know, we are completely out of works of George Browne at this point . . . and I wonder if you can do anything to remedy the situation in the near future," he wrote in 1956. In 1955, George ended his association with Grand Central and had them return the works they had been unable to sell, works that were promptly sold through Crossroads or directly by the artist.

The only other gallery that George Browne dealt with was the Canadian Art Galleries in Calgary. In 1951, while he was living in Seebe, George bought painting supplies from the Canadian Art Galleries and sold paintings through them. His friendly association with J. D. "Jack" Turner, the gallery's director, continued after the Brownes moved to Connecticut. Over the years, George consigned thirty-three paintings to the Canadian Art Galleries, a number of which were commissions Turner had obtained for him. Every one of the oils Turner received was sold, often within a month of their receipt; and like Terrill, Turner frequently wrote the artist asking for more. The selling commission received by the Canadian Gallery was slightly less than that charged by Grand Central and Crossroads; however, the occasional problems of getting pictures through Canadian customs and the necessity of packing them for shipment presented some difficulties. George, nevertheless, valued his cordial relationship with Turner and always sent him some paintings each year, the largest consignment being seven pictures in 1956.

Throughout his career, George was concerned about the financial aspect of his work. He worked a prodigious schedule to produce as many paintings as possible, for he felt constant pressure to provide for his wife and children, and the sale of paintings was his sole source of income.

George apparently enjoyed keeping his parents

informed as to how his painting was going. In March 1949 he wrote:

> *I just finished two more pictures and destroyed it! One of them that is, the other is O.K. In fact they both were, but the one I destroyed couldn't pass the final test. When I finish a picture I ask myself 'is it worth the price I'm asking?' The answer was 'no' so I'll destroy it, but I'm going to transfer it as it's a good idea.*
>
> *Gosh, I'm all fired up over this painting business. It gets more intriguing every day. Just when you think you've got one stage of it licked and go on to the next, bang, it's first stage gets you in the back! It's the darned birds which gave me trouble this time.*

Although he maintained high standards for his work and destroyed paintings that he thought were of inferior quality, George was always looking for ways to speed up the production process to meet the insistent demands of his dealers. He made daily notes of the progress on each canvas and took obvious pleasure in the completion of a painting in a relatively few days.

Early in 1949 George wrote his father, "My new method of painting landscape first is a great help in keeping the landscapes from having that tired look and, as my weakness is landscape, it helps me improve and perfect them before being distracted by the problem of the ducks; also a picture goes much faster with this method, it eliminates much of the difficulty of trying to paint an even sky between wing feathers, never completely satisfactory, but get a good sky first, then you have something to shoot at. Pictures painted with this new method have more the landscape quality and aren't quite so illustrative."

In response to his father's comments about his "new method," George wrote: "I still have lots of bad moments about this, but it seems to me the more of a system I employ during construction the more I can forget the technical details and concentrate on the artistic and fine work of the picture." He also said, "I'm getting more fun and interest out of my painting than I ever have before. Believe it or not, I actually would rather paint than hunt these days." Later that year he wrote:

> *Boy, Ba, my painting is really going swell. I'm just beginning to realize a few of the fundamentals, and what a big thrill painting really is! I've found I can really turn the work out when I have to! The new method really pays off. I've completed four canvases this month, also seven sketches. The big saving in time this new method provides is in the elementary stage of the picture. So far I've not found a real shortcut to the actual painting of a picture. I don't suppose such a thing exists, but by streamlining the technical details I can help.*

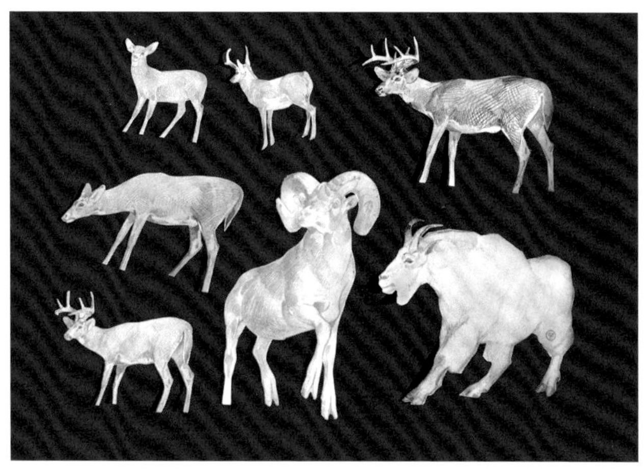

ABOVE AND OPPOSITE: *Cutouts George made for painting layouts*

George was an innovator, continually looking for ways to improve his technique and his production. A family friend in California who sometimes watched George work in his studio has said, "George painted birds upside down to improve concentration on specific colors and shapes—not what he thought form should be but what he actually saw—to ensure realism and objectivity." The practice of painting a subject upside down was abandoned, but the fact that he would experiment with it is evidence of his openness to original approaches.

George kept dozens of manila envelopes stuffed with photographs of animals he had clipped from newspapers and magazines for reference purposes. He also followed a practice he developed himself, the use of cutout silhouettes of birds and animals to try out various composition options. He made many hundreds of these cutouts, which depict all of the animals found in his paintings in a variety of poses and sizes. Many of the cutouts are detailed pencil drawings of the subjects. Having painted the background landscape for a scene of, perhaps, canvasback

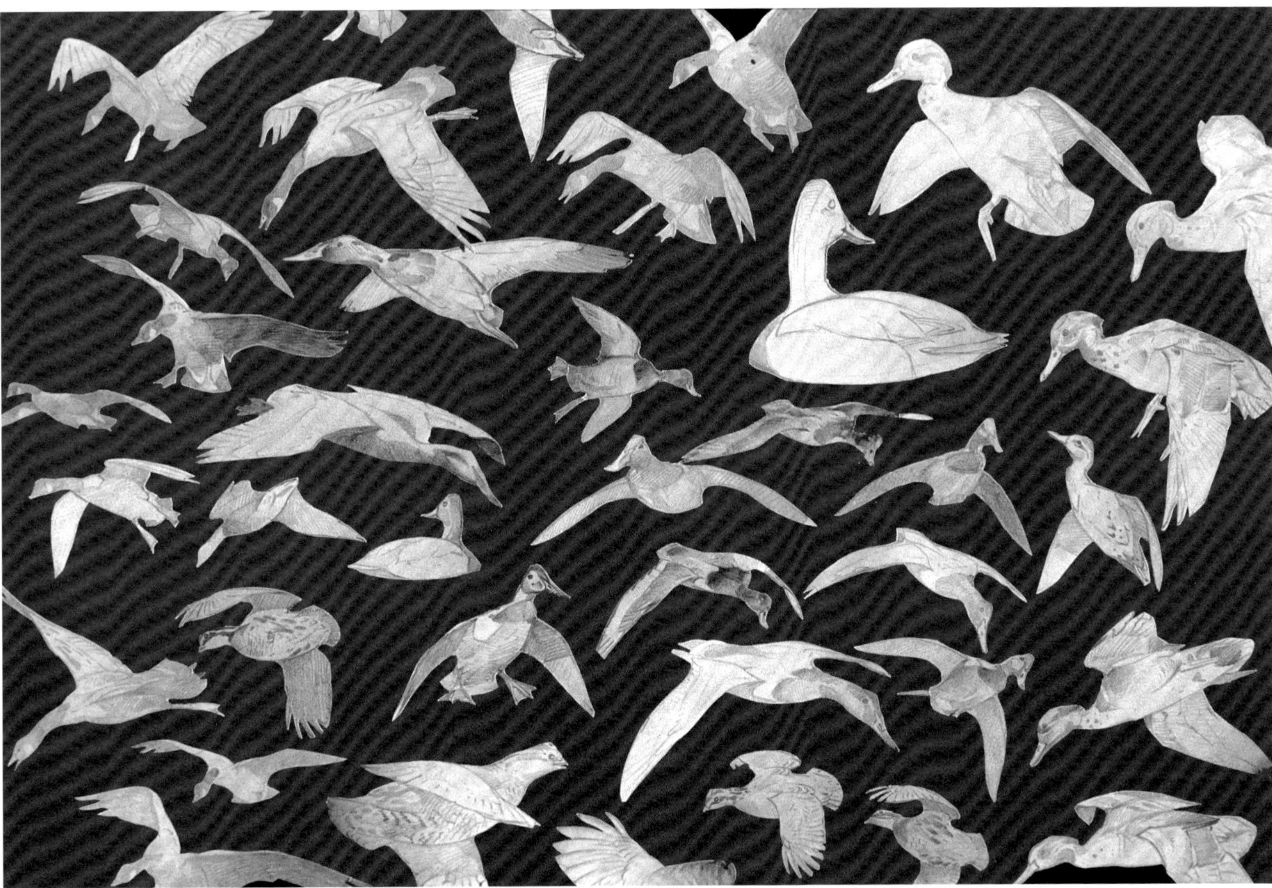

ducks in flight, he would take his canvasback cutouts and move them about on the canvas until he had achieved a satisfactory design. He would then overpaint the landscape with the birds in the positions where he had placed the cutouts. For reference on feather colors and patterns, George had oil sketches of ducks and upland birds he had shot pinned to the walls of his studio.

George may have adapted some of his painting practices from his Alberta neighbor, Carl Rungius. Rungius's biographer, William Schaldach, wrote, "[Rungius's] studio is well stocked with sketches on rectangles of canvas, usually 9 x 11 inches in size, and every season he adds to the collection. Besides the landscape studies for background there are innumerable small oil sketches of particular animals which have been shot and drawn for future reference."

In 1951, concerned as always with production rate, George wrote his parents:

> *It used to take me 18 days to paint a 25 x 30; now I do the same type of canvas in between 9 and 12 days. It used to take me between 25 and 35 days to do a 30 x 40. This last one, which is by far my finest, I did in 16 days. I cannot account for this speed up really; it worries me in a way. My only explanation is that I think I flounder less with a picture than I used to.*
>
> *I am very careful that I don't start a picture unless I am absolutely sure it is a nockout* [sic] *and a good composition. I'm beginning to find out how little I know and how much I've got to learn about composition, but it surely is the secret to a good picture, provided a man has the knowledge and ability to paint a good picture.*
>
> *Another idea I've worked on this winter, it is probably not new, and that is paint several pictures of the same subject at once. This may sound like cheating in a way, but* if *the final results are* good, *why not? Boy,*

this has really paid off for me. 2nd better than 1st, 3rd better than 2nd.

Throughout his career, George kept precise records of his work on each painting. An 18 x 24-inch oil that he painted in the winter of 1951–52, "Mallards in Alberta," on which he worked off and on over a period of five months, took a total of seventeen days to complete. His notes are as follows:

Dec. 13th	Pencil Sketches
Dec. 17th	Sketches
Dec. 28th	Sketches
Jan. 15th	Sketch
Jan. 20th	Sketch
Feb. 4th	Cut outs
Feb. 5th	Ink Lay in
Feb. 7th	Oil Lay in Landscape
April 8th	Lay in birds
April 9th	Lay in Figures
April 11	Ducks
April 13th	3 duck
April 15th	1 and 2 Duck
April 20th	Sky flock
April 21st	Sky foreground
April 24th	Distant Flock
April 25th	Landscape Flock
Completed 17 days	Sold

A larger work, a 24 x 36-inch oil, "At the Crossing," on which he worked in the summer of 1957, took but nine days.

July 6th	Cut outs
July 7th	Ink Lay in
July 10th	Oil Landscape Lay in
July 11th	1—2—3rd bird
July 12th	1st bird
July 13th	2nd & 3rd Birds
July 15th	Sky
July 16	Landscape
July 17	Foreground
Completed 9 Days	Sold

At the same time that he was working on "At the Crossing," he was painting another 24 x 36-inch oil, "The Channel Entrance."

1. June 29	Sketches	
2. June 30	Cut outs	
3. July 2	Cut outs	
4. July 4	Ink lay in	Oil Lay in
5. July 7	Oil lay in	Ducks
6. July 8	Completed 1st Bird	
7. July 9	Completed 2, 3 & 4th Bird	
8. July 14	Completed Birds	
9. July 15	Landscape	
10. July 17	Landscape	
July 18	Landscape	
Completed 11 Days	Sold	

A comparison of his work notes shows that, whereas George spent an average of twelve days on his paintings in 1952, he was able to complete his pictures in an average of seven and a half days by 1957.

A sad note is struck by the last page of work notes that appears in his studio record book:

Canvas Size 22″ x 32″

	Mule Deer
1. March 2	Sketches
2. March 3	Sketches
3. March 4th	Sketches
4. March 5th	Cut outs
5. March 6th	Oil Lay in
6. March 7th	Bucks
7. March 8th	First Buck
8.	
9.	

This painting was left unfinished when George died.

George was so concerned with the matter of time invested relative to value received for his paintings that he actually computed the square inch of canvas to sale price ratio for paintings of various sizes.

He also calculated annual figures from 1950 through 1956 for days worked, number of paintings sold, total gross income, average income per picture sold, profit per days worked, and average income per day, per week and per month.

George's goal initially was to turn out two oils each month; however, he eventually was able to increase his production to an average of three paintings a month. He also painted numerous sketches, which were essentially studies to be incorporated into his formal pictures. Although there were no completed paintings in his studio at the time of his death, there were numerous sketches—landscapes depicting mountains and valleys, upland game cover, marshes and lakes and studies of big game animals, ducks, geese and upland game birds. Each of these sketches represents an effort to work out

Square Inch of Canvas to Sale Price Ratio

Sale Price	Profit (after Commission)	Size	Sq. Ins.	Price Per Sq. In.	Profit Per Sq. In.
$ 400	$ 266	18″ x 24″	432	93¢	60¢
$ 300	$ 200	15″ x 20″	300	$1.00	66¢
$ 1100	$ 734	30″ x 40″	1200	$91	61¢

Year	Days Worked	No. Sold	Gross Income	Gross Per Picture	Profit Per Days Worked	Income Per Day	Income Per Week	Income Per Month
1950	208	22	$4,445.32	$202	$22	$12.25	$85.75	$367
1951	226	22	$4,389.21	$199	$19	$12.00	$84.00	$360
1952	205	21	$5,289.30	$252	$25	$14.40	$100.80	$432
1953	209	22	$6,431.67	$292	$30	$17.60	$123.20	$528
1954	176	25	$7,050.30	$282	$40	$19.30	$135.10	$579
1955	190	29	$7,154.98	$246	$38	$17.60	$137.50	$596
1956	188	33	$10,271.49	$311	$54	$28.14	$197.52	$855

a particular problem of composition, light and shade, seasonal colors and the like; and some of these informal sketches have noteworthy artistic quality.

George was an observant person, and he studied mountains, marshes, coverts and meadows out of his determination to "get it right" in his studio when he would incorporate in a painting what he had seen in the field. Upon occasion he would make written field notes to serve as references for paintings at some time in the future. An example, undated, is as follows:

Bird: Canada Geese 13
Background: Timbered Ridges
Lighting: Sun just set, Early twilight
Distance: 35 yds. over River
General Impressions: Birds noticeably flying fast. General color tone cold. Black areas noticeable lack of detail. Head and body unaffected by motion of wings, but base of neck and chest rise and fall alternately with wing beats. Chests cool whitish gray, check marks buckskin color.

More light areas visible on geese in profile than when coming and going. Flock seemed dense, birds between 6 and 8 ft. apart on average.

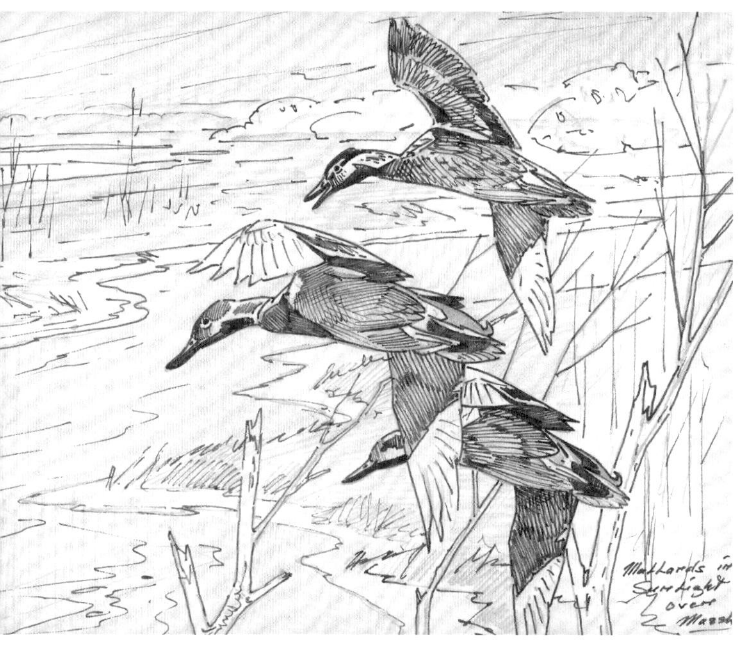

LEFT: *Sketch by George*—Mallards

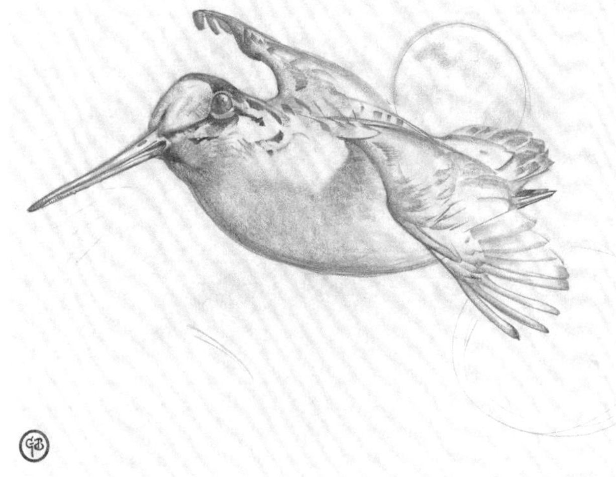

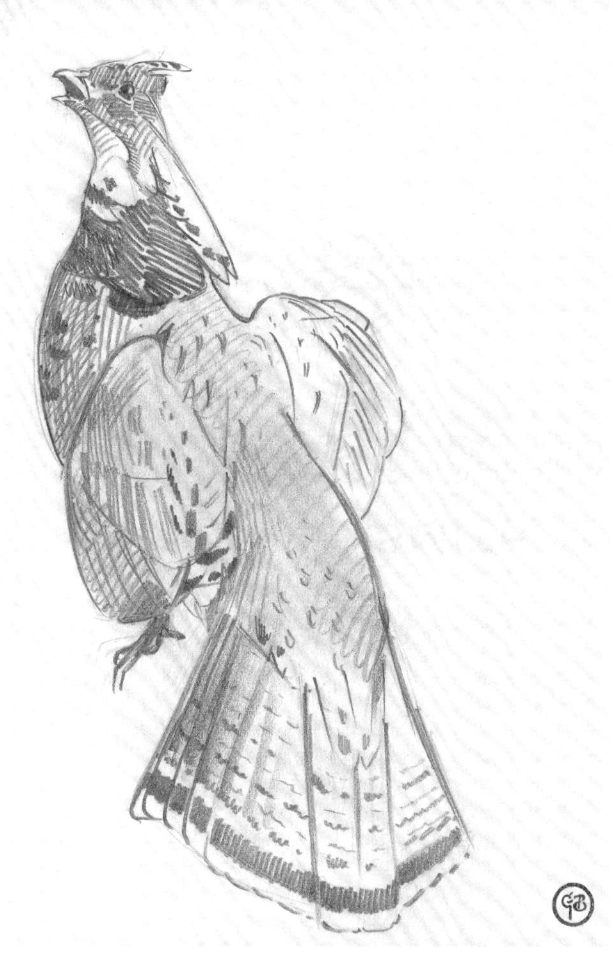

ABOVE: *Sketch by George*—Woodcock

RIGHT: *Sketch by George*—Grouse

Recognition by those whose opinions he valued as well as financial rewards were both important to George, but he truly loved the activity of painting. He would, he is quoted as having said, "rather paint tomatoes on soup labels than not paint." He also admitted that he had chosen to be a painter of wildlife in part at least because he would be able to spend much of his time out-of-doors. Having chosen his career, George became a consummate professional. Tibby wrote that his working day "averaged between twelve and fourteen hours, allowing scant time for sleeping and eating and still gave him a solid sense of fulfillment. This sense was, of course, fortified by the enthusiastic response to his work."

Tibby also commented on her late husband's attitude toward his work: "Browne thought of himself specifically as a painter rather than as an artist, as he'd been conditioned to be suspect of the long-haired, self-absorbed prototype of 'the artist.' As a matter of fact, he all but shaved his head as a symbol of his absence of 'artistic temperament.'"

Tibby wrote: "It was surely his good fortune . . . that he was able to combine his love of the out-of-doors and of fishing and hunting with his work, to the ire of the IRS, which granted, after an audit of our accounts, that indeed we could take as a deduction half the expenses for our extraordinary Irish setter and the cost of shotgun shells, all as business expense!"

Belmore Browne's approach to painting has been called "dilettantish," almost as if painting had been merely an avocation; and his family was sometimes in financial straits. His wife Agnes on occasion had to badger him to get him to his easel, and there were times when she had to resort to selling inherited items of value to make ends meet. Agnes commented sympathetically on Belmore's occasional lack of dedication to painting, their principal source of income: "B was finding it very difficult to give his whole time to serious mountain pictures, but he always had no end of courage & grit, & so I kept on never losing faith that *some* day he would produce something fine."

George Browne, however, was determined that his wife and children would not live with the stress he had experienced as a child. While his father at times had to be coaxed to paint, George worked at painting all day, every day, unless special circumstances warranted a temporary break in this working regimen.

George made an interesting observation on his father's work, contrasting it to his own, in a 1958 letter to a Canadian friend who had been a patron of both artists:

> *I feel that Father was a great mountain painter, but he belonged to a school of thought which advocated straight landscape as the ultimate artistic endeavor. I feel that this philosophy cost him dearly and that it is the reason that his work was not more saleable. It has certainly been my experience that figures enhance the landscape and a picture with some drama and a story is, everything else being equal, much more interesting. Thus it has been our experience with Father's pictures that those with pack horses, animals or a story of some kind have sold readily, whereas the pure landscapes have required a specialized market.*

Sketch by George—Pheasant

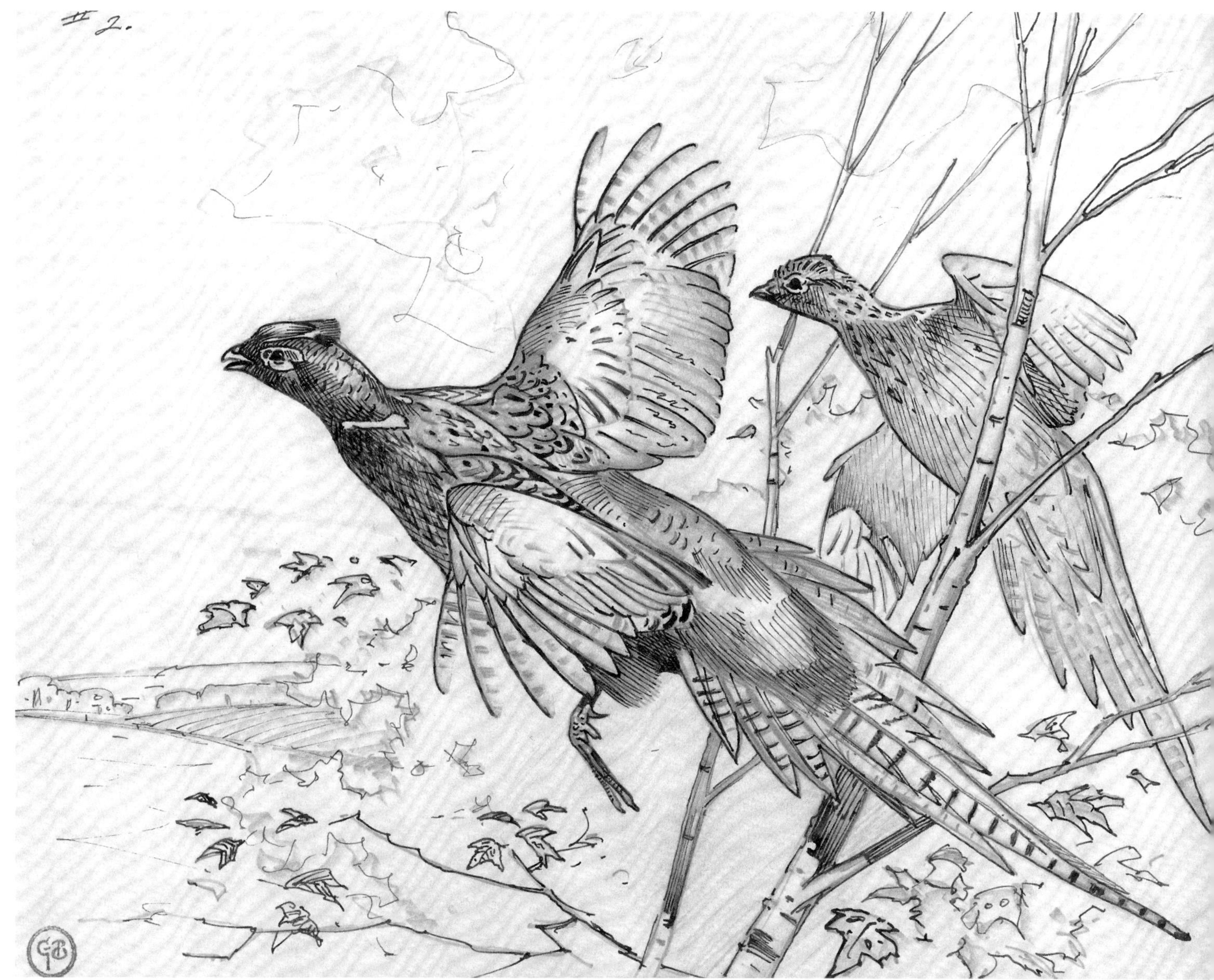

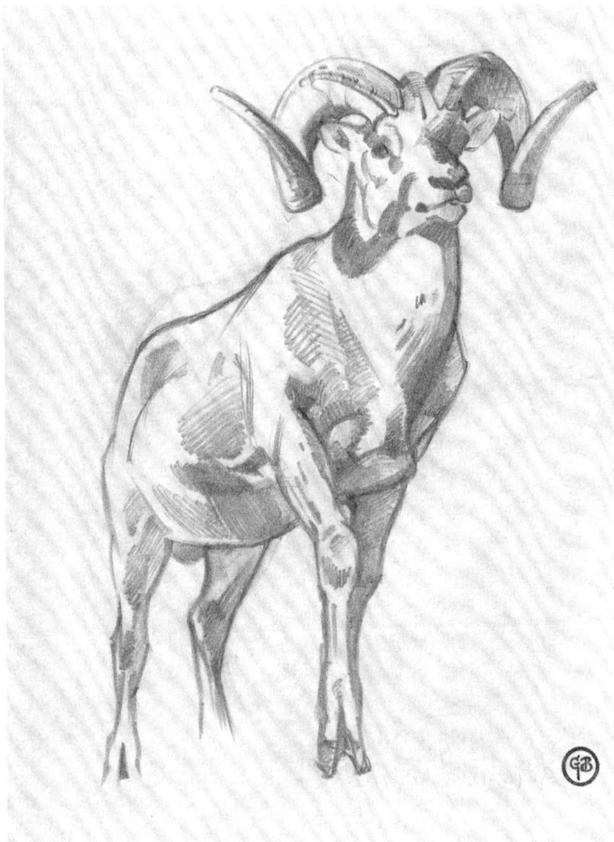

Sketch by George—Big Horn Sheep

It would be grossly unfair to a man whose achievements as a painter, a writer, an explorer and a sportsman are truly noteworthy to suggest that Belmore Browne was anything less than an accomplished artist. He was among the first and the most important painters of Alaska and the western Canadian provinces and the animals native to the region. His work, furthermore, was the foundation upon which his son George based his own work. Belmore was the master who took on an apprentice and provided the training, the encouragement and the inspiration that enabled his student to become a master in his own right.

Perhaps Belmore, who had once enjoyed the distinction of having paintings selected for inclusion in national exhibitions and juried shows, painted with an underlying desire to impress the New York critics and have his work hung in the Metropolitan Museum. George, on the other hand, simply wanted to impress Ralph Terrill's customers and have his work on the cover of the Crossroads of Sport catalogue. George referred to himself as a painter; Belmore thought of himself as an artist.

Commenting on the painting styles of her father and her brother, Evelyn Browne wrote:

> *It is interesting that George's subject matter followed what seems to have been an inherited passion for fishing and hunting. George was a superb outdoorsman, and in this respect, as well as in his artistic career, he followed in the footsteps of his father. I should like to make it clear that—although George was obviously influenced by his father and his environment—his paintings were in no way like father's. From the beginning they were individual and distinctly George.*

Not only was Belmore George's teacher but father and son frequently worked side by side with their drawing pads and at their easels. Nevertheless, as Evelyn observed, her brother's paintings were "individual and distinctly George."

It is in the choice of subjects that the work of the two artists differs most obviously. Belmore was essentially a painter of pure landscape—typically, a panoramic vista with a vast open middle ground and majestic, rugged mountain peaks in the far distance. Rarely is there any sign of human intrusion in Belmore's wilderness scenes. When man is present, he is dwarfed by massive mountains or, occasionally, huge animals. The wilderness, for all its awesome beauty, is an inhospitable place, an adversary that presents a challenge to man.

George's scenes, with the exception of some of his earliest works done when the influence of his father was strongest, are of the habitat of the animals that were his subjects, generally waterfowl and upland game birds. The country he painted was friendly to man. Nature was not an adversary, but a friendly host. Man is not an alien in a foreign land; he is in his natural environment; and although humans are rarely seen in George's paintings, the scenes are presented as if seen by a hunter who is there by implication.

As to technique and style, George's oils are painted with a lighter palette than his father's. They are also generally more detailed, painted with greater precision, yet with a characteristic impressionistic softness. Belmore's works, by contrast, are painted boldly, with broad brush strokes. His pictures are strong and rugged, like the country that he depicted.

George grew up in a cabin in Alberta, riding out into the wilderness on pack train trips as soon as he was able to sit a horse. He never felt threatened by anything he encountered there, for his remarkably capable father was always in control, and the woods were George's playground. Belmore, however, was raised in "civilization"—dressed in velvet and silk, attended by servants in commodious apartments in New York City and the cultural centers of Europe. The wilderness of the Pacific Northwest, which he first encountered at the age of eight, was something very different from the familiar, something to which he was instinctively drawn, yet something that was formidable and challenging. Perhaps the difference in their earliest experiences with the wilderness is reflected in the fundamental difference of mood that is sensed when comparing their works.

Although both Belmore and George had monocular vision, each having lost the sight of one eye in shooting accidents, any limitation they may have experienced in depth perception is not evinced in their paintings. Characteristically, neither of them seemed greatly troubled by an injury that might have been devastating to other artists. One family story shows that Belmore even managed to turn their disability to advantage: A pair of high-quality Zeiss binoculars in a pawn shop window caught Belmore's eye. He examined them and found them to be excellent, but the price was more than he felt he should spend. He continued to think about them after leaving the shop, however, and after walking a few blocks, he had an idea that would enable him to rationalize the expenditure. He reversed his steps and bought the glasses. When he got them home, he divided the binoculars with a hacksaw and, keeping one half for himself, presented the other monocular to his son.

Sketch by George—Antelope

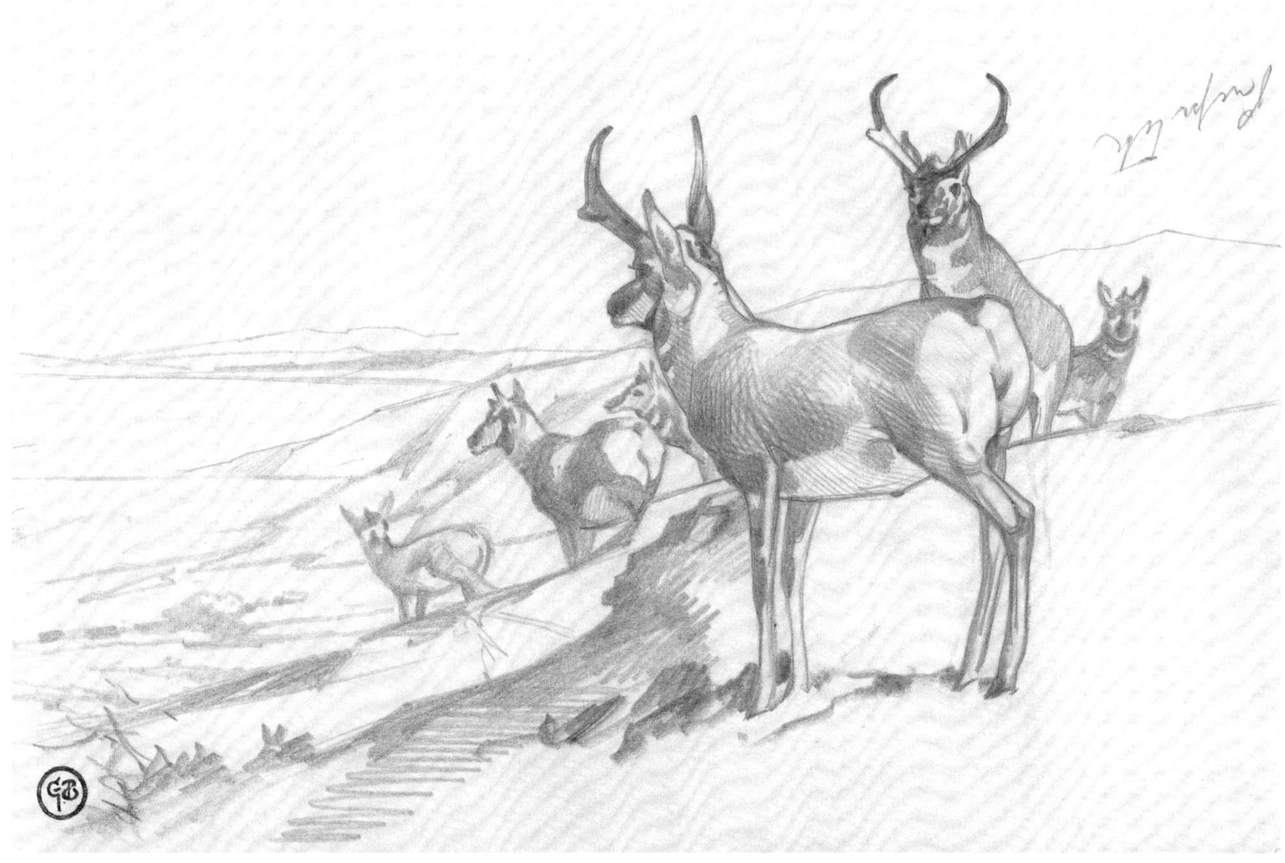

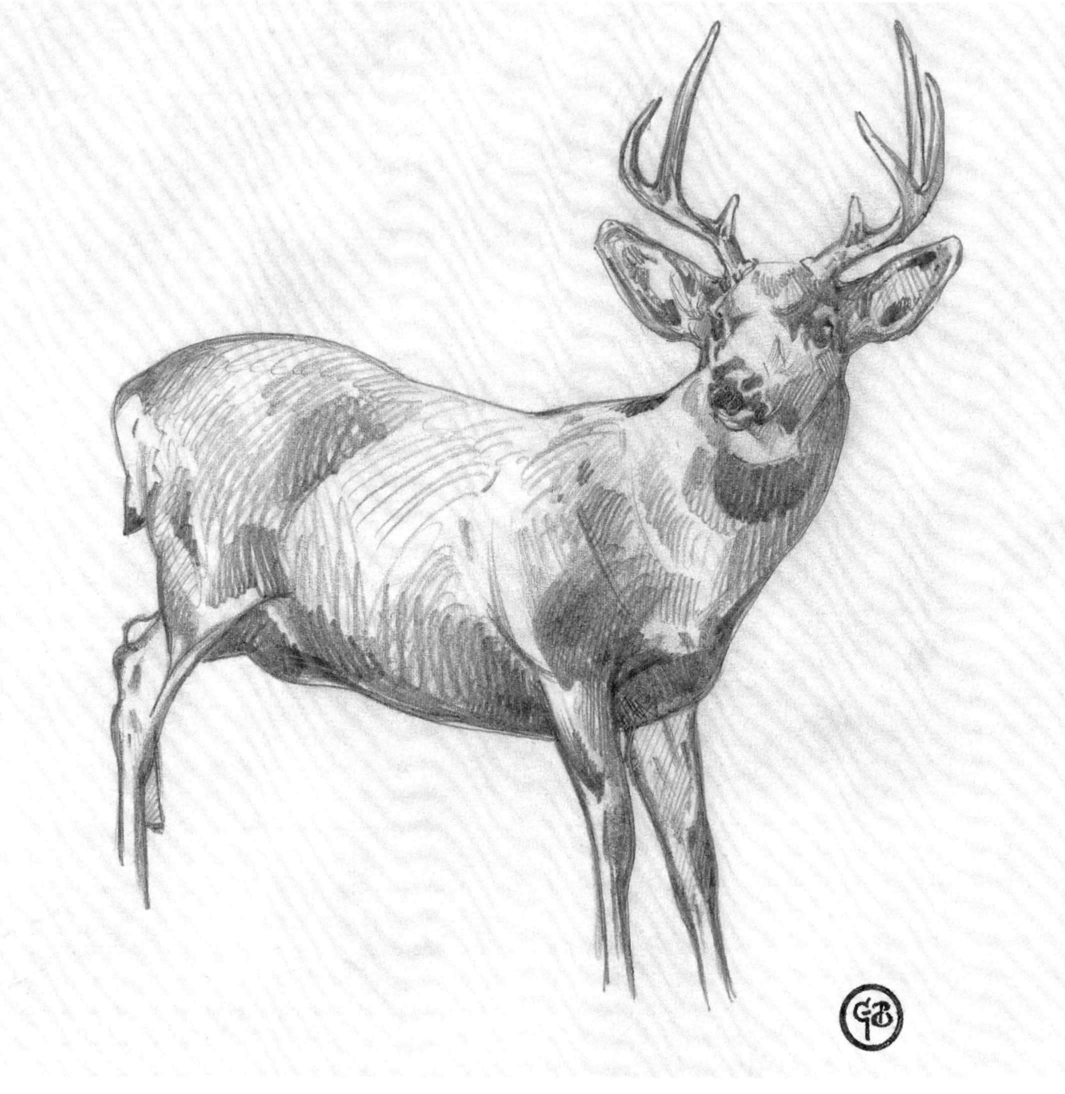

Sketch by George—Whitetail Buck

The measure of respect George had for his father is clearly indicated in a letter he wrote his mother in February 1944:

> *Ba differs from the much publicized type of out door man, like Dr. Clark, Roy Andrews and Brad Washburn, in the fact that his publicity has come through sincerity, and his true love of the out of doors has overpowered the temptation of money and publicity offered by the large metropolitan areas of this country. Men who have accomplished a very few sensational feats of exploration or mountaineering rely on these few trips into the wilderness, coupled with much lecturing and publicity, to maintain their standing as authorities on the out of doors. Ba possesses all these men have and all they lack. To the public he is a great out of doors man, but to the men who know the out of doors, like Dan Beard, Washburn, etc. Ba is the best of them all. He is, in fact, a pioneer who is still an active wilderness man.*
>
> *Although Ba's experience has been mostly confined to North America, he has acquired*

knowledge and the ability to meet any situation, which I think is most unusual. He has lived the life, done it himself. His accomplishments have not only been sensational, but hazardous and laborsome. He is proficient in almost every type of wilderness work and has proved his ability to adapt his knowledge and good judgement to any type of association with the wilds or with civilization. On top of all this, he is a wonderful teacher.

George's sister Evelyn shared his feelings of love and respect for their father, feelings she expressed in a tribute that summarized the accomplishments of this remarkable man:

Belmore Browne left behind him a wealth of proof that he was one of our greatest outdoorsmen and mountain artists. He also has left a host of friends, old and young, wherever his trail led him. He was powerful and resourceful on the trail, yet infinitely kind and gentle of nature. His patience was at times unbelievable, yet no one could fight more gallantly than he to defend what he felt to be the truth.

His career spanned the entire modern development of Alaska from before the Gold Rush to the present. He saw Anchorage develop from a forested bluff on the shores of Cook Inlet to a thriving frontier metropolis of 40,000. He shot a moose on what is now the main street of Fairbanks. He dogteamed and rafted a thousand miles from Seward to the Yukon in six months, and he made a four-engine airplane flight from Minneapolis to Alaska in a dozen hours. He went up the winding Susitna in a stern wheeler, fought the Chulitna's rocky rapids in an open boat and floated down the Stikino in a Tlingit canoe. He panned for gold on the gravel bars of the Kantishna and hunted seals and whales in didarkhas with the Aleuts. He hunted sheep from the wilderness of Denali to the Cassiar and the Athabasca, and tracked bear from the Alaska Peninsula to Kodiak and the Matanuska.

Because of this thrilling accomplishment, spread over nearly three-quarters of a century, Belmore Browne attained unsurpassed accuracy and authenticity in his painting and his writing. His was a rich, full eventful life and, still more, he had what all men most desire: a devoted wife and a happy family.

George's appreciation of his parents' contribution to his becoming the man he was is expressed in a letter he wrote his mother a few months after joining the army:

There is one thing about me, mother, that you may think terrible, but it is never the less true. There is one thing I love more than you, or Ba or myself or anyone and that's the wilderness and all that goes with it, but it is for this reason I am so fond of you and Ba. You have all your married life gone without so that Ba and I could live the life we love so much, something almost no other woman would do, and Ba has been part of the wilderness life itself to me. He represents it and has presented it to me in his paintings and in his tolerance and patience with my feeble efforts to follow in his footsteps as an artist and out door man.

Tibby wrote, "Of course it should be noted that as a result of George's great number of interests in common with his father, and too, of having this compelling man as parent, pal, shooting companion and teacher, an intimacy, admiration and bond had developed transcending the usual father-son relationship."

Tibby also commented on George Browne's devotion to sporting activities, noting that "fishing and shooting were his relaxation, inspiration and spiritual refreshment."

"He spent several weeks a year in the field acquiring familiarity with various parts of the country as applicable to the painting of various upland and shore birds," she wrote. The ultimate sportsman, "George prided himself in deriving the multi-faceted satisfaction from the hunt: the bird in the hand, the sketch of the same, the meal of the same and finally the use of the feathers of the same for fly tying."

George was by nature a meticulous record keeper, and he maintained accounts of his hunting activities that were as detailed as his studio records. In the early 1950's in Seebe, for example, he made a map of the local grouse habitat on which he noted every ruffed grouse he

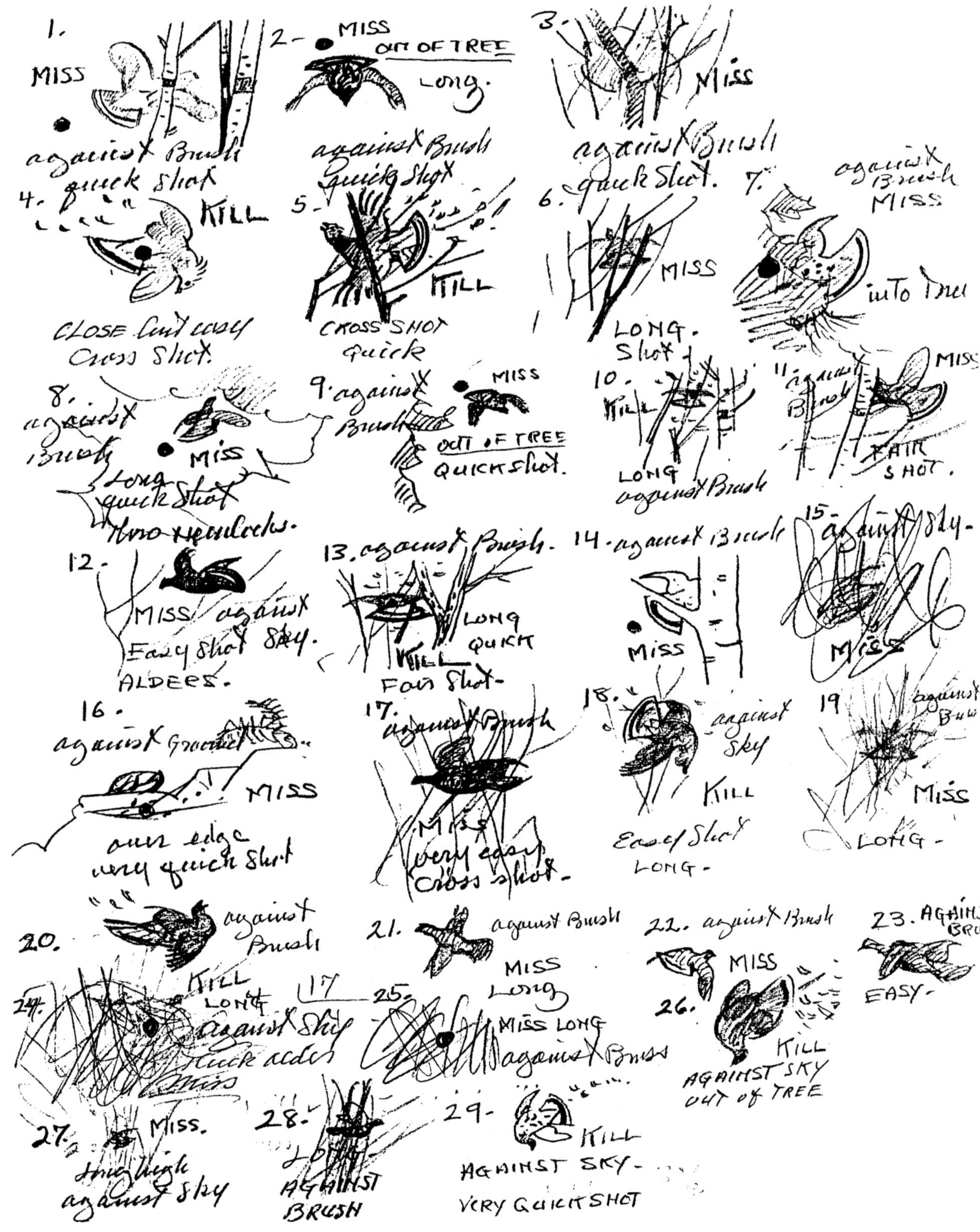
1. MISS against Brush quick shot
2- MISS OUT OF TREE Long. against Brush Quick Shot
3- Miss against Brush quick shot.
4. KILL CLOSE but easy Cross Shot.
5. KILL CROSS SHOT quick
6. MISS LONG. Shot
7. against Brush MISS into tree
8. against Brush MISS Long quick shot thro hemlocks.
9. against Brush MISS OUT OF TREE QUICK shot.
10. Kill LONG against Brush
11 against Brush MISS FAIR SHOT.
12. MISS against sky. Easy shot ALDERS.
13. against Brush. LONG QUICK KILL Fair Shot.
14. against Brush MISS
15. against sky. Miss
16. against Ground MISS over edge very quick shot
17. against Brush Miss very easy Cross shot.
18. against sky KILL Easy Shot LONG.
19 against Brush MISS LONG.
20. against Brush KILL LONG
21. against Brush MISS Long
22. against Brush MISS
23. AGAINST BRUSH EASY.
24. against Sky Quick action Miss
25. MISS LONG against Brush
26. KILL AGAINST SKY OUT OF TREE
27. MISS. high against sky
28. LONG AGAINST BRUSH
29. KILL AGAINST SKY. VERY QUICK SHOT

OPPOSITE: *Sketches by George—grouse as seen when shot*

flushed—a blue dot for a bird he missed, a red dot for a kill. This record was complemented by a set of sketches that depicted each grouse as he had seen it when he shot.

Whenever possible, George was able to combine his vocation with his principal avocation. In 1953 he wrote some friends, "After I left you I spent two days, on the way home, painting grouse and woodcock cover in Vt. and got some really good sketches. However, there were a couple of covers I could not resist and allowed myself an hour of hunting each day. My luck held out and fortune smiled on me and I picked up three grouse and two woodcock." George never hired a guide or joined a hunting or fishing club, for if he did not have the company of his father or his wife or good friends, he preferred to go it alone.

Evelyn Browne wrote of her brother's devotion—indeed, *passion* is perhaps not too strong a word—for the outdoors and sporting activities:

> *George was a superb outdoorsman and in this respect as well as in his artistic career he followed in the footsteps of his father. He never lost his love of fishing and his earliest drawings were of fish. When he was old enough to shoot a shotgun, he went into duck hunting in a big way. In the prairie fields and marshes of Alberta to the sloughs and open water of San Francisco Bay he hunted and painted ducks. George's wildfowl paintings exhibit a masterly knowledge of the habitat and the individual qualities of each species, whether it is the endearing quality of the little buffleheads poking around in a sheltered cove or the majestic sweep of a noisy flock of hundreds of Canada geese dropping in to take over an Alberta cornfield with snow on the distant Rockies in the late fall, George knew what he was painting with scientific accuracy and he had the transcendent ability to render what he saw in paintings of unparalleled and arresting beauty.*

In a letter to his parents written during his army years, George wrote, "I am the happiest person in the world because I have discovered that painting means more to me than almost anything and it is one thing I am never going to give up but will work harder and harder at it as the years go on."

"George's tenacious application to his work," Tibby noted, "came from a deep urge to paint and to be able to stand with the best." He loved his profession and he wanted the recognition he believed he deserved.

George aspired to membership in the National Academy, to which his father had been elected an associate. In 1957, he submitted an autumnal composition of duck and deer at a pond near Norfolk; it was, however, rejected by the entry committee. Ogden Pleissner, who was a National Academician, told him, "George, you'll never make it [into the National Academy] with nature."

In January 1958, two months before his death, George entered into correspondence with *Life* magazine concerning the possibility of *Life*'s publishing a page or two of his paintings. Commenting on his work, George wrote:

> *While I do some landscape work, my subject matter lies largely in the field of wild life in habitat, for it has been in this area that I have derived considerable public response; therefore [it is] a subject I feel most likely to interest you. I feel that my work differs from that of some of our very excellent bird illustrators in that it lies in the fine arts realm and in that it has been purchased exclusively by private individuals for hanging in homes and public buildings.*
>
> *It has been my thought that this work would be more "newsworthy" and that it would have more impact if it were presented as relatively unknown, and it has therefore been my plan during the past ten years to withhold it from excessive publicity until I felt it worthy for publication in* Life. *I have painted approximately twenty-five major oils each year for the past ten years and have sold virtually all of them. They have not been reproduced in magazines or books, neither have they been submitted for public exhibition.*

Unfortunately, perhaps because of his death, nothing came of this initiative.

George also wrote Ralph Terrill in January 1958, to complain that he had been "billed behind" several other artists who did not give the Crossroads of Sport exclusive right to their works in New York City as he did. "I shelved all other work toward the end of 1957," he wrote, "in order to give Crossroads first attention, and I must say that you delivered the goods in every way, but I do feel that I could occasionally be better represented in the Catalogue." He went on to say, "I know that in past years you have featured other artists [other than Pleissner] on your Catalogue cover: Rouseau, Rungius, Jacques, etc., and if you could possibly justify it, I would certainly like my chance."

Terrill responded immediately: "I will try, in next year's catalog, to see that you get more of a break than you feel you got this year, because I certainly want your sporting stuff exclusively, and I think to date our sales justify it." He concluded by suggesting, "When next you are in New York, let's arrange a luncheon and sit down and talk it over, for I certainly don't want you unhappy with your connection here." In a subsequent letter, Terrill agreed to meet with George on March 13, a date that George later cancelled in order to join a group of friends for a weekend in the Adirondacks.

Epilogue

A GREATNESS UNFULFILLED

Having joined an informal gathering of conservation-minded sportsmen for a weekend of conversation and recreation in the Adirondack region of New York State, George Browne was accidentally shot and killed on March 14, 1958. The men had been amusing themselves by shooting at inflated balloons that were blown out on a frozen lake by an erratic wind. A man who was inexperienced in the use of firearms mishandled a hang-fire. The gun discharged and the bullet struck George in the neck. He died within an hour.

The loss to the world of sporting art occasioned by George's abrupt, tragic death was as nothing compared to the loss felt by his widow and their two young children, recently settled in rural Connecticut. The tributes to George and the messages of condolence came from many men who admired the artist but admired the man even more—messages that spoke of George's strength and stamina, but also of his integrity, his kindness and his gentle nature. These were of some consolation, and Tibby did not lack for friends and supporters. A resilient and loving woman, she eventually re-married, bore two sons to her husband, Hugh Robinson, and lived out a full, productive life as a wife, a mother and an activist for civic and educational causes in Norfolk.

The pages that had displayed George's paintings in the annual Crossroads of Sport catalogues up through 1958 were subsequently devoted to the work of other rising sporting artists, and as decades passed, George Browne's name became unknown to all but those who remembered his work from the 1950's and the fortunate people who had bought or inherited his pictures.

Among those best able to evaluate the paintings of George Browne and to compare his work to that of his contemporaries and the artists who have followed him is Bill Webster, of Wild Wings, who has written, "[George] came out of the clear blue sky, and he was ahead of his time. Had he lived, he'd be recognized as one of the best wildlife painters ever."

"Clearly," Webster continued, "in the eyes of his peers and the vast majority of sporting artists since his death, he set the bar at a height that really hasn't been equaled, and may never be."

Bob Fraser, one the country's most knowledgeable dealers in sporting art, has written, "When I look at a duck painting by George, I am immediately transferred there with the duck; I am on its level, whether it be a power stroke, setting wings or a flight pattern. To me that is the greatness of George." Fraser went on to say that George was one of the few American artists—and he mentioned specifically Winslow Homer and A. B. Frost—who could "enable his viewer to feel what the individual duck exhibited in the painting." Fraser is unequivocal in his evaluation: "George Browne is the greatest artist of the 20th century. When you look at what else has been done in this era, no one can touch him."

Perhaps this present publication and the several exhibitions of Belmore and George Browne paintings that are being planned will serve to complete the re-discovery process. George Browne certainly deserves the position that he craved and had earned among America's premier sporting artists.

The memorial resolution from George's colleagues on the Camp Fire Club's Conservation Committee included this elegiac poem written by George's friend Victor Skiff a few hours after George died:

This man; artist by vocation, hunter by choice,
chose as well to paint what he knew best.
Learned the grammar of the woods, to know its voice
and heart, made his own translations meet the test
of running water, scales of fish, a woodcock's
practiced poise
against the rising draft of wind. The rest,
untranslatable, but known to him: to love the noise
of summer rising urgent from a hidden nest,
regard the rush of partridge wings, rejoice
in what cannot be painted, manifest
the solemn mystery and joys
of beauty in his life; its secrets in his breast.

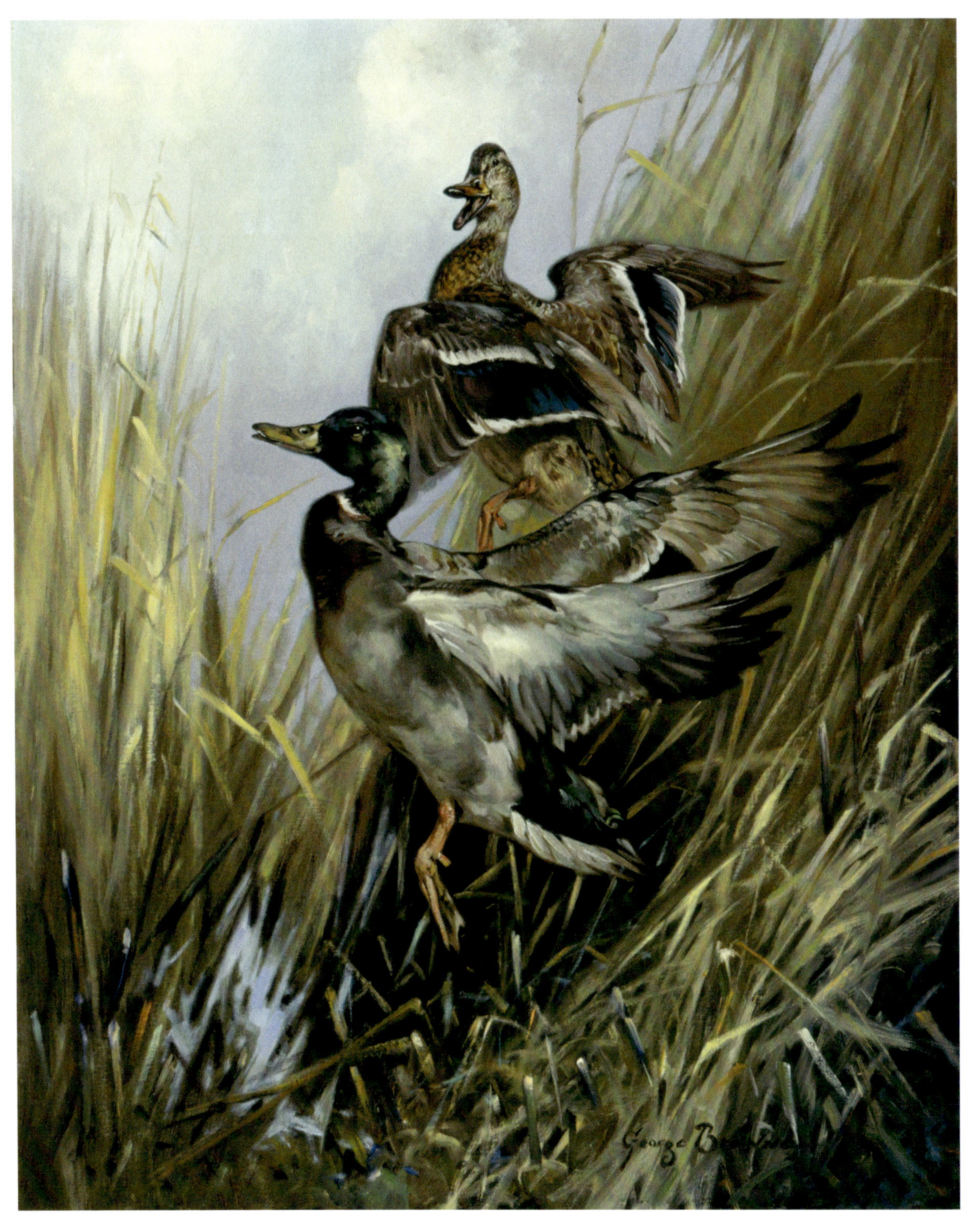

PLATE 14
George Browne
Startled Mallards 1949
oil on canvas, 30 x 25 in.
Private Collection

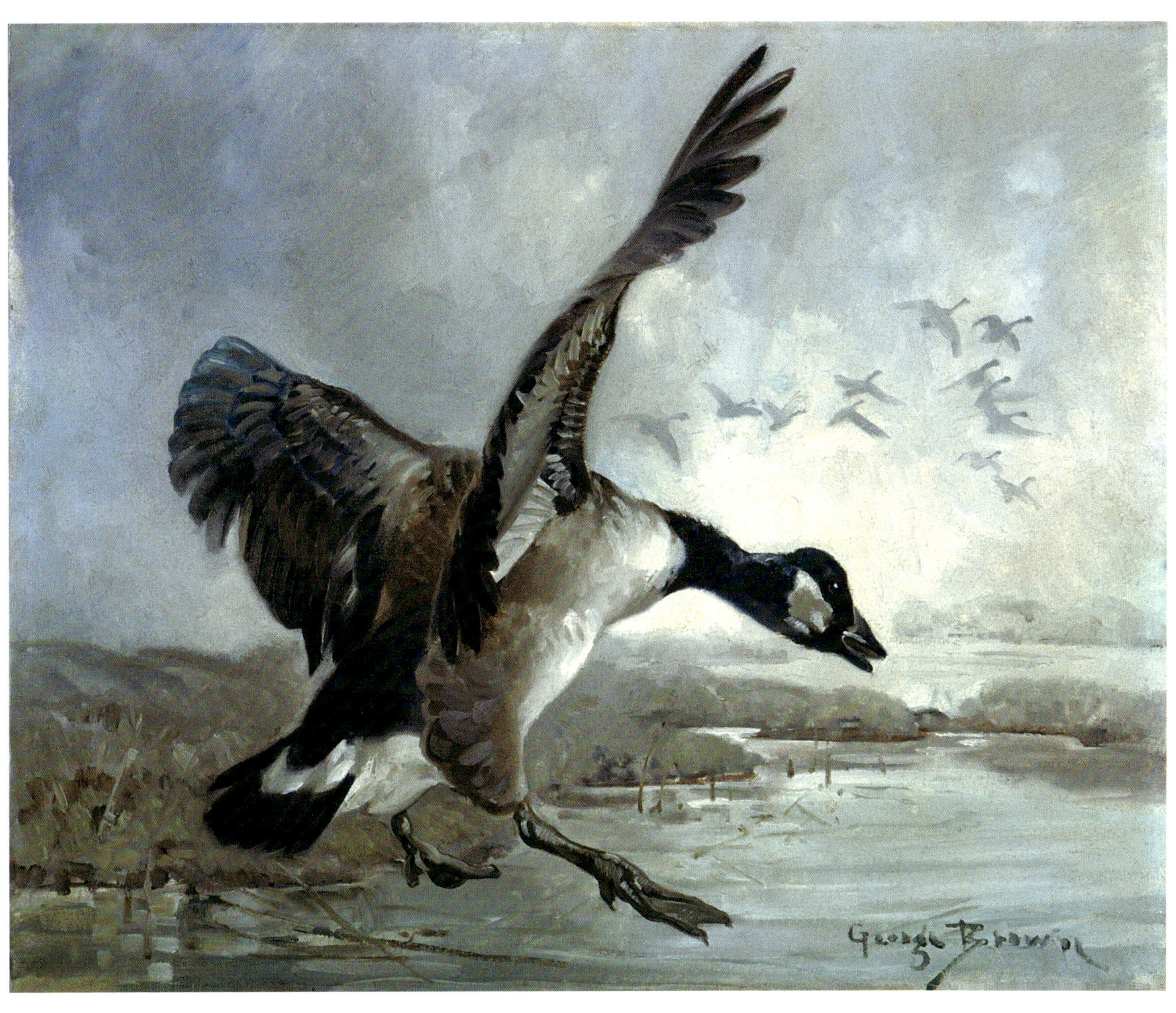

Plate 15
George Browne
Hutchinson Goose 1949
oil on canvas, 18 x 21½ in.
Private Collection

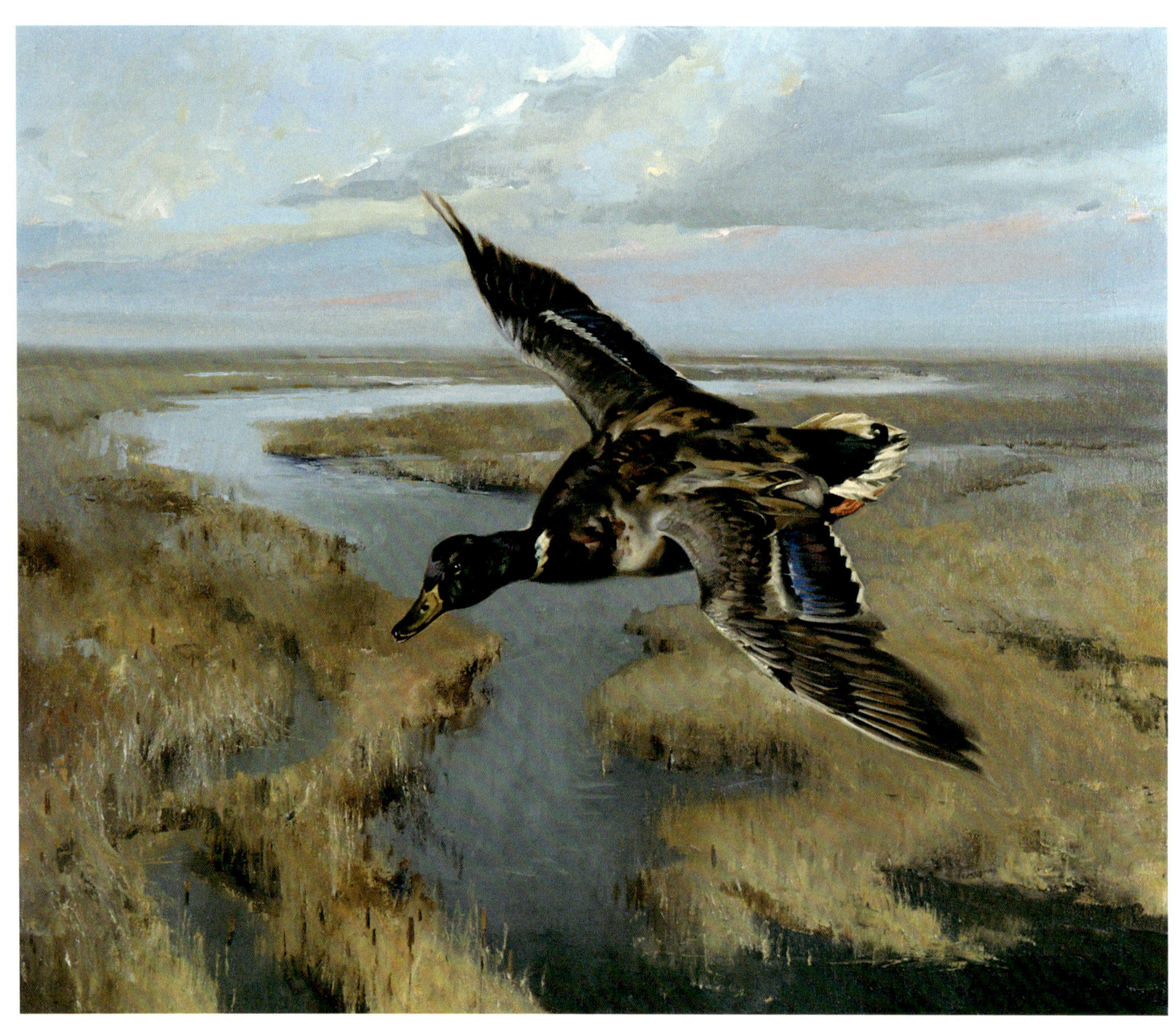

Plate 16
George Browne
Mallard in Flight 1948
oil on canvas, 26 x 31 in.
Private Collection

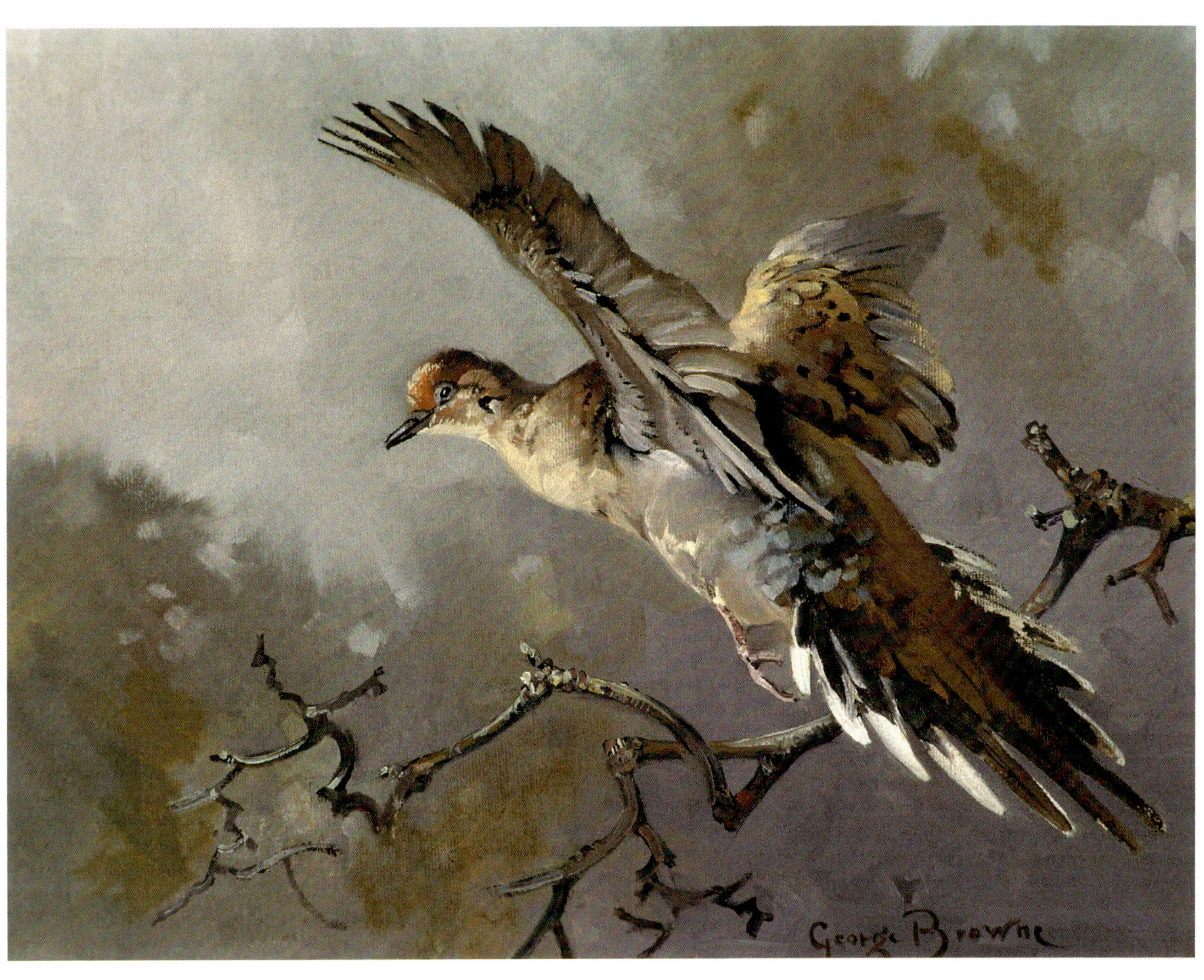

PLATE 17
George Browne
Mourning Dove 1942
oil on canvas board, 11⅞ x 16 in.
Leigh Yawkey Woodson Art Museum

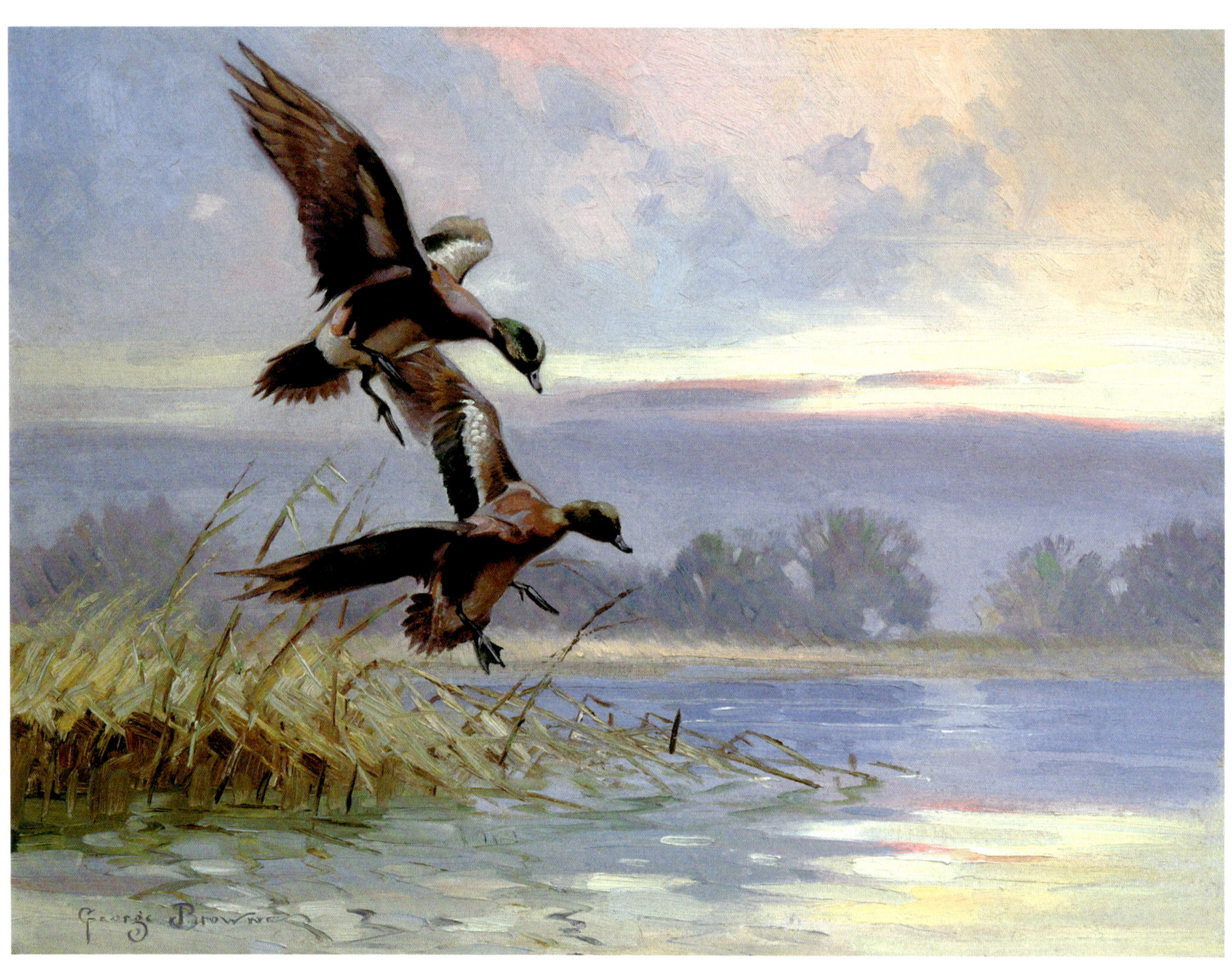

PLATE 18
George Browne
Widgeon
Date unknown
oil on canvas board, 12 x 16 in.
Bell Museum of Natural History/American Museum of Wildlife Art Collection

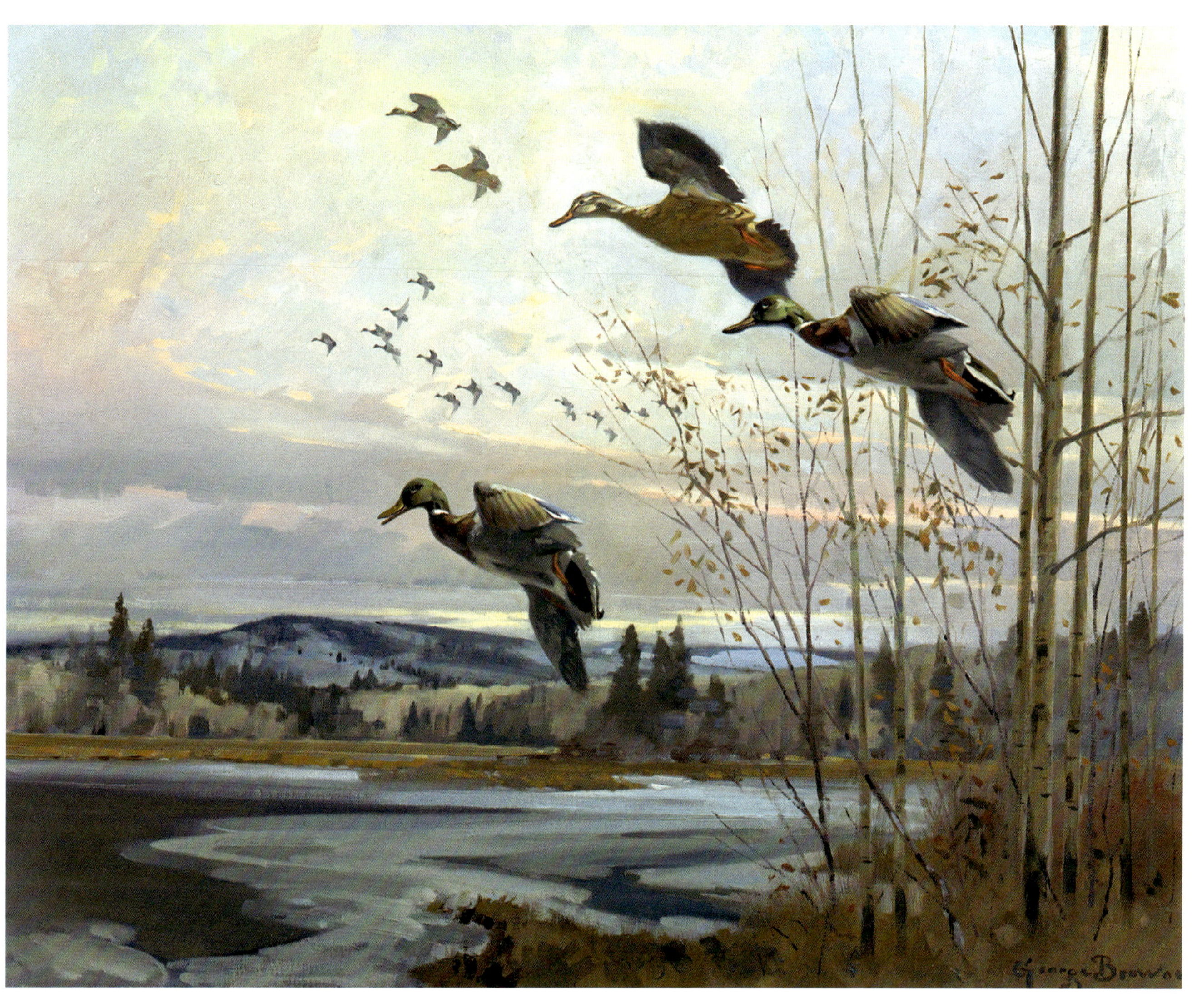

PLATE 19
George Browne
Foothills in November
Date unknown
oil on canvas, 20 x 25 in.
J.N. Bartfield Galleries

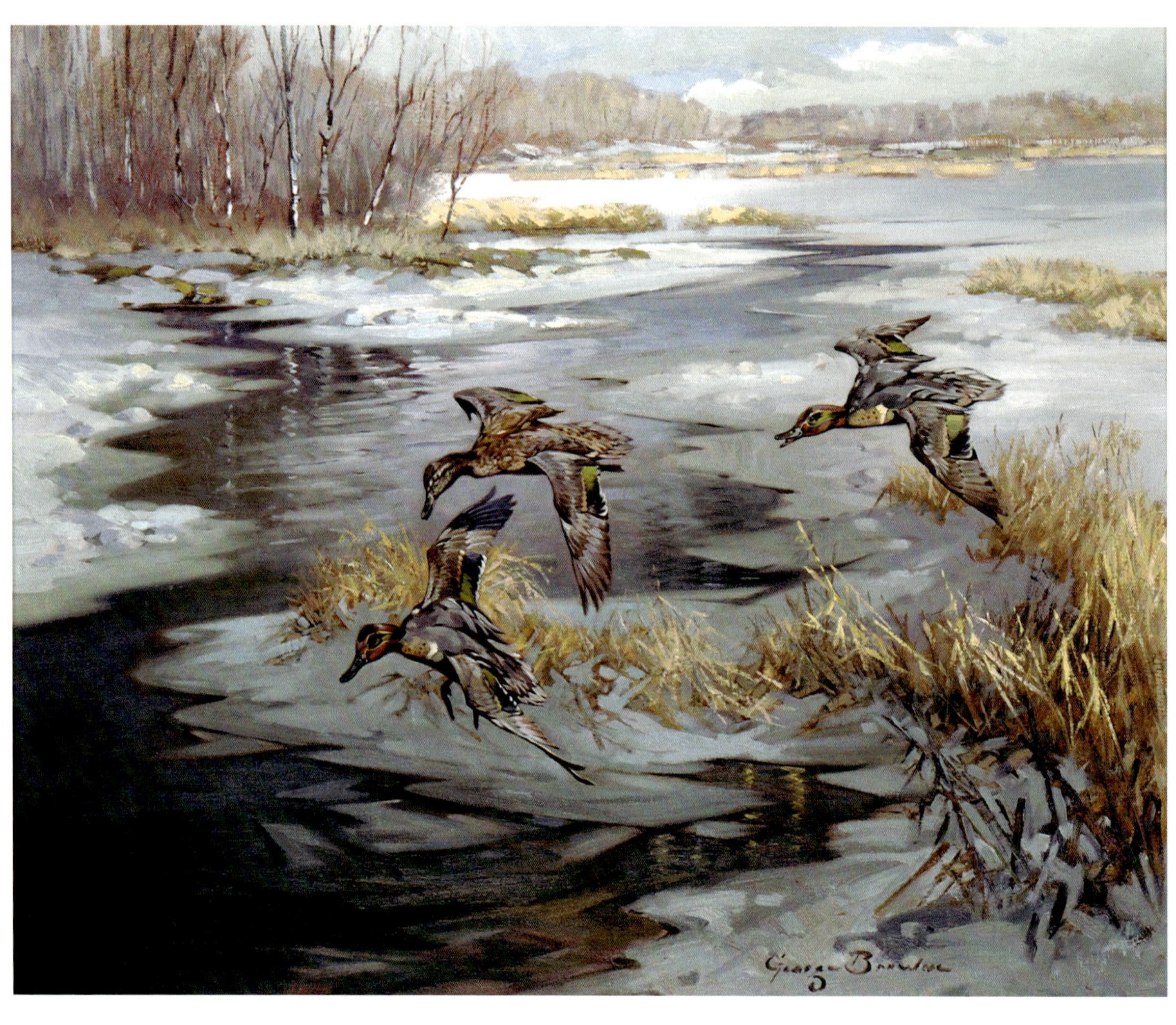

PLATE 20
George Browne
Greenwings in Cold Weather
Date unknown
oil on canvas, 20 x 30 in.
Len Braarud Fine Art

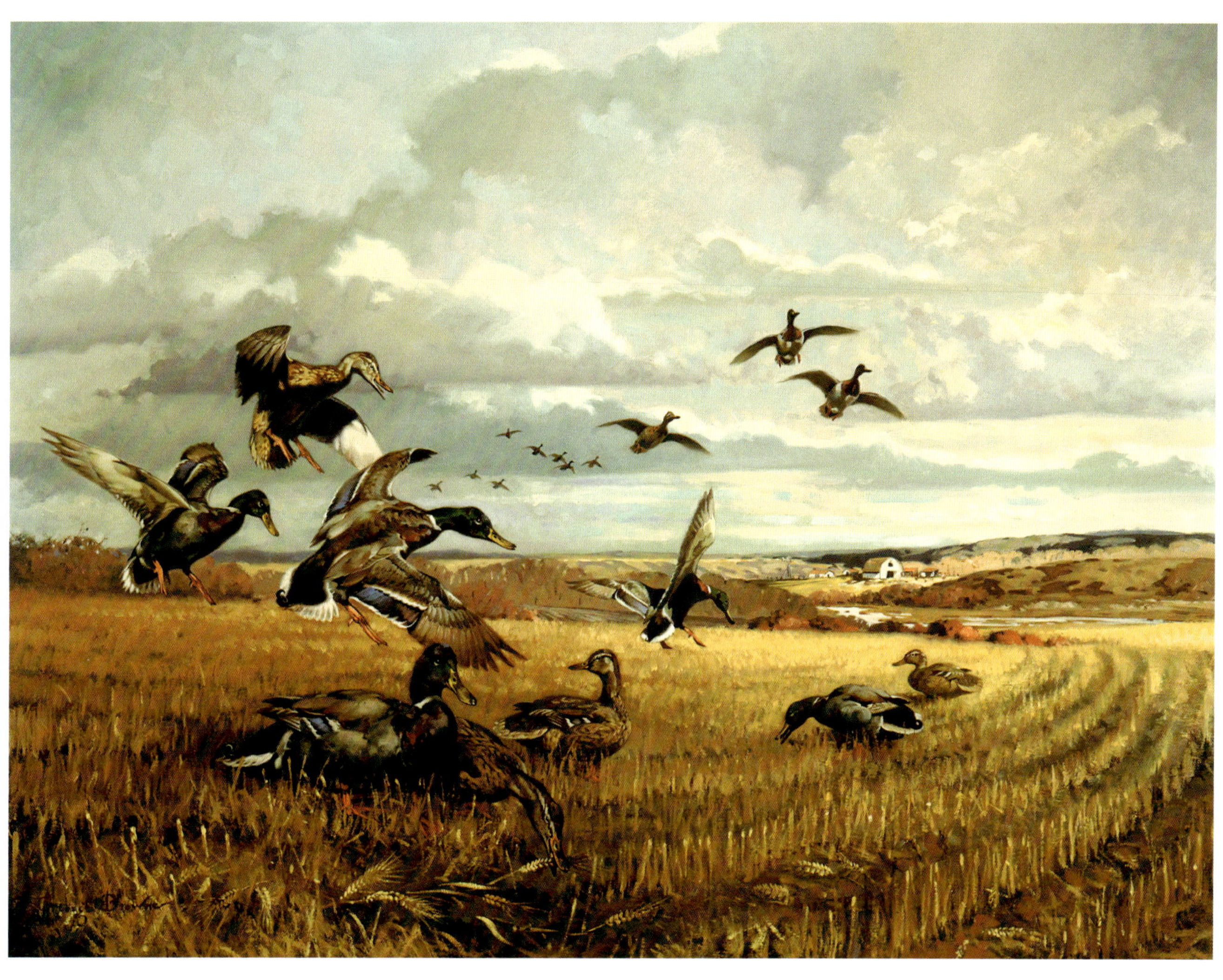

PLATE 21
George Browne
Mallards Gleaning the Stubble 1951
oil on canvas, 30 x 40 in.
Private Collection

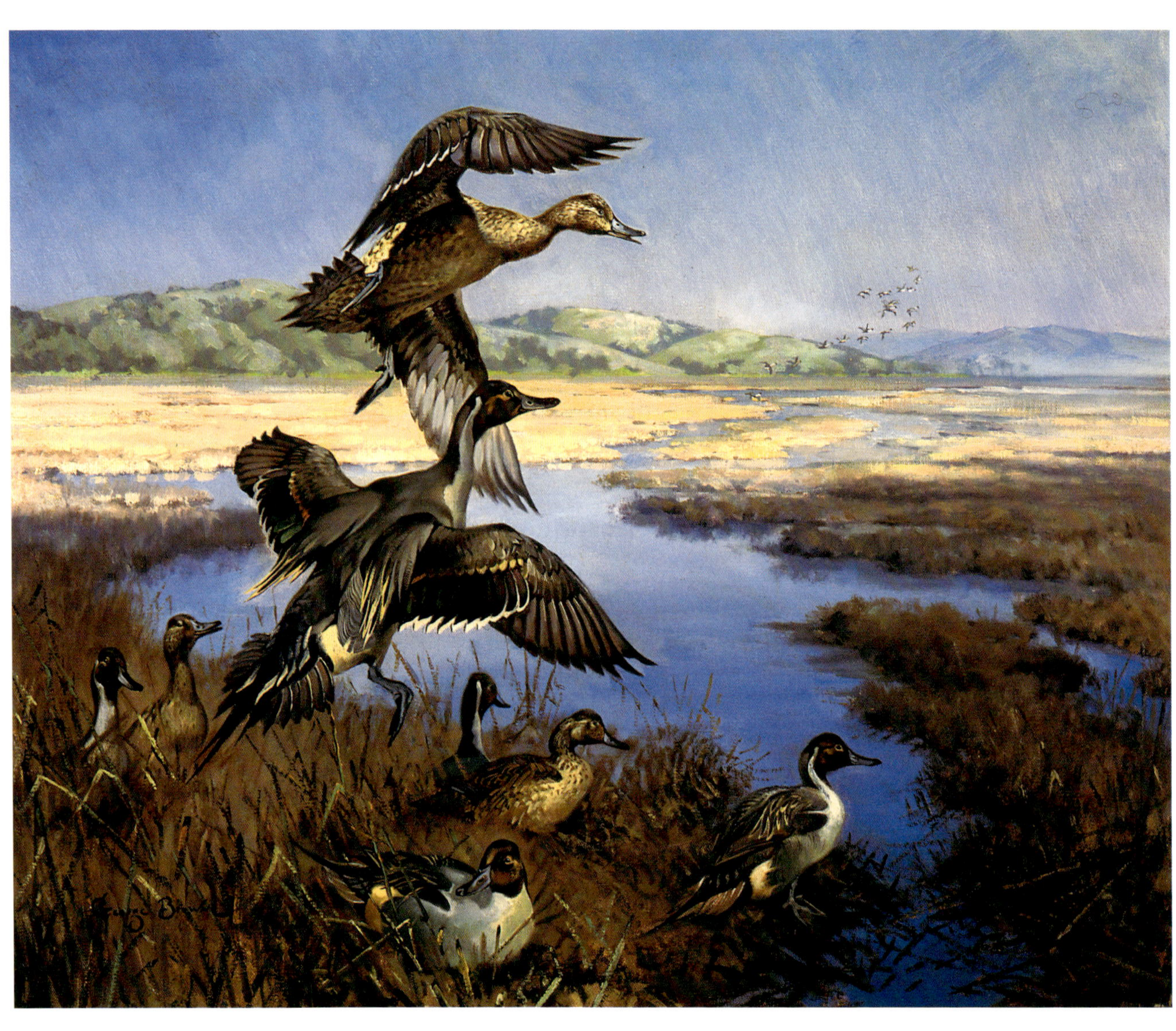

PLATE 22
George Browne
Pintails At Sunrise
Date unknown
oil on canvas, 25 x 30 in.
Collection of Hugh Robinson/Drummond Gallery

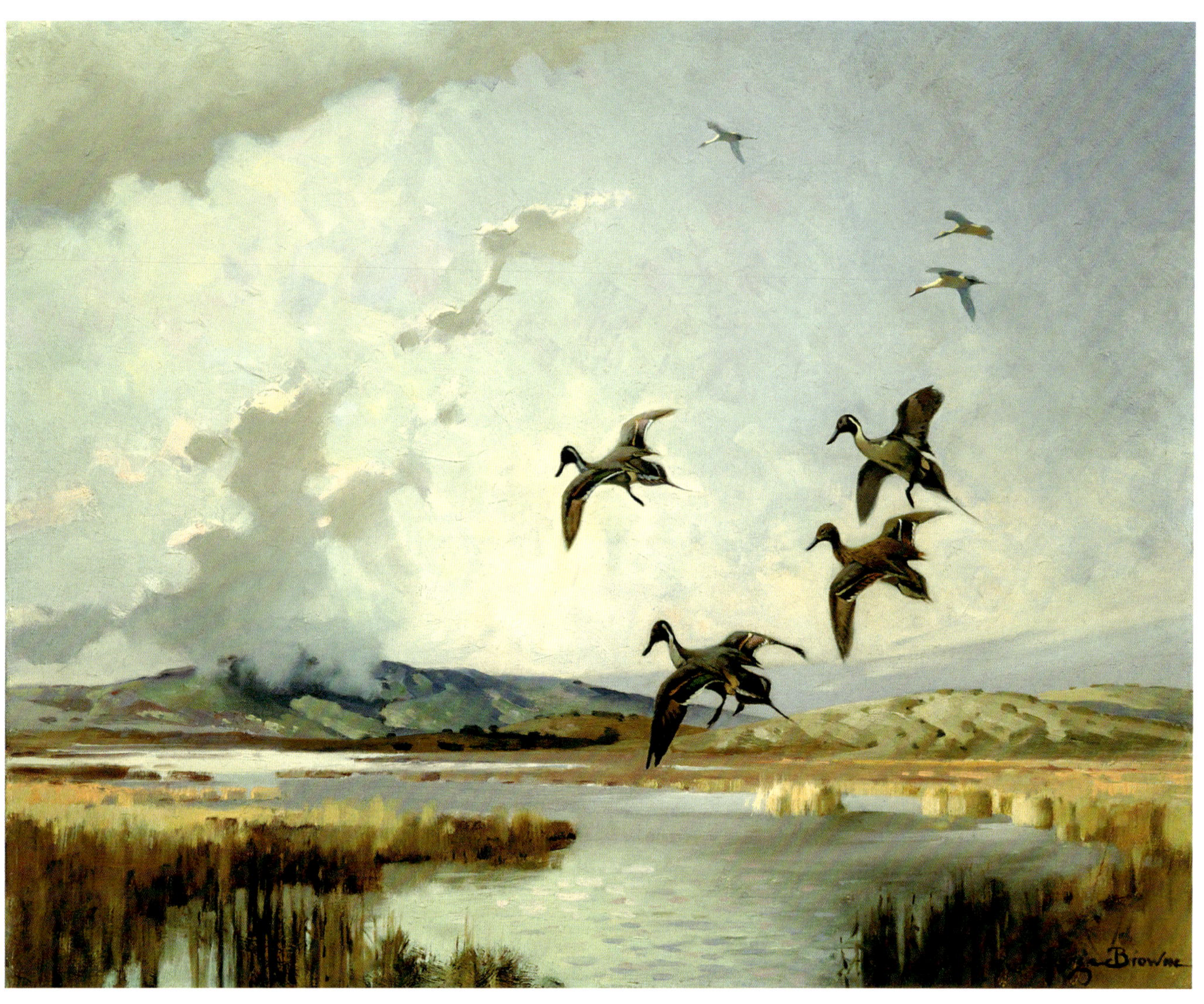

PLATE 23
George Browne
Pintails
Date unknown
oil on canvas, 16 x 20 in.
Bell Museum of Natural History/American Museum of Wildlife Art Collection

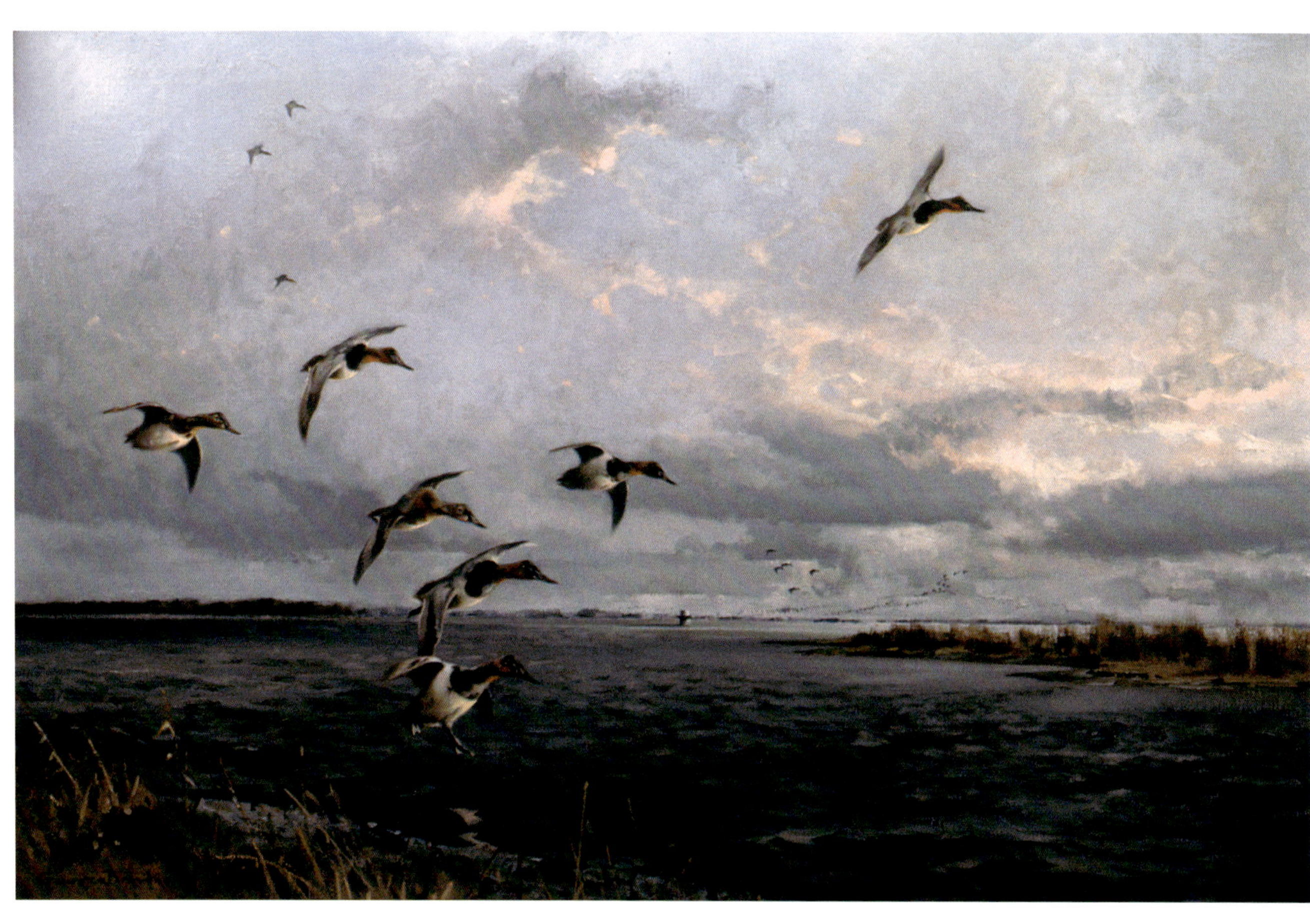

PLATE 24
George Browne
Newfoundland Point
Date unknown
oil on canvas, 24 x 36 in.
Ward Museum of Wildfowl Art/Permanent Loan Private Collection

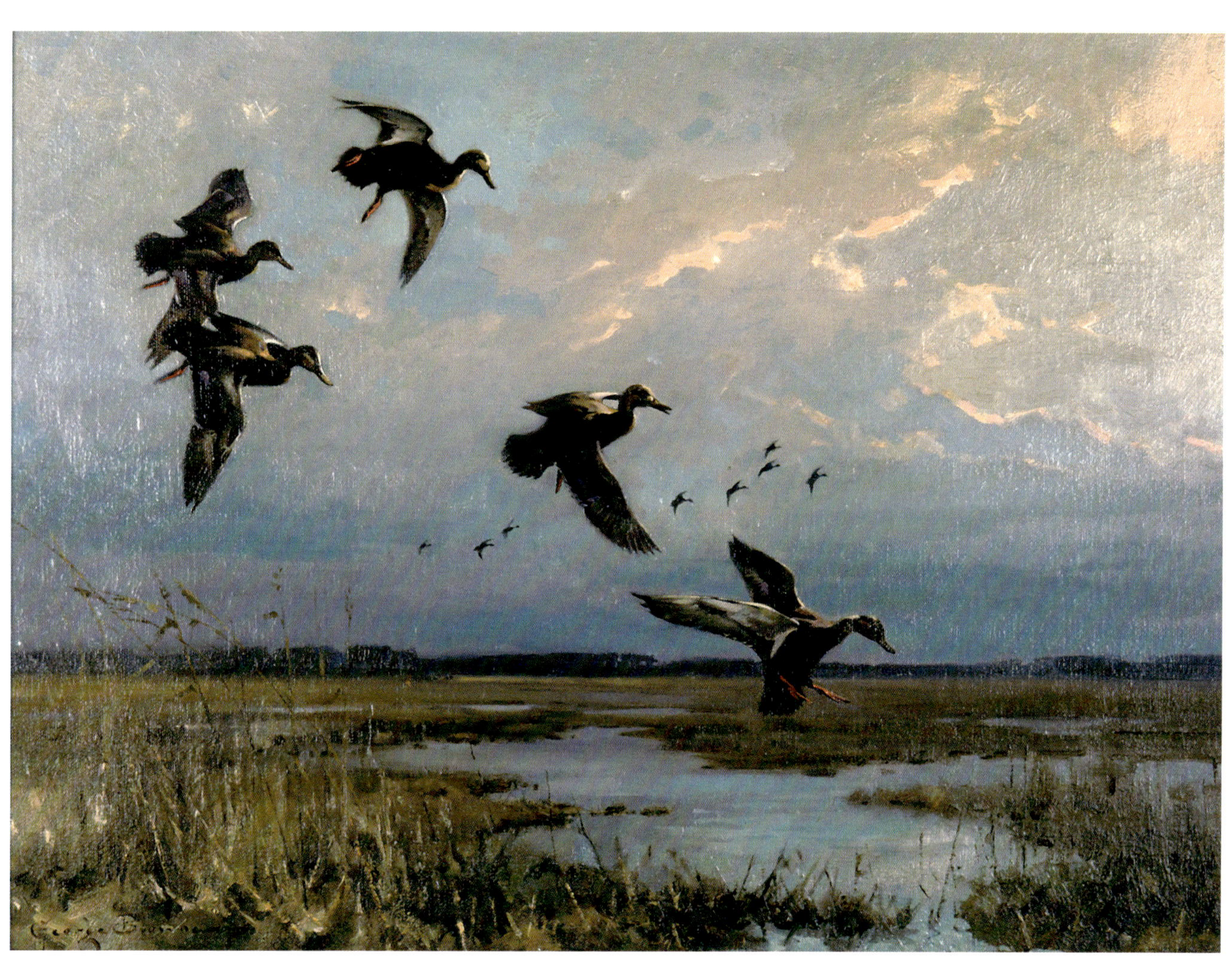

PLATE 25
George Browne
Black Ducks 1928
oil on canvas, 16 x 20 in.
Drummond Gallery

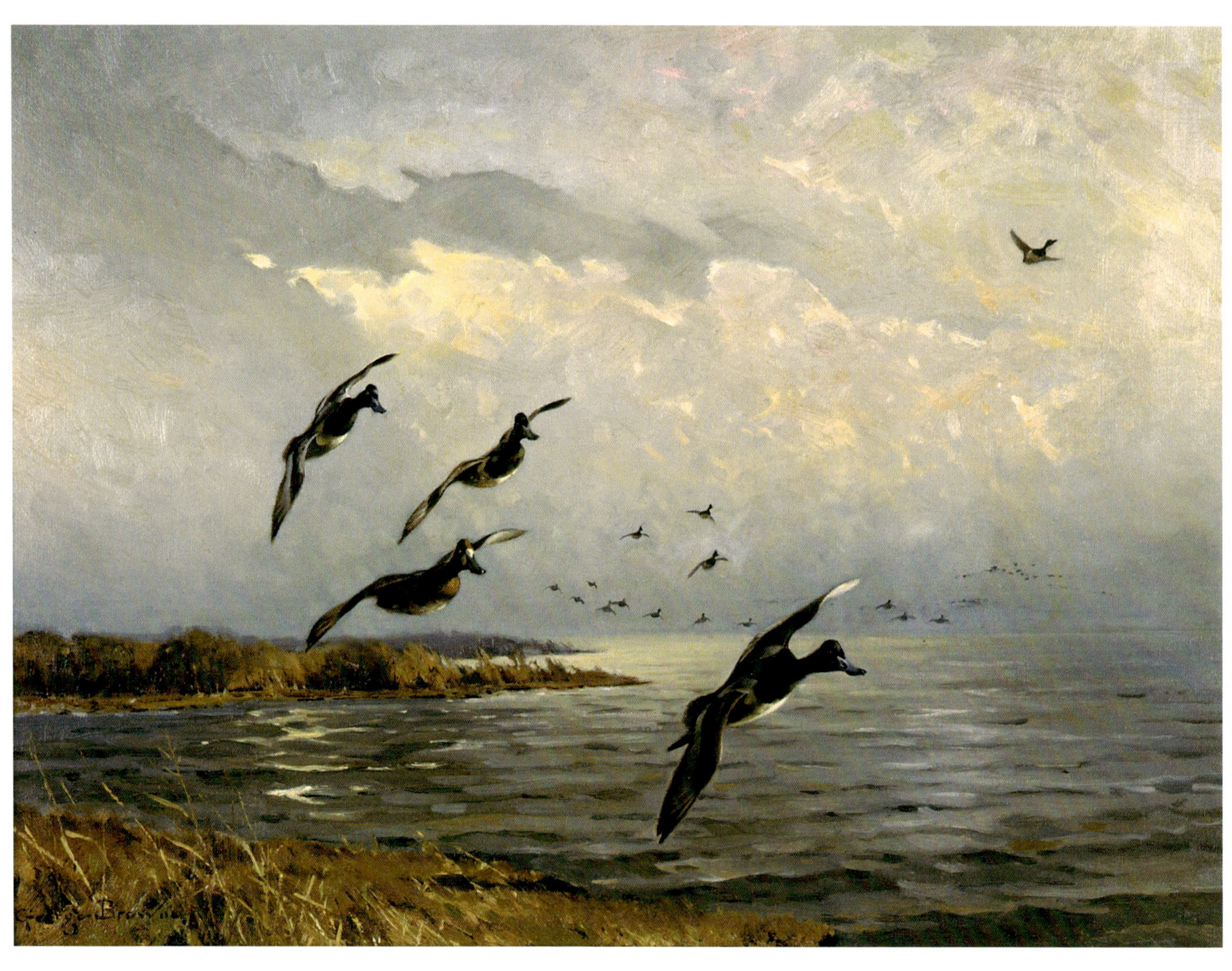

Plate 26
George Browne
Blue Bills
Date unknown
oil on canvas, 16 x 20 in.
Drummond Gallery

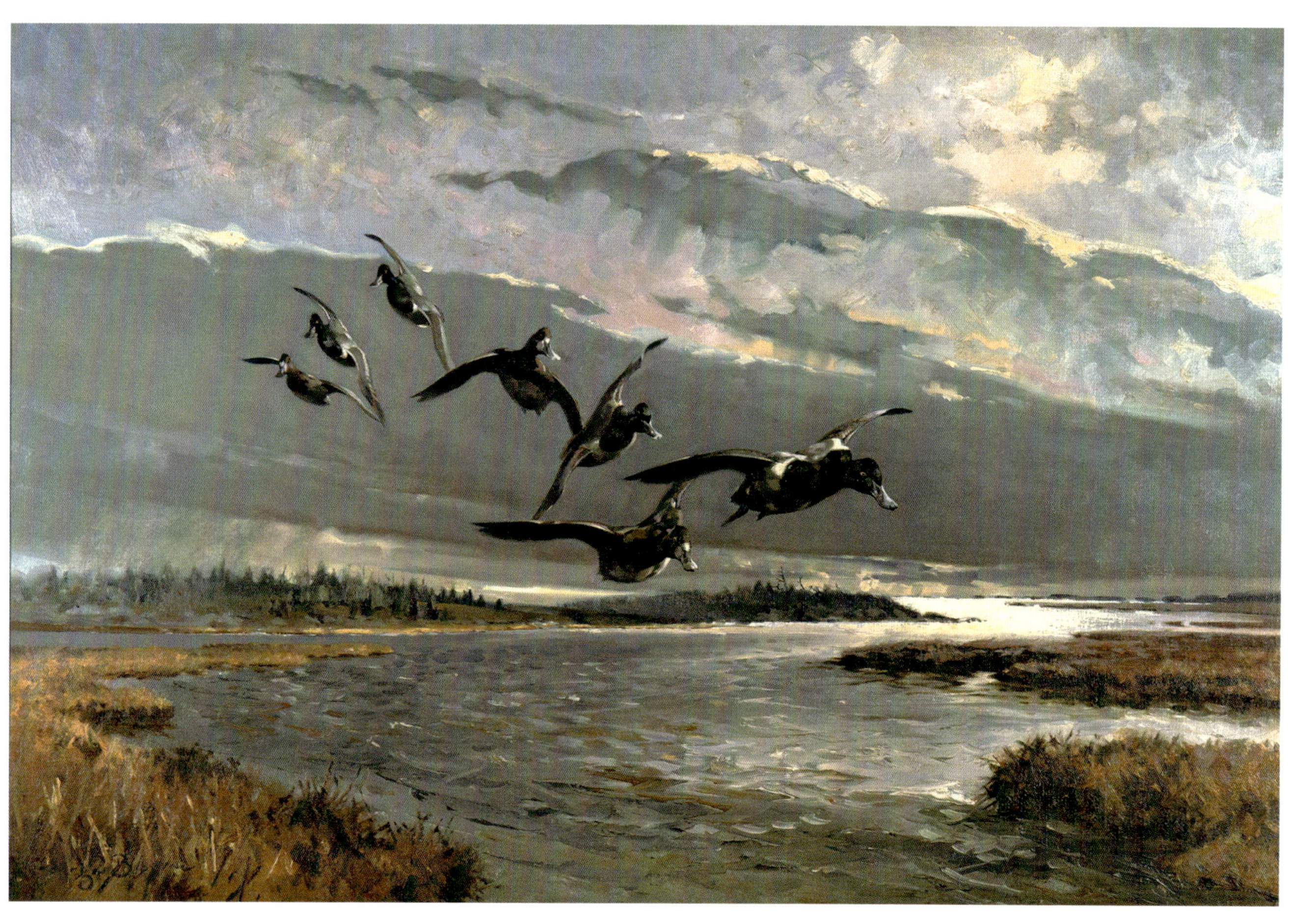

PLATE 27
George Browne
Broadbills Before the Squall 1956
oil on canvas, 19½ x 29 in.
Private Collection

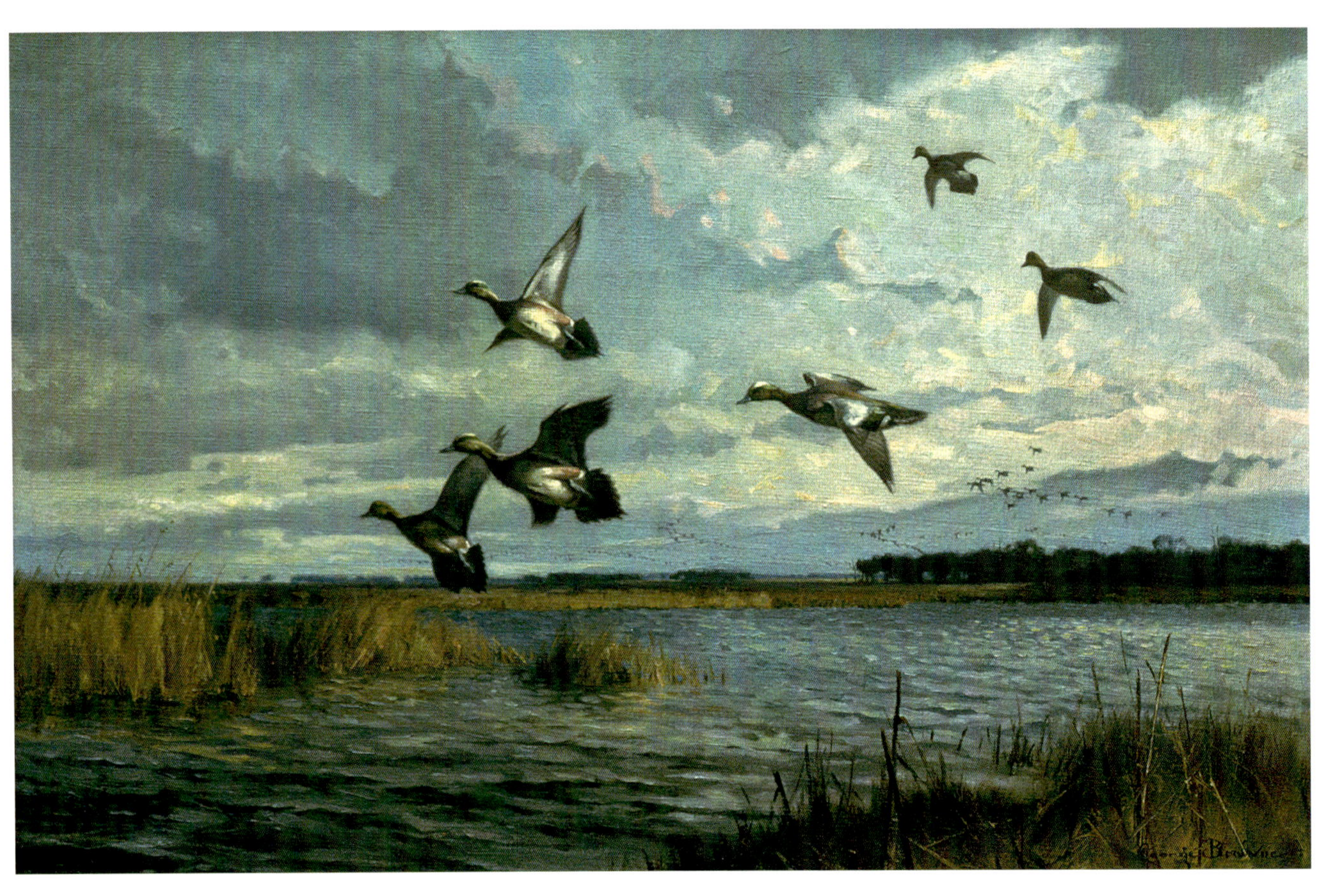

PLATE 28
George Browne
Baldpate Widgeon
Date unknown
oil on canvas
Robert Fraser Sporting and Southern Art

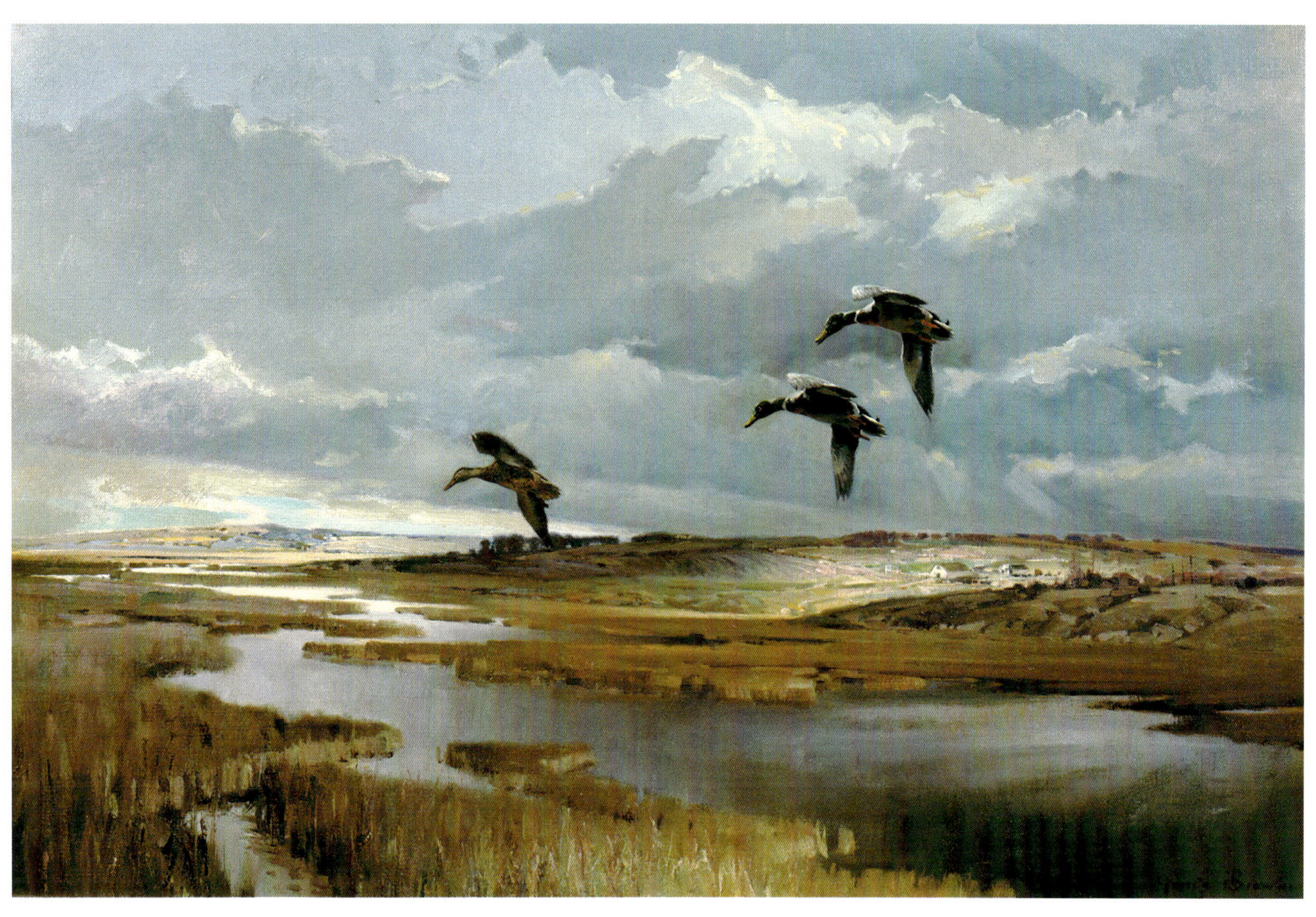

Plate 29
George Browne
The Farm Marsh
Date unknown
oil on canvas, 24 x 36 in.
Sportsman's Edge Ltd.
Crossroads of Sport catalogue 1982

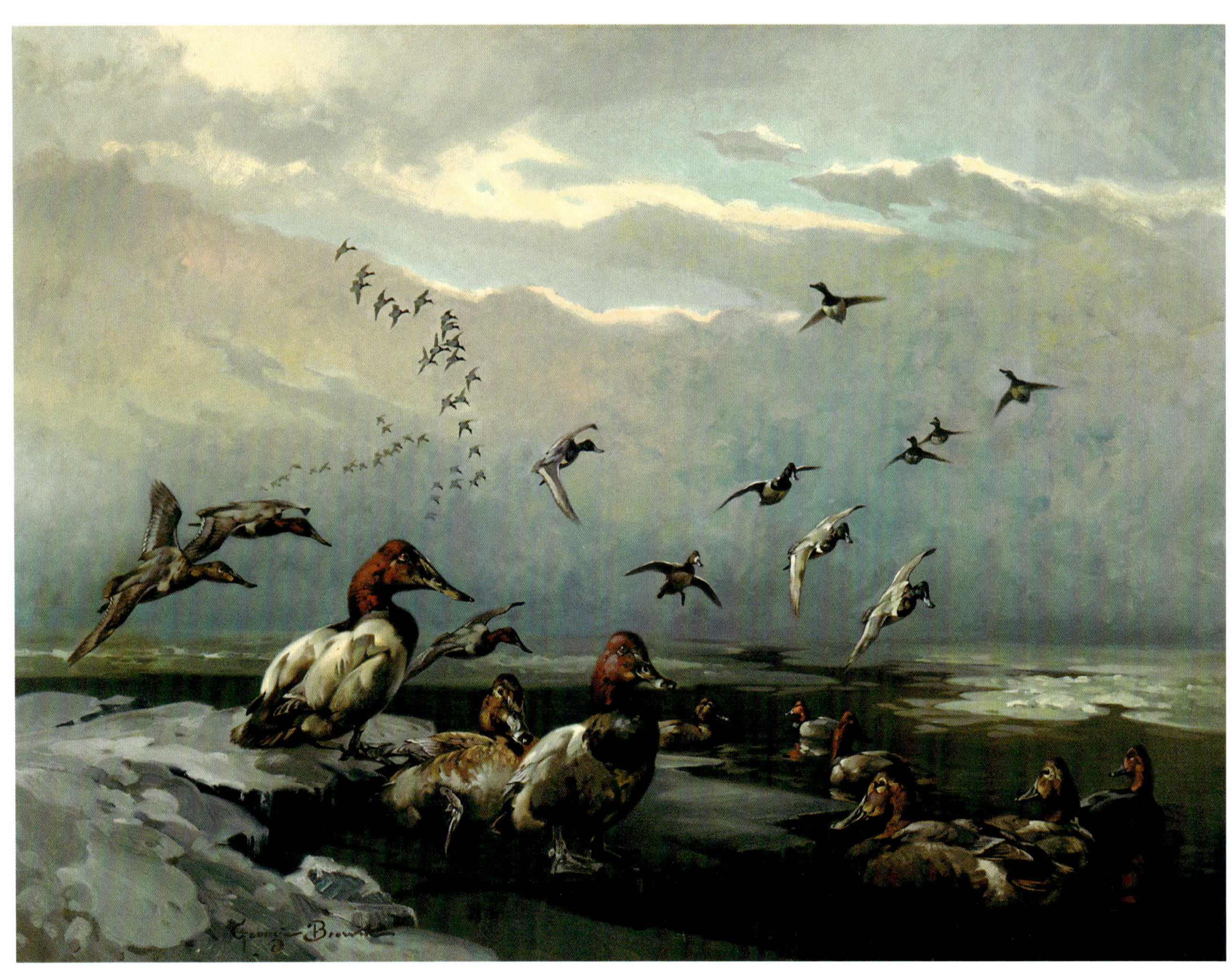

Plate 30
George Browne
Winter On The Bay 1942
oil on canvas, 30 x 40 in.
Private Collection

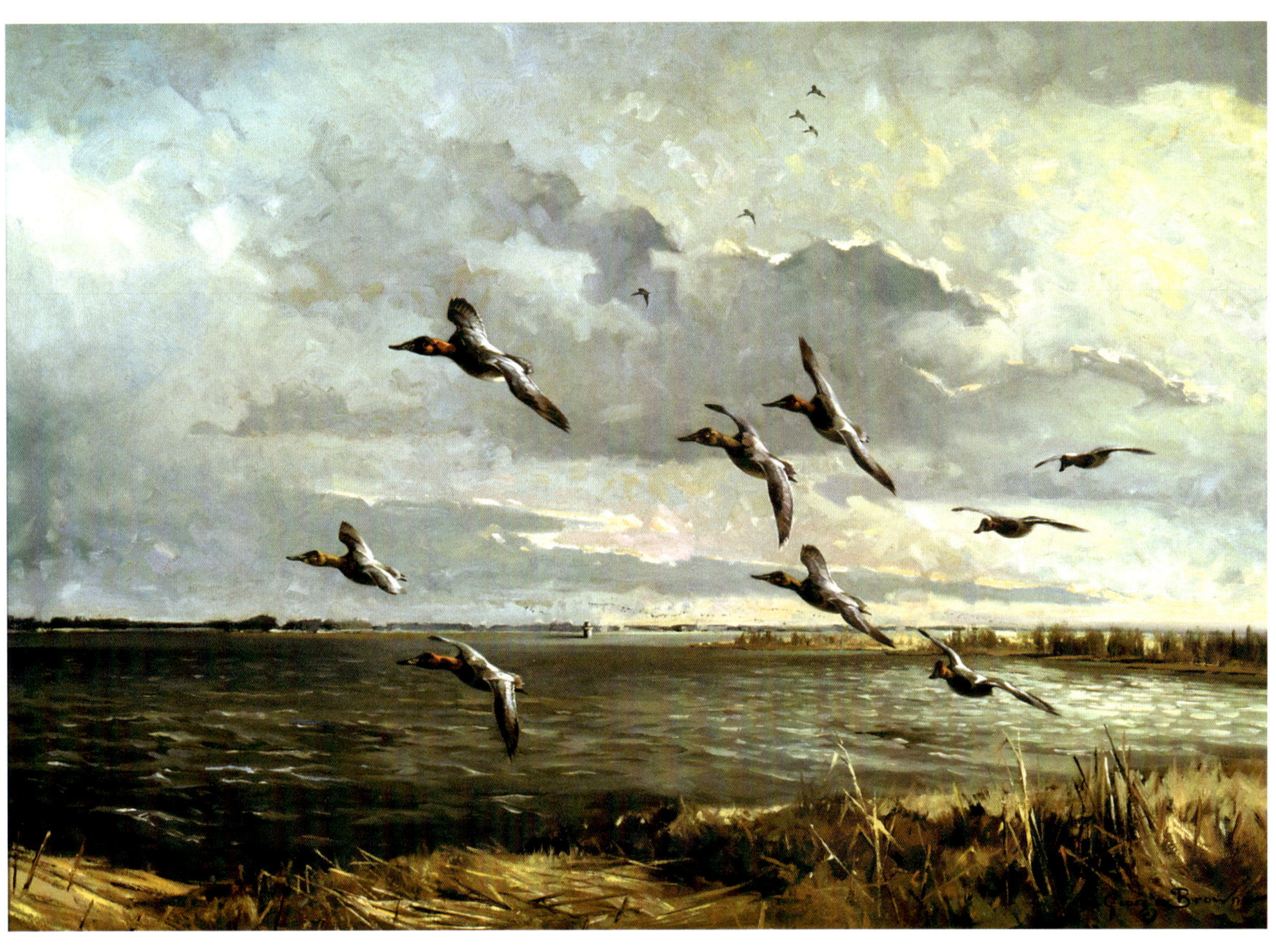

PLATE 31
George Browne
Canvasbacks Swinging the Channel 1950
oil on canvas, 24 x 36 in.
Private Collection

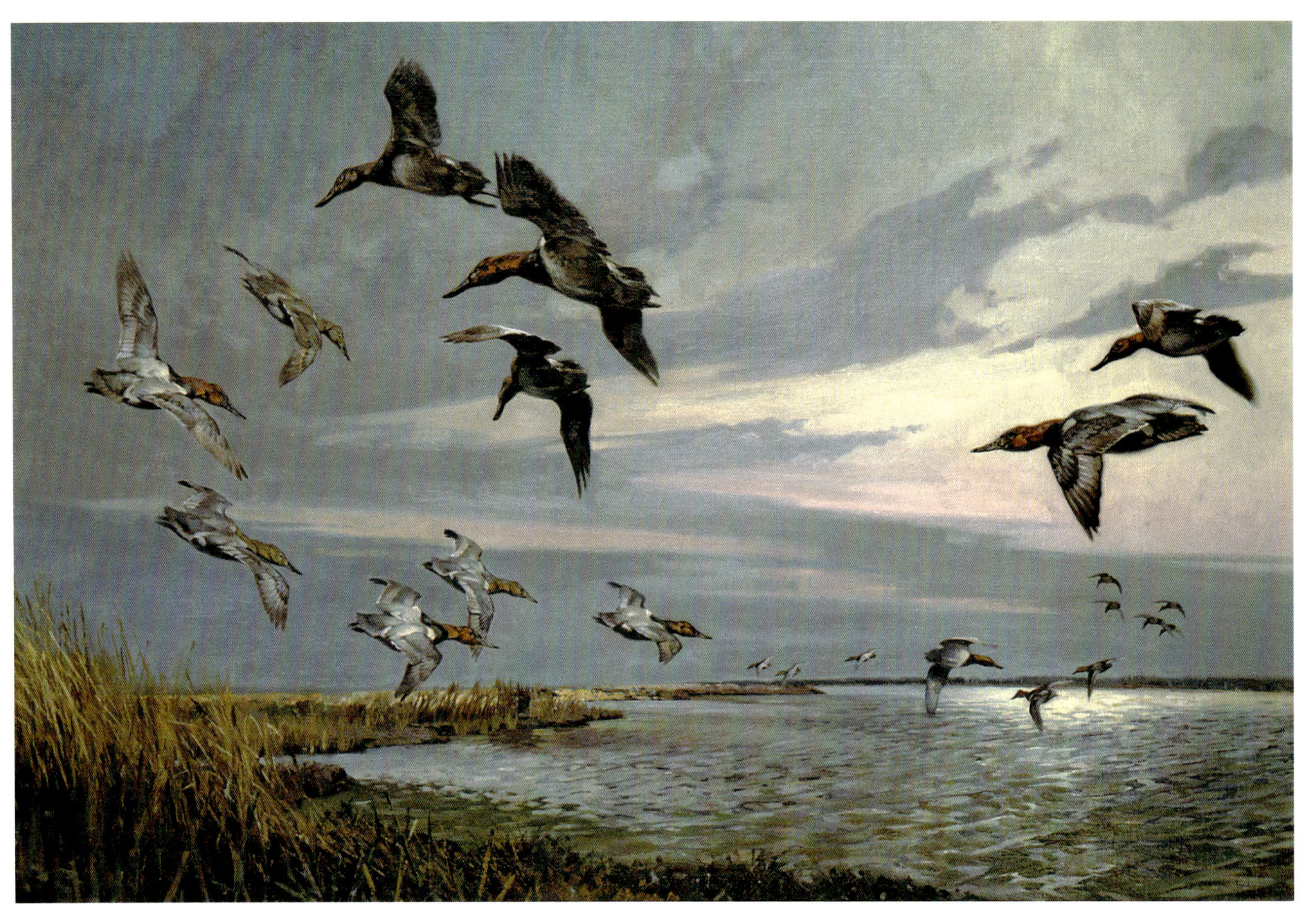

PLATE 32
George Browne
Cove Blind At Mubulo—Canvasbacks
Date Unknown
oil on canvas board, 22½ x 34½ in.
Bell Museum of Natural History/American Museum of Wildlife Art Collection

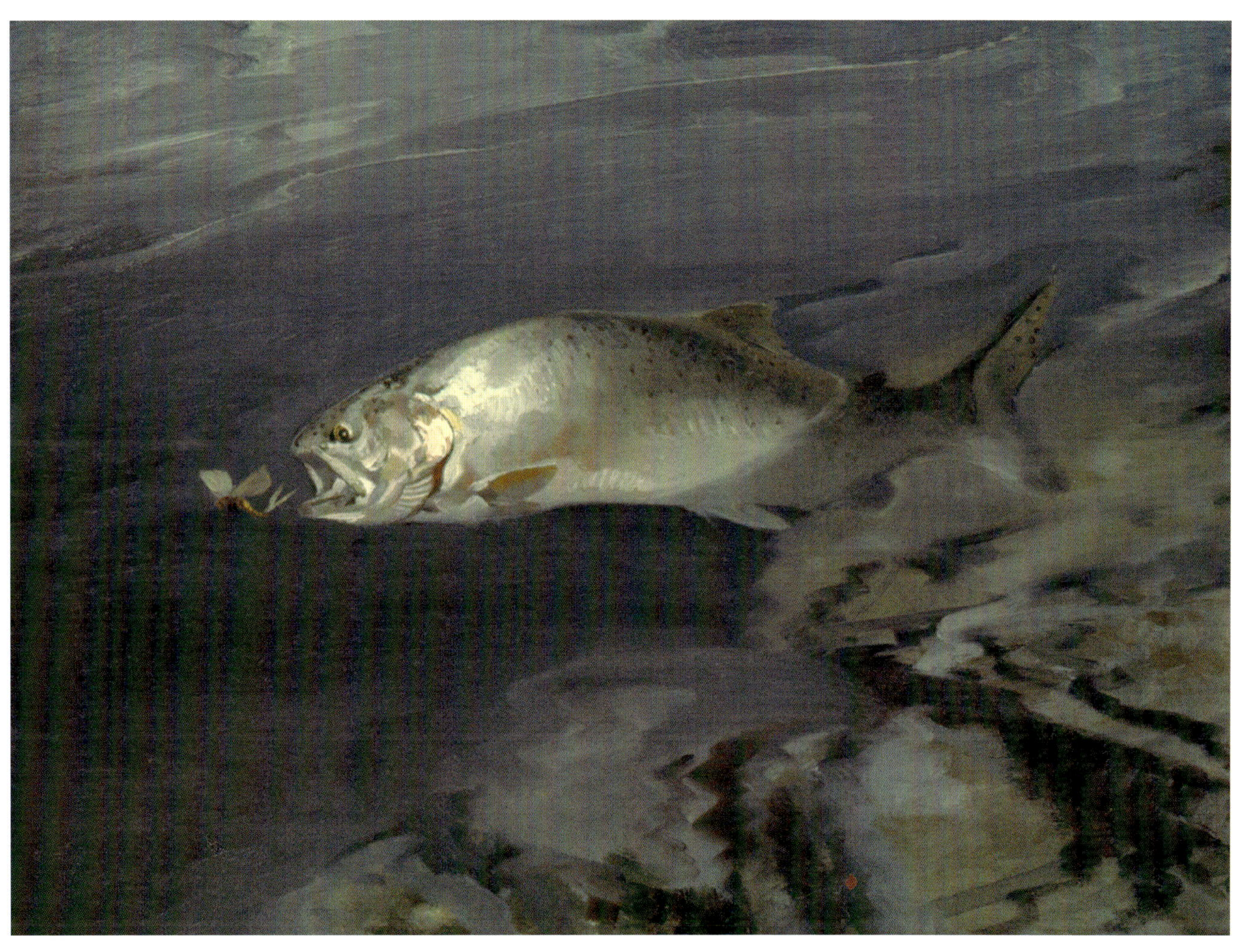

Plate 33
George Browne
Cutthroat Trout (unsigned) 1945
oil on canvas, 12 x 16 in.
Private Collection

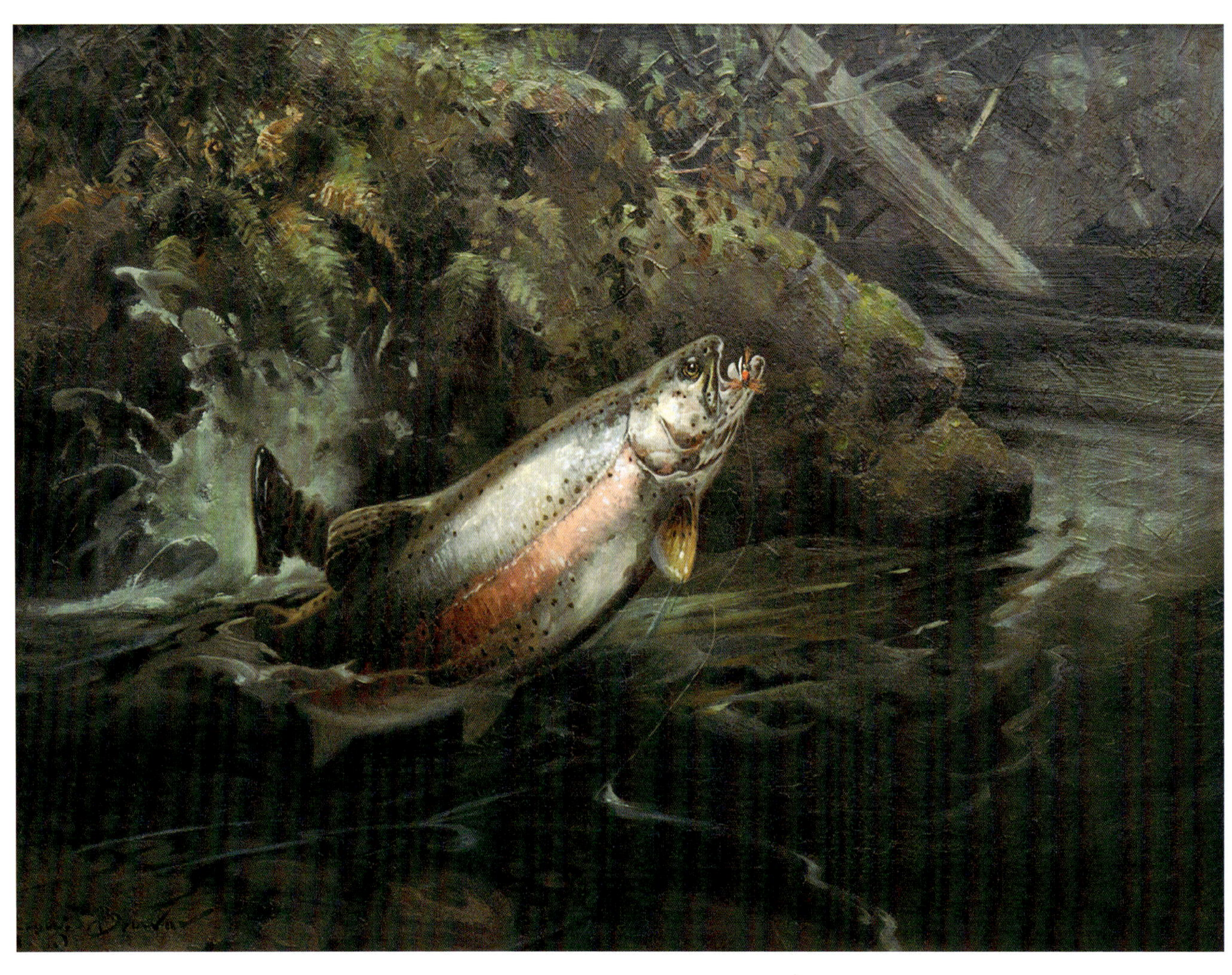

PLATE 34
George Browne
Rainbow Trout 1941
oil on canvas, 12 x 16 in.
Robert Fraser Sporting and Southern Art

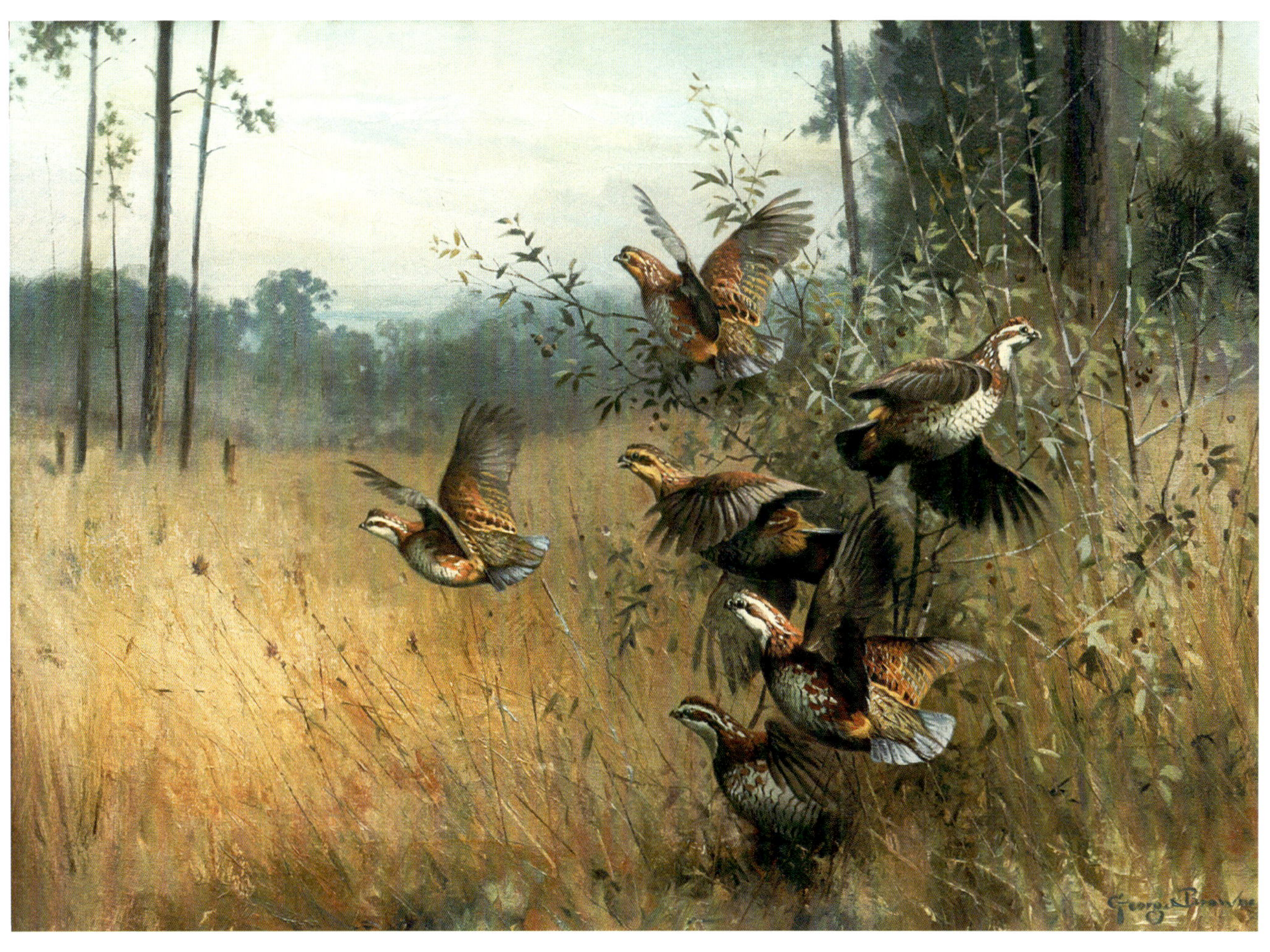

PLATE 35
George Browne
Bobwhite
Date unknown
oil on canvas
Robert Fraser Sporting and Southern Art

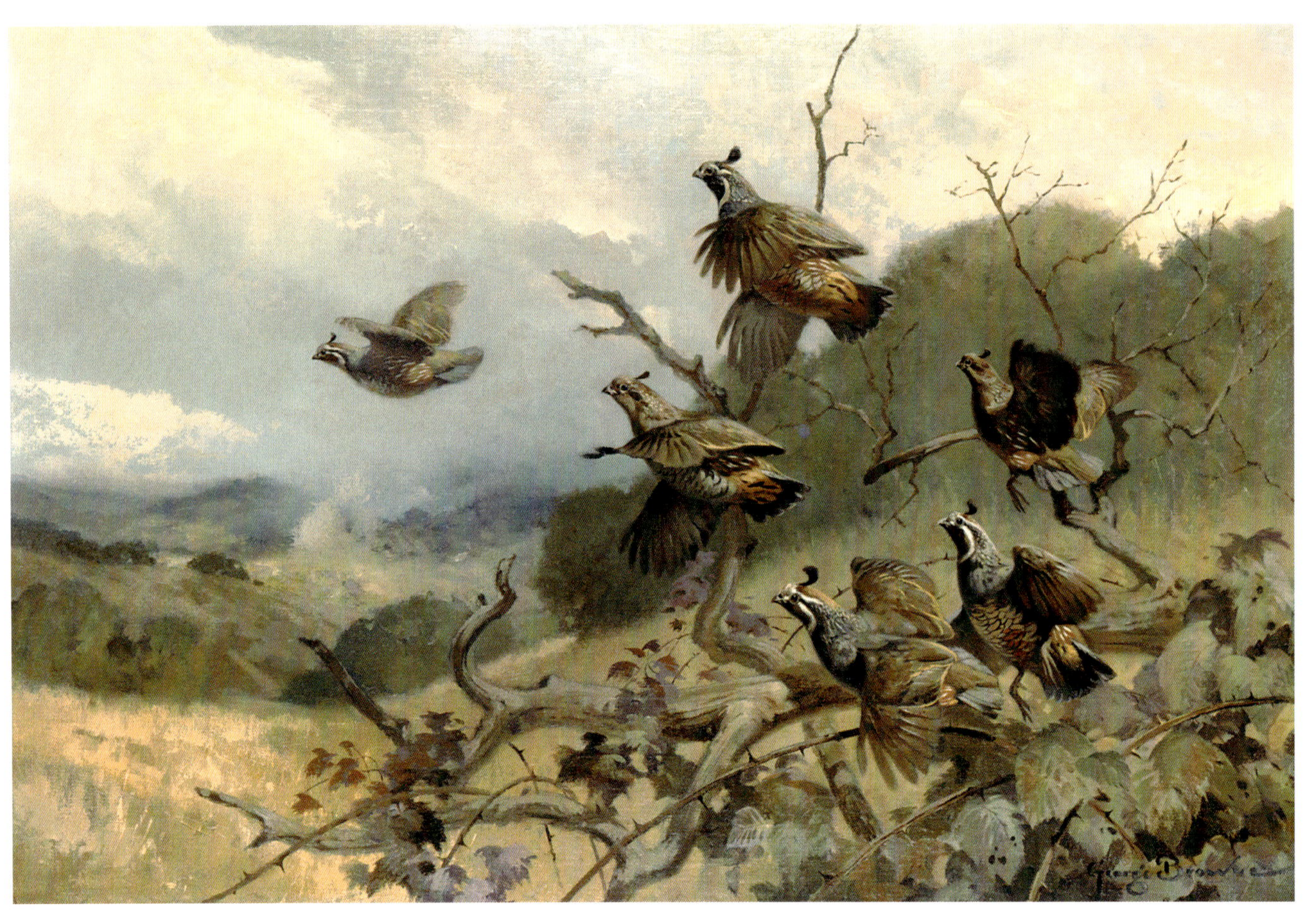

Plate 36
George Browne
Roosting Cover 1956
oil on canvas, 20 x 30 in.
Len Braarud Fine Art

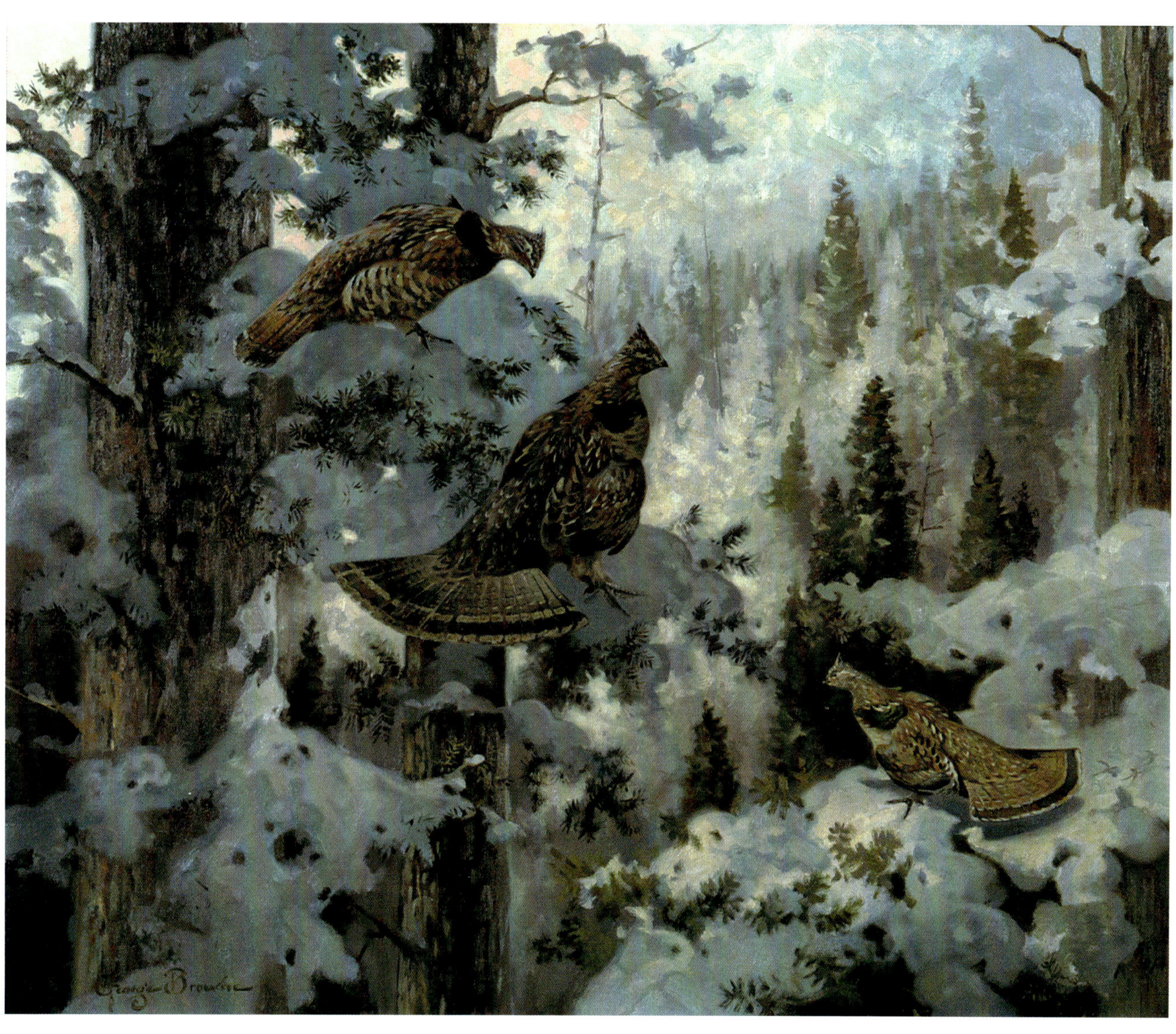

Plate 37
George Browne
Winter's Morning (Ruffed Grouse)
Date unknown
oil on canvas, 24 x 30 in.
Sportsman's Edge Ltd.

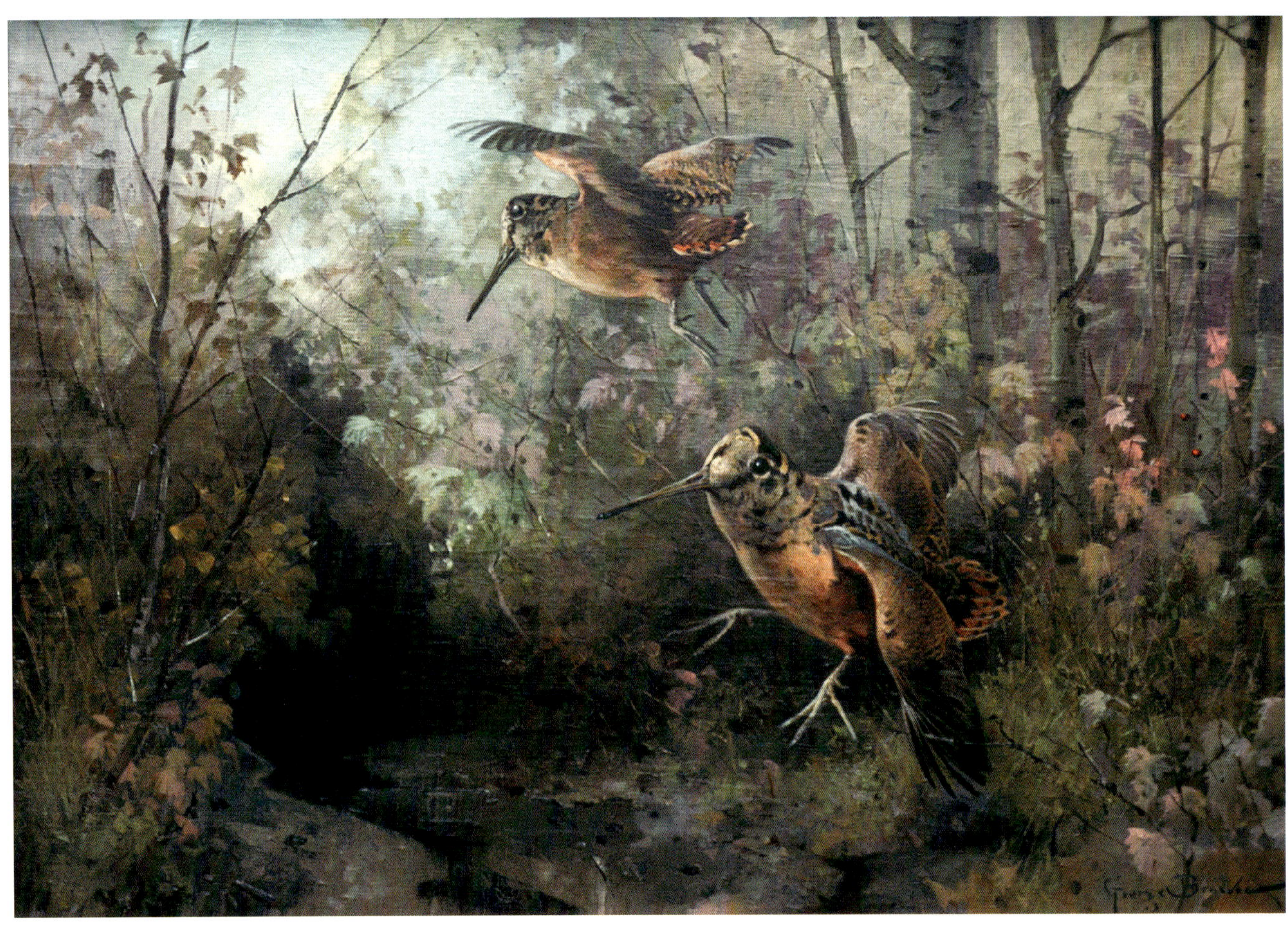

Plate 38
George Browne
Woodcock 1957
oil on canvas, 18 x 26 in
Robert Fraser Sporting and Southern Art

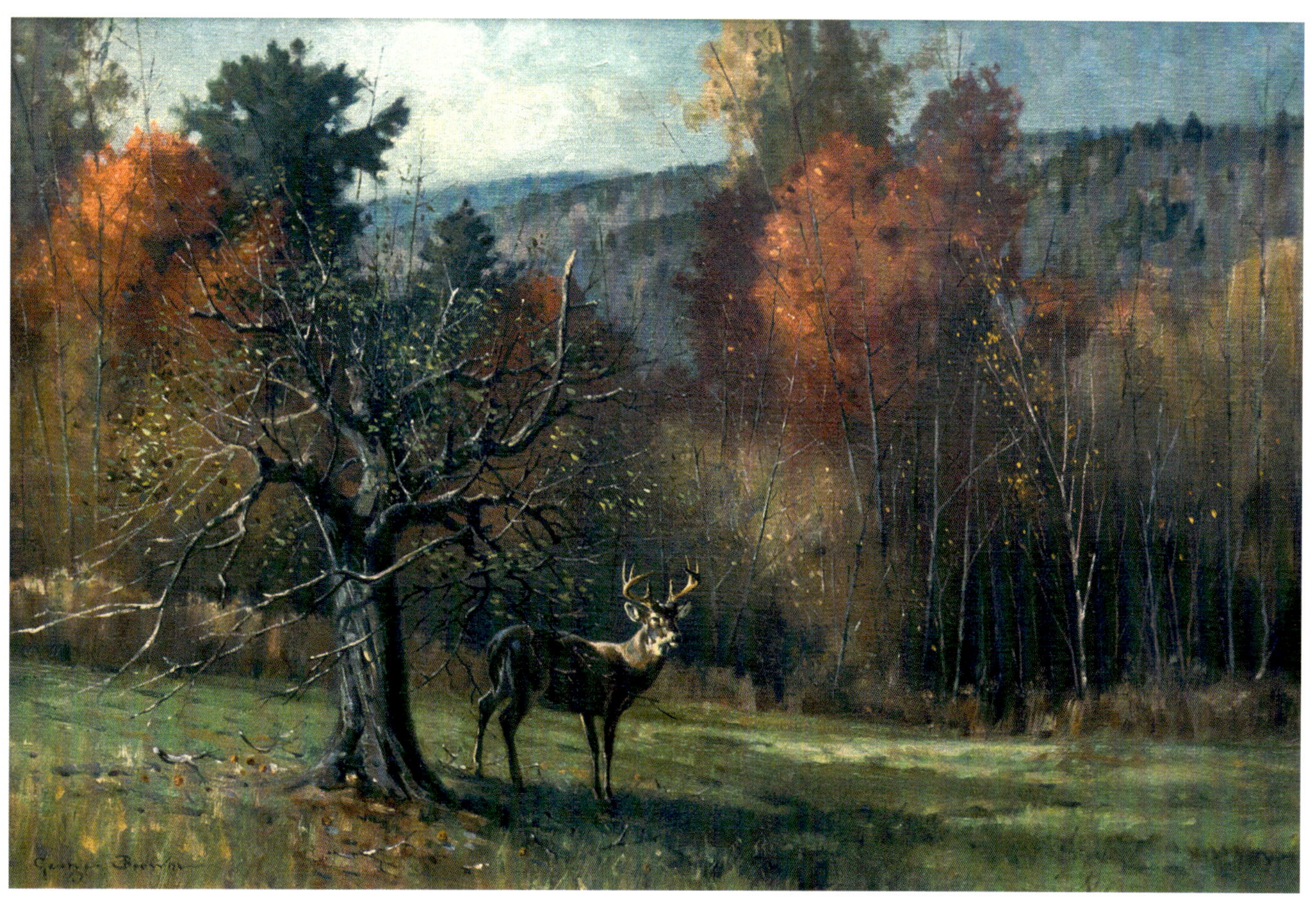

PLATE 39
George Browne
Whitetail Deer
Date unknown
oil on canvas
Robert Fraser Sporting and Southern Art

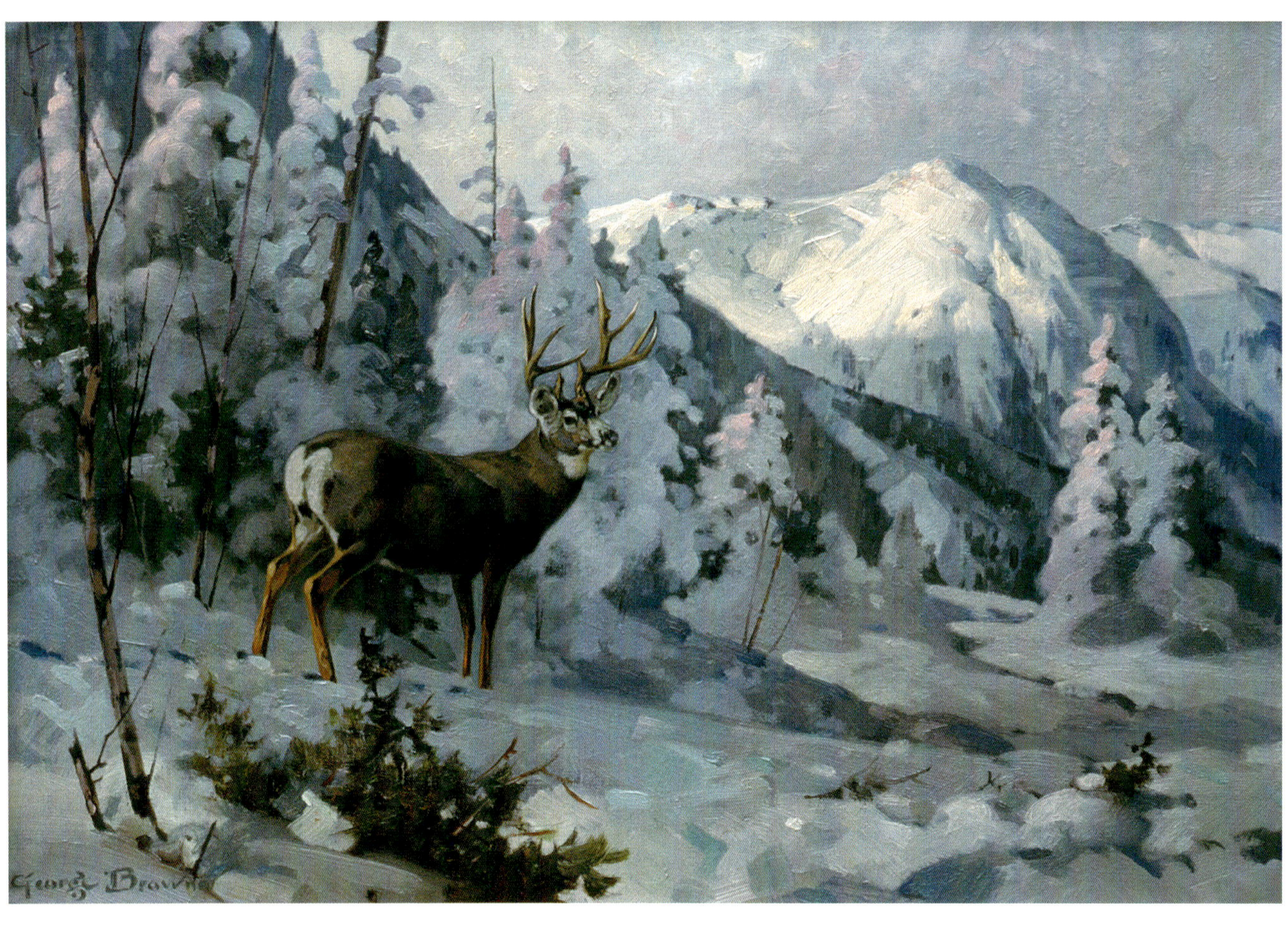

PLATE 40
George Browne
Mule Deer 1956
oil on canvas, 20 x 30 in.
Robert Fraser Sporting and Southern Art

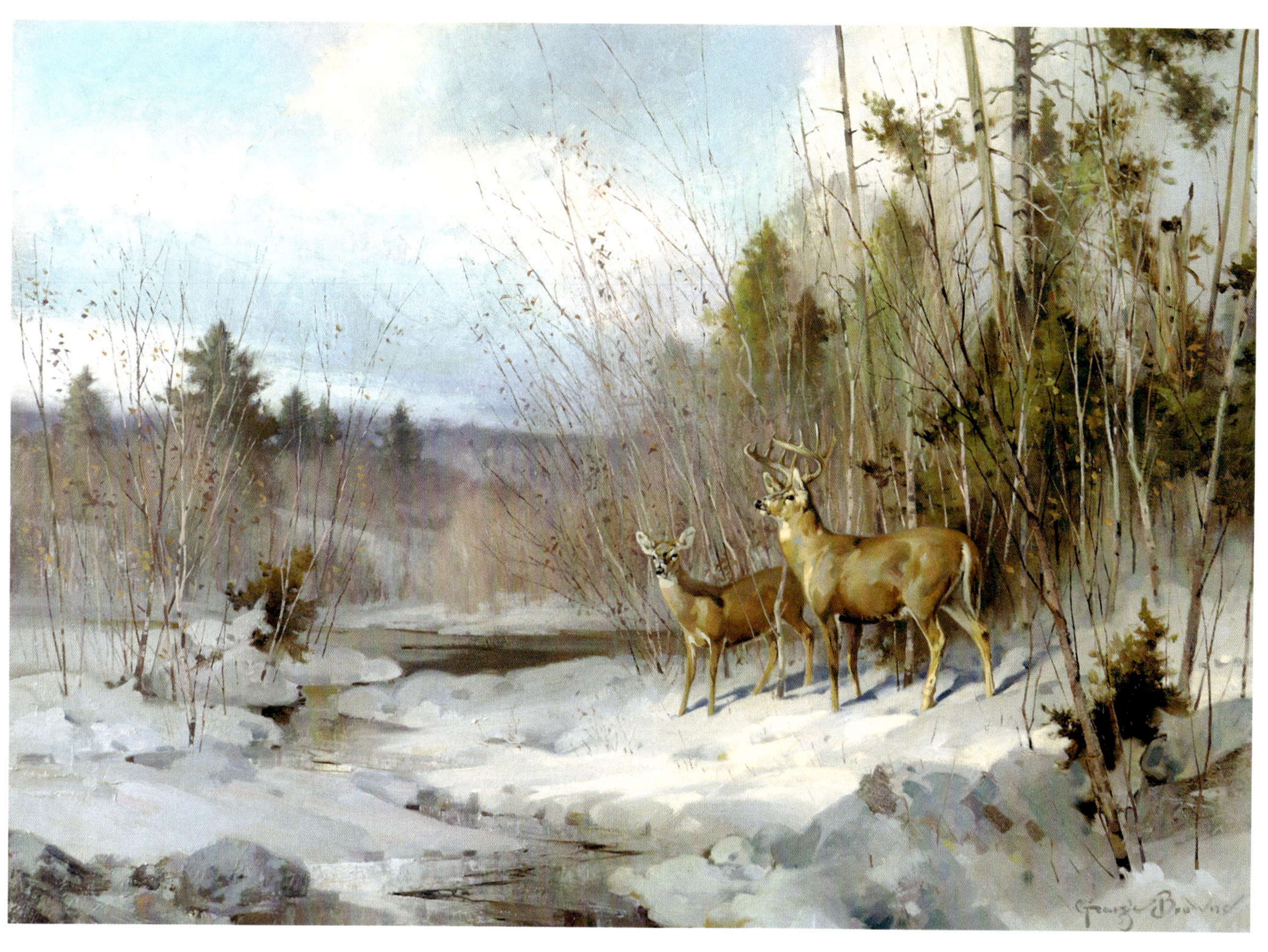

PLATE 41
George Browne
At The Crossing 1957
oil on canvas, 22 x 32 in.
J.N. Bartfield Galleries

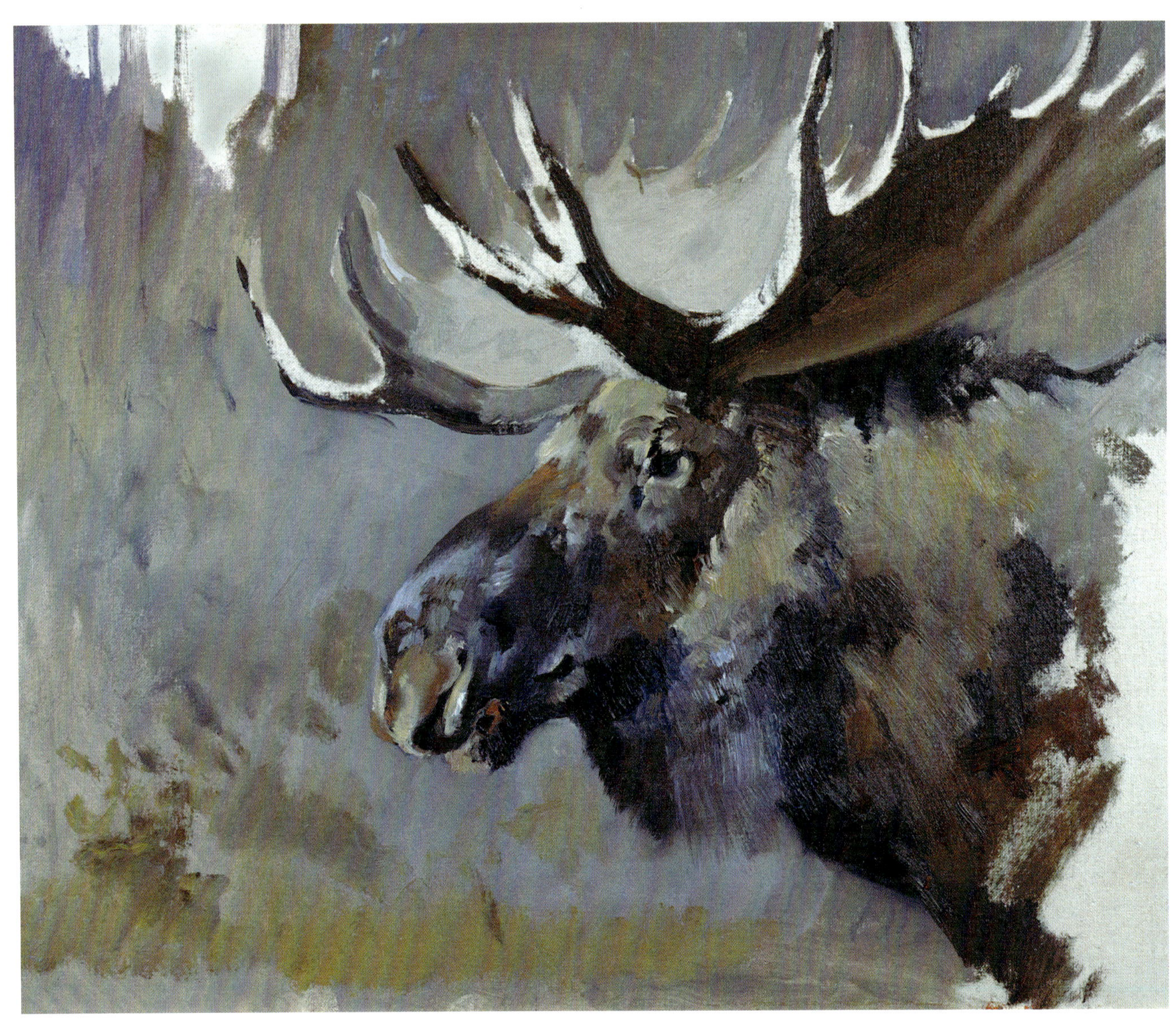

PLATE 42
George Browne
Bull Moose 1947
oil on canvas, 16 x 20 in.
J.N. Bartfield Galleries

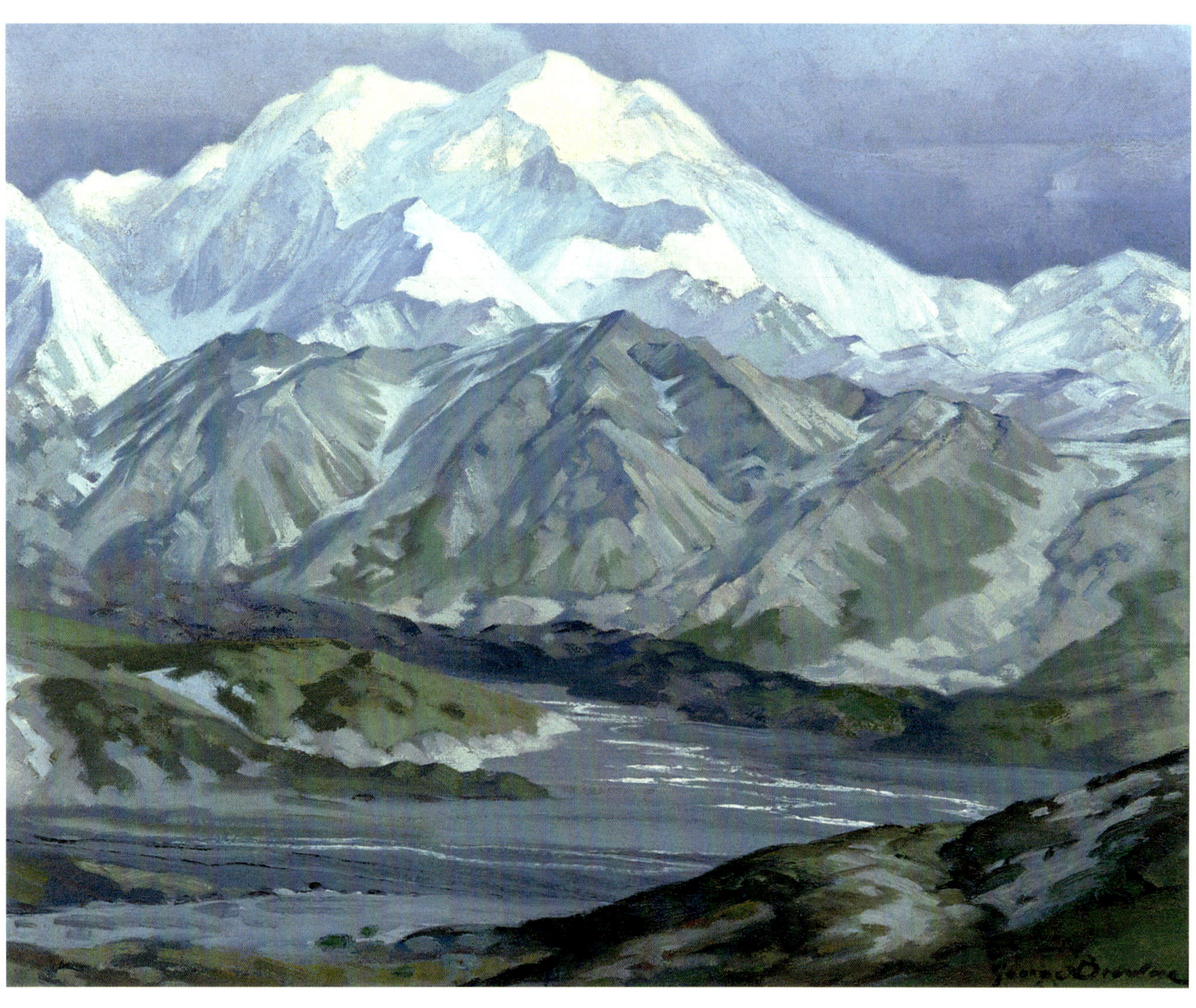

PLATE 43
George Browne
Mt. McKinley From The Kontishna 1947
oil on canvas, 16 x 20 in.
Robert Fraser Sporting and Southern Art/Len Braarud Fine Art

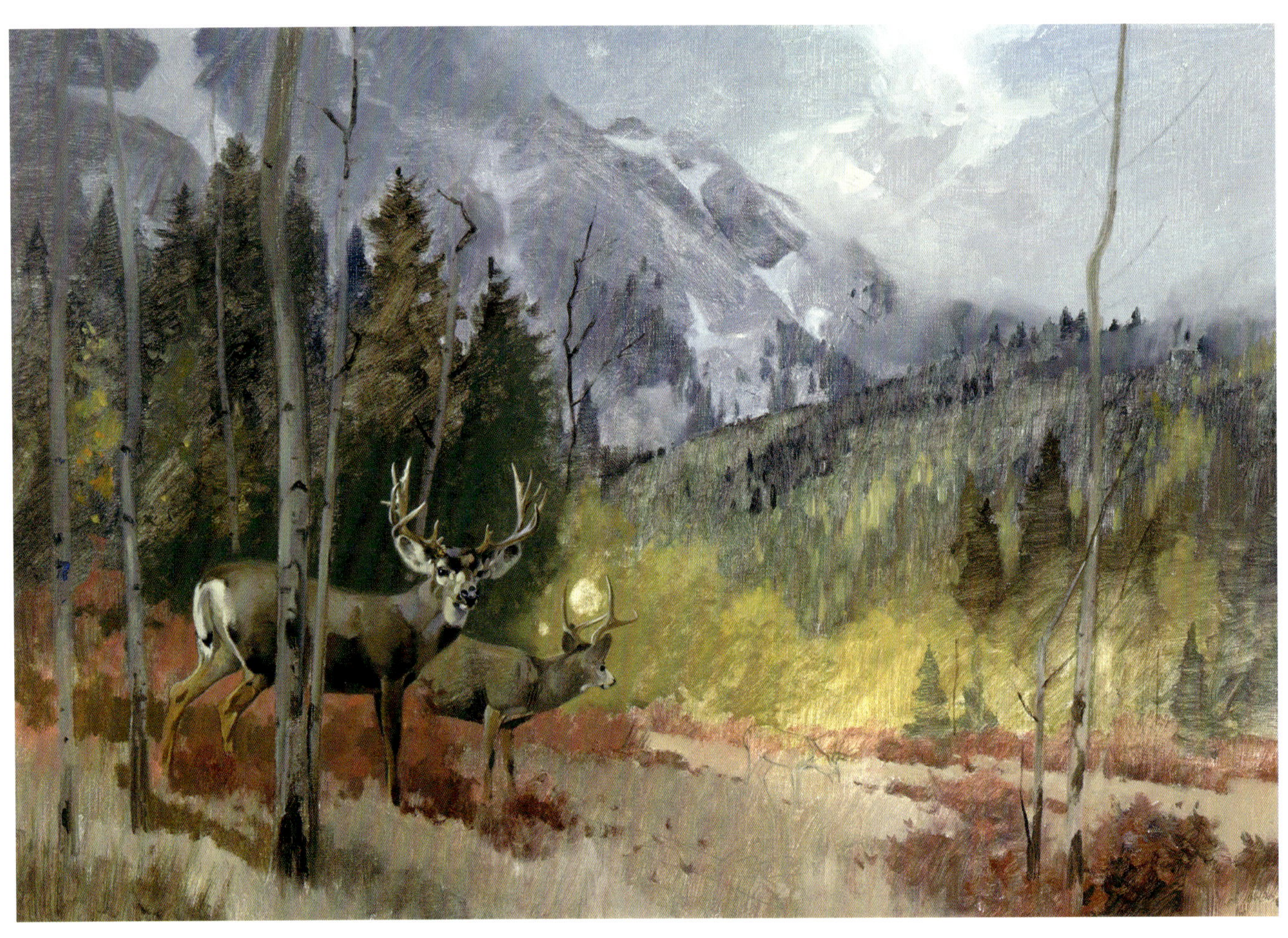

PLATE 44
George Browne
Mule Deer 1956
oil on canvas, 22 x 32 in.
Collection of Hugh Robinson
Last painting by George—unfinished

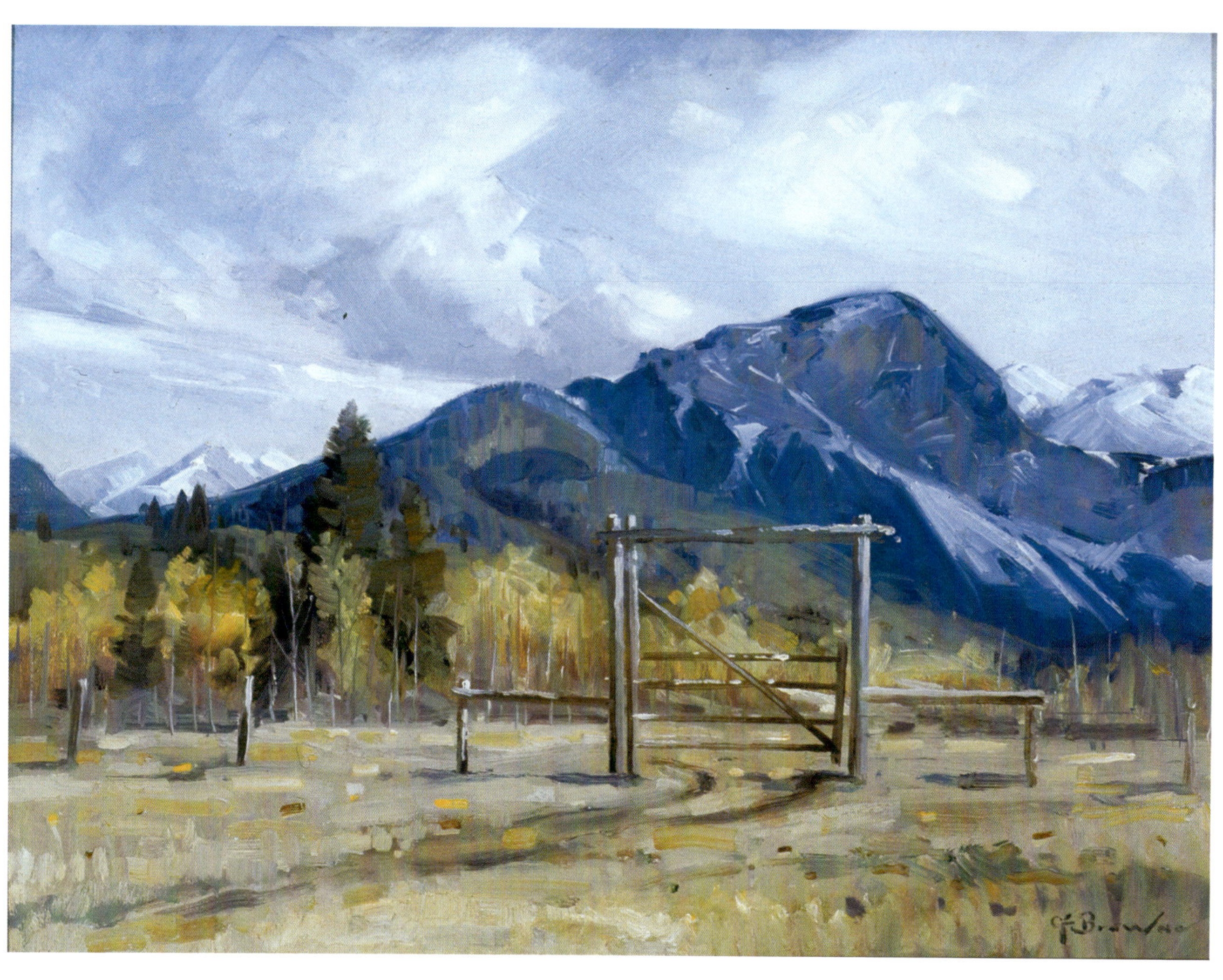

Plate 45
George Browne
Alan Ranch, Seebe Alberta 1956
oil on canvas, 12 x 16 in.
Thomas Nygard and J.N. Bartfield Galleries

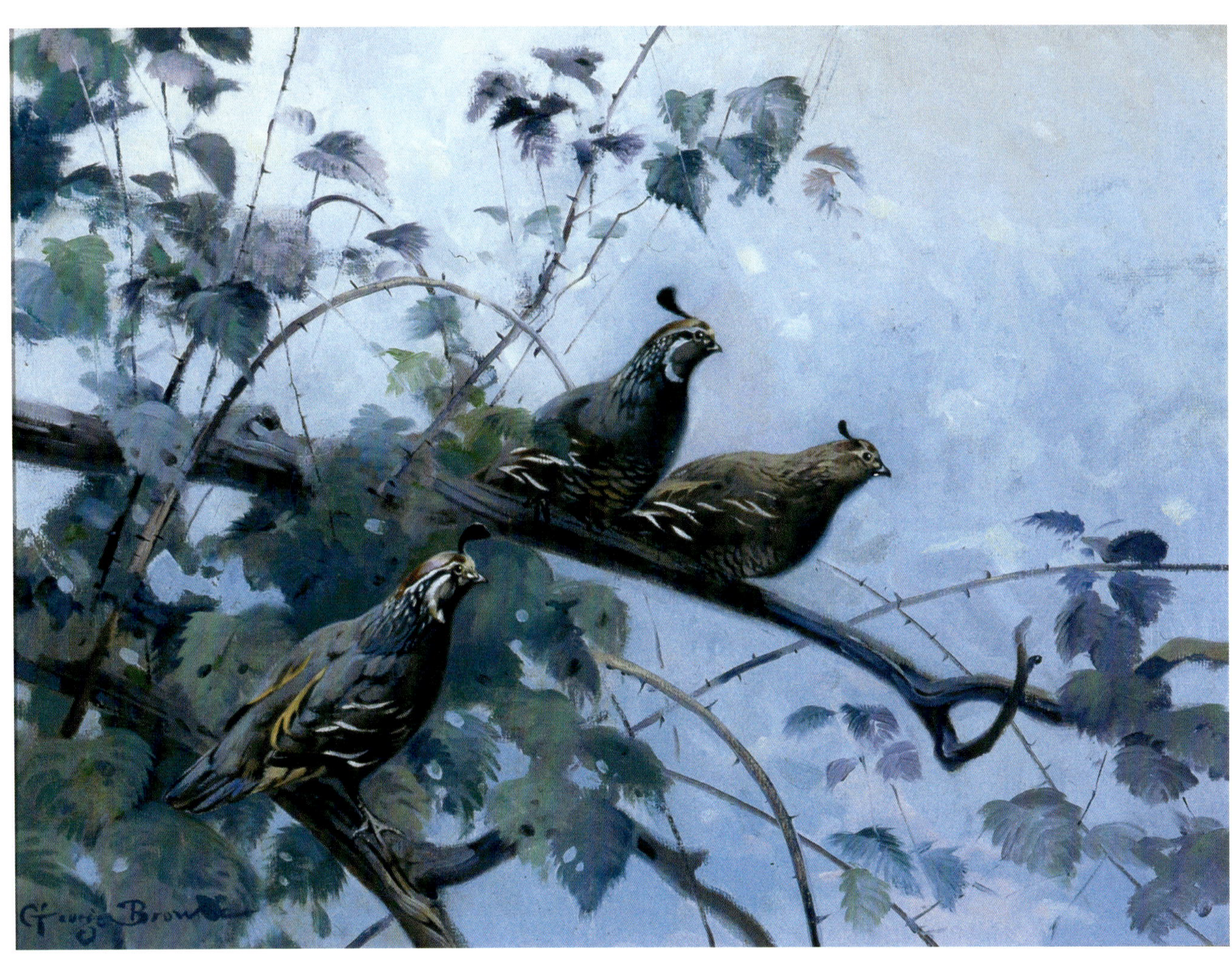

PLATE 46
George Browne
California Quail 1955
oil on canvas, 12 x 16 in.
Thomas Nygard and J.N. Bartfield Galleries

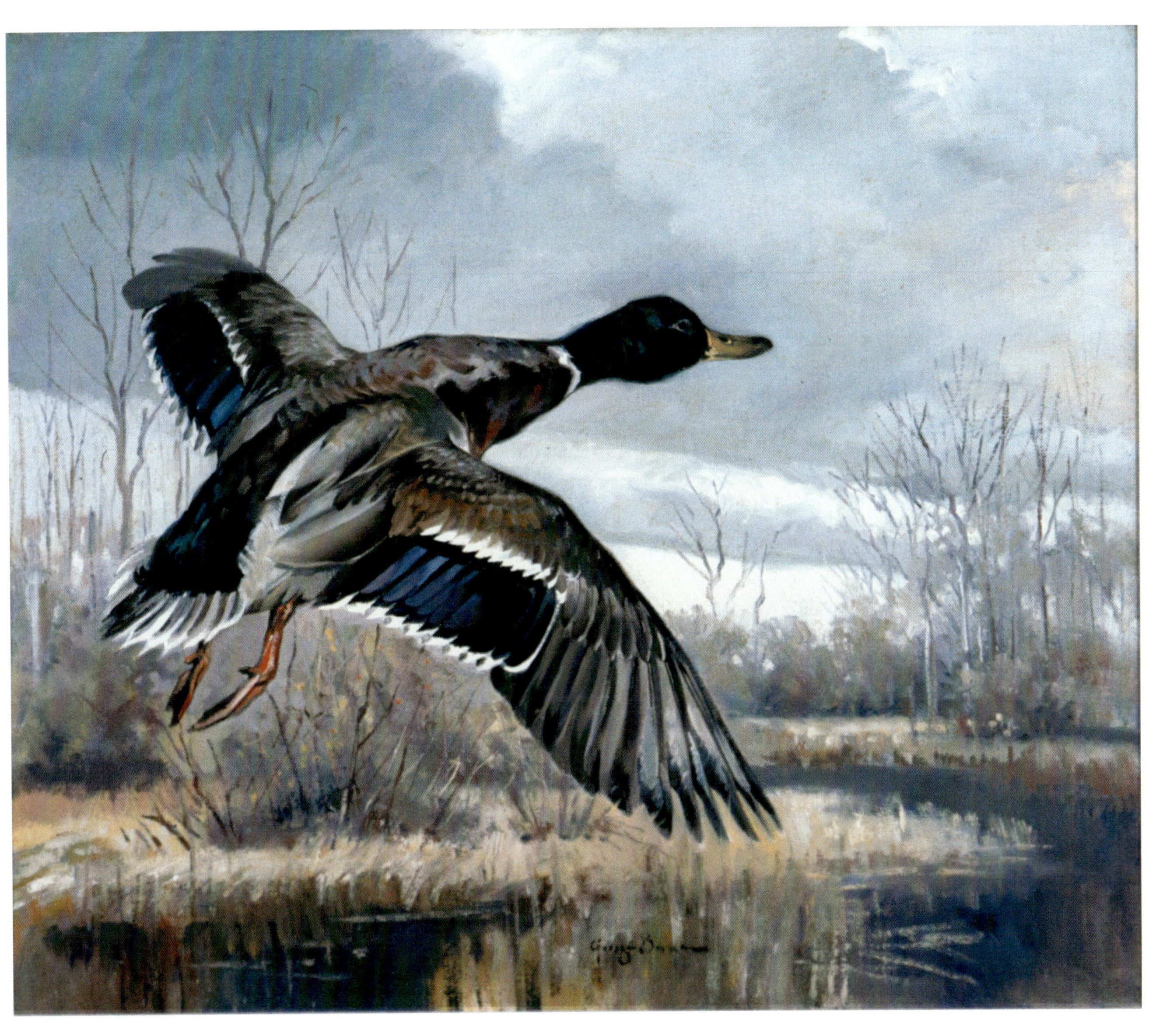

PLATE 47
George Browne
Mallard Going Out 1948
oil on canvas, 25 x 30 in.
Thomas Nygard and J.N. Bartfield Galleries

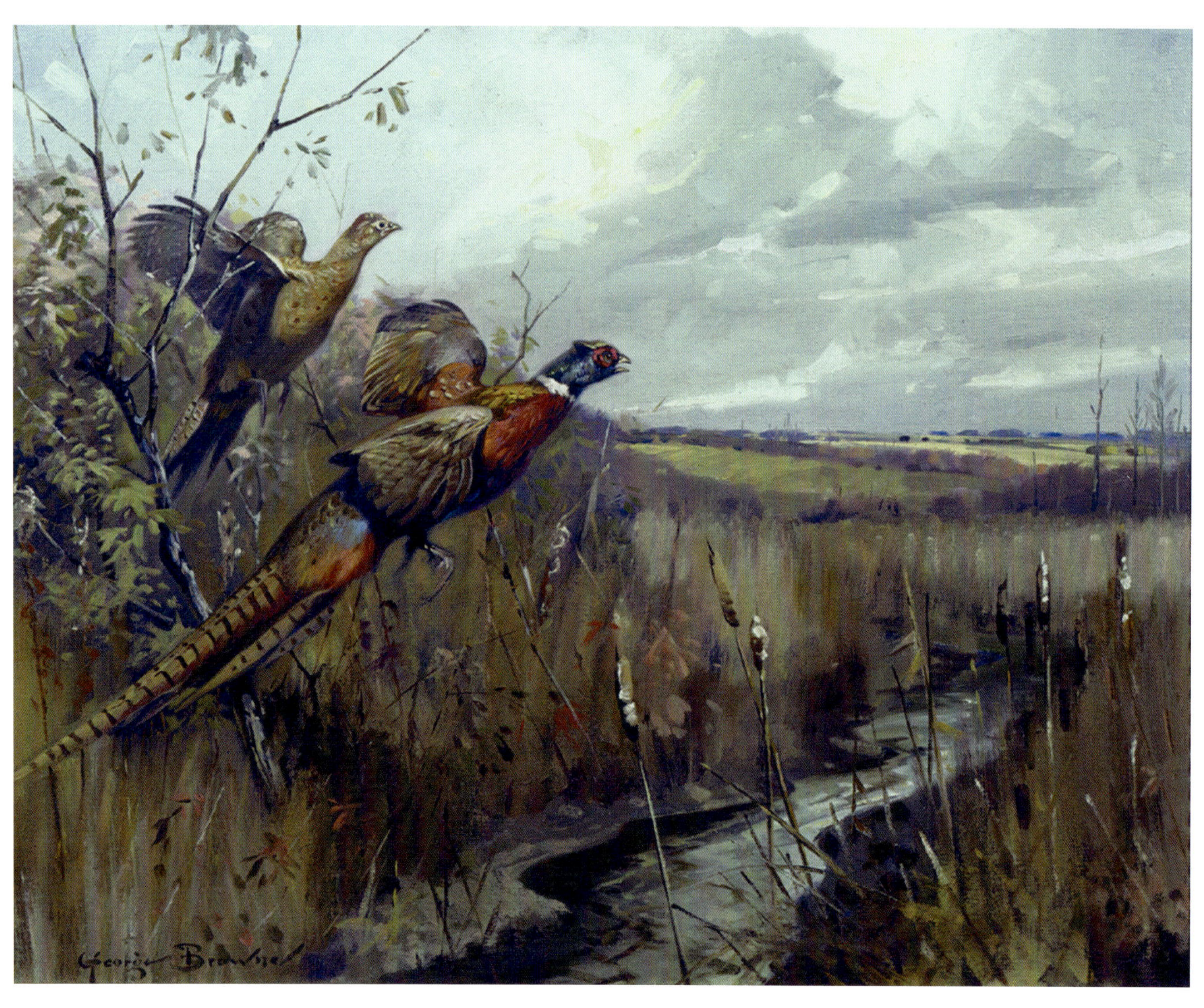

PLATE 48
George Browne
Pheasants Rising 1952
oil on canvas, 20 x 30 in.
Private collection

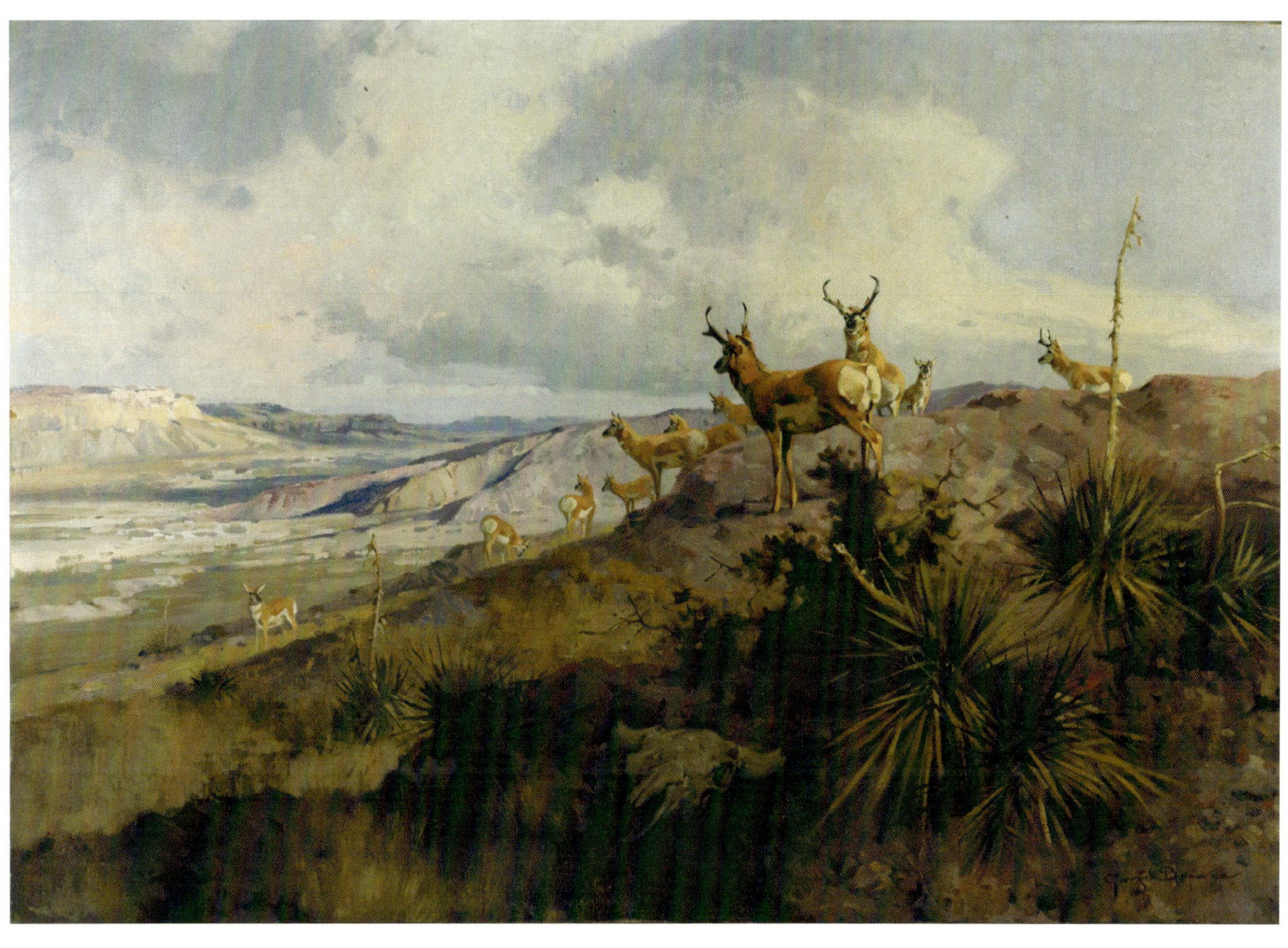

PLATE 49
George Browne
Prairie Longhorns 1958
oil on canvas, 22 x 32 in.
Thomas Nygard and J.N. Bartfield Galleries

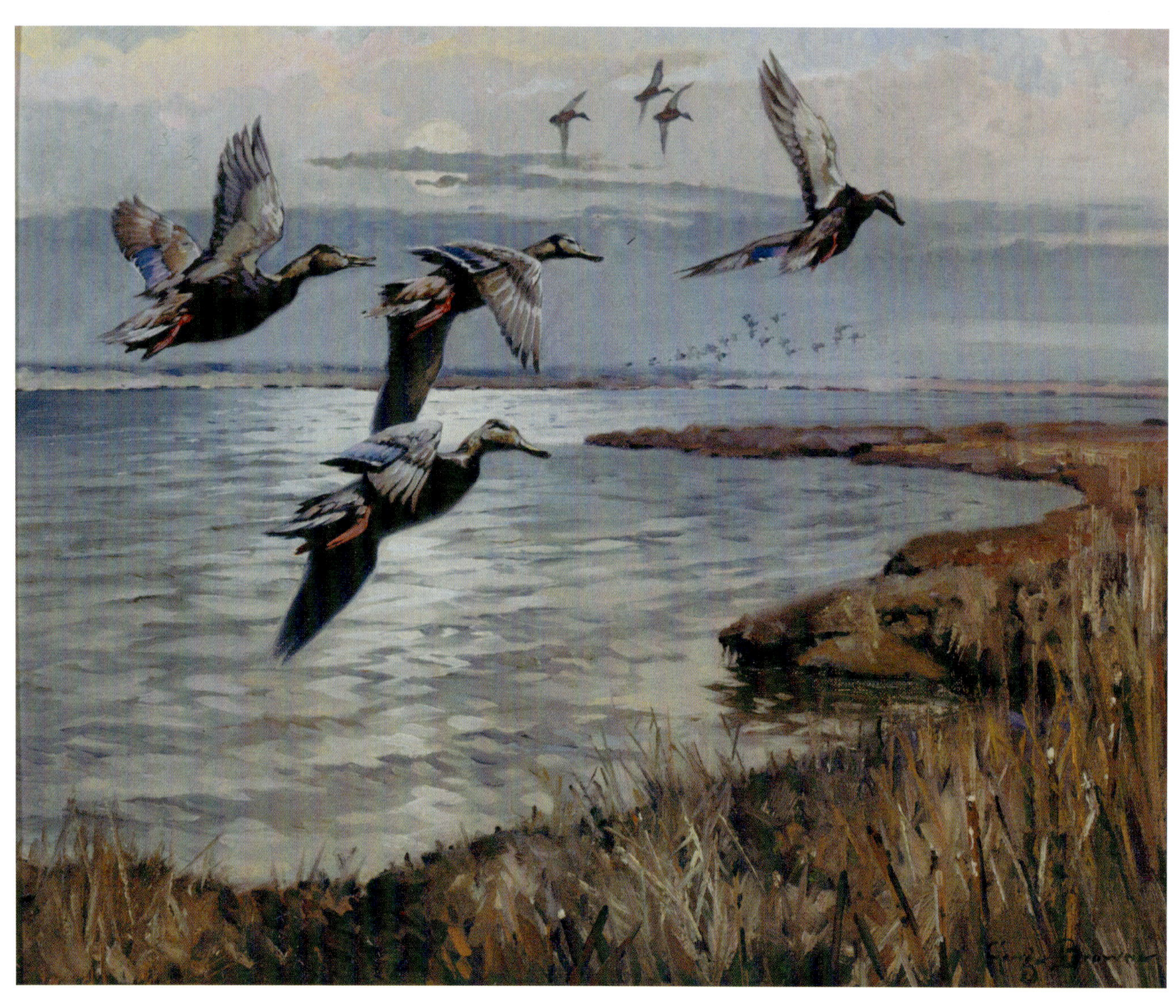

PLATE 50
George Browne
Swinging The Cove 1954
oil on canvas board, 16 x 20 in.
Steven B. O'Brien, Jr. Fine Arts

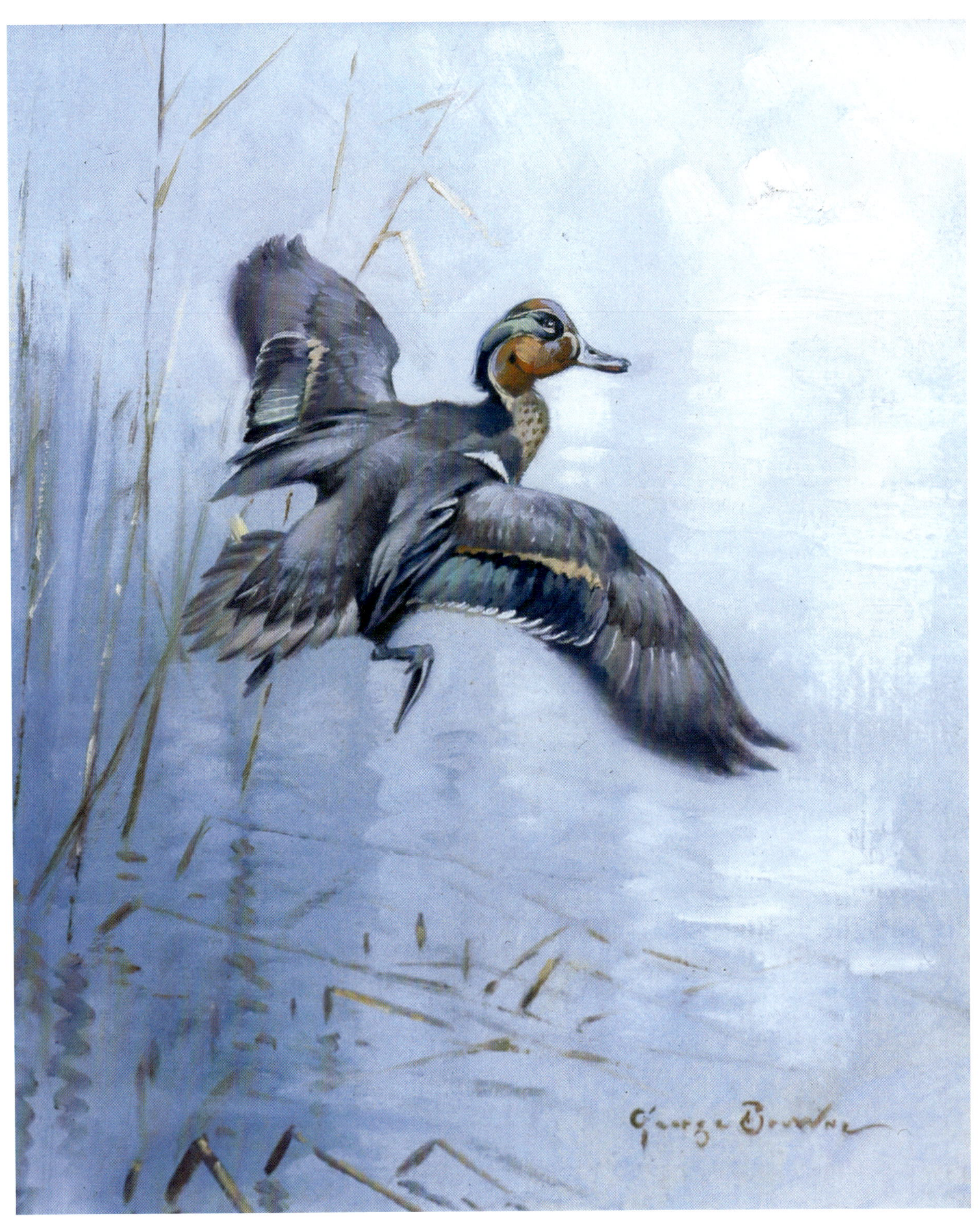

PLATE 51
George Browne
Teal Date unknown
oil on canvas, 14 x 12 in.
Thomas Nygard and J.N. Bartfield Galleries

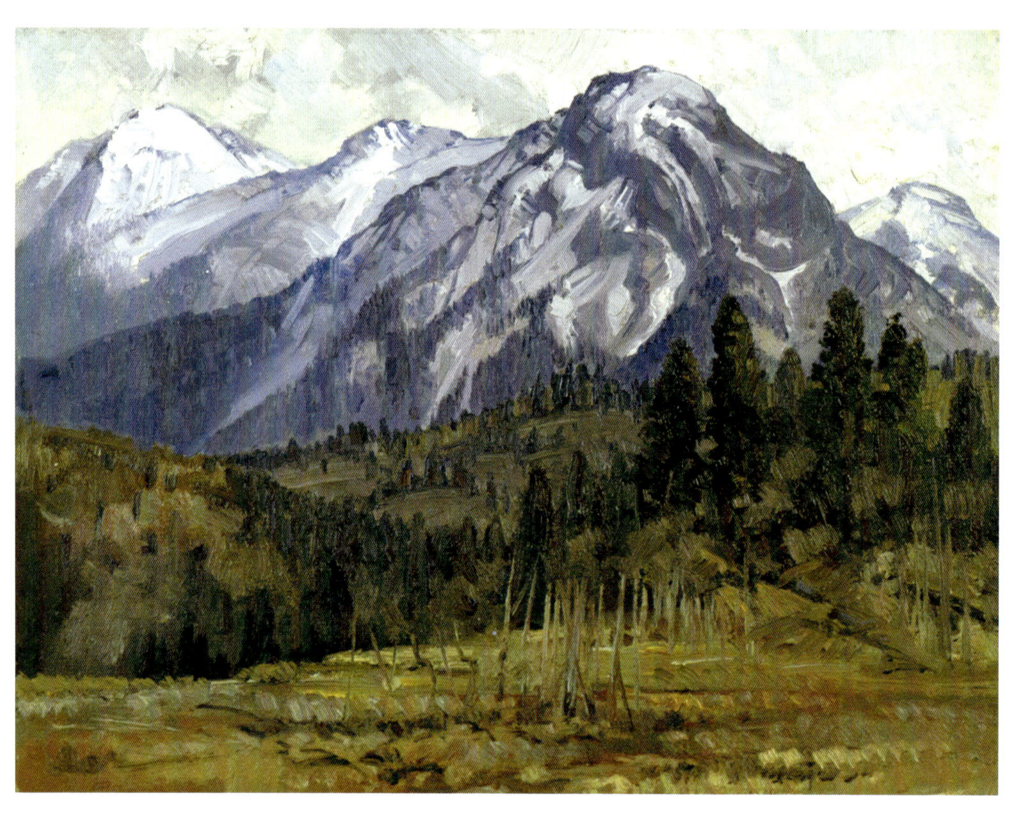

PLATE 52
George Browne
Blue Mountain
Date unknown
oil on board, 12 x 16 in.
J.N. Bartfield and Thomas Nygard Galleries

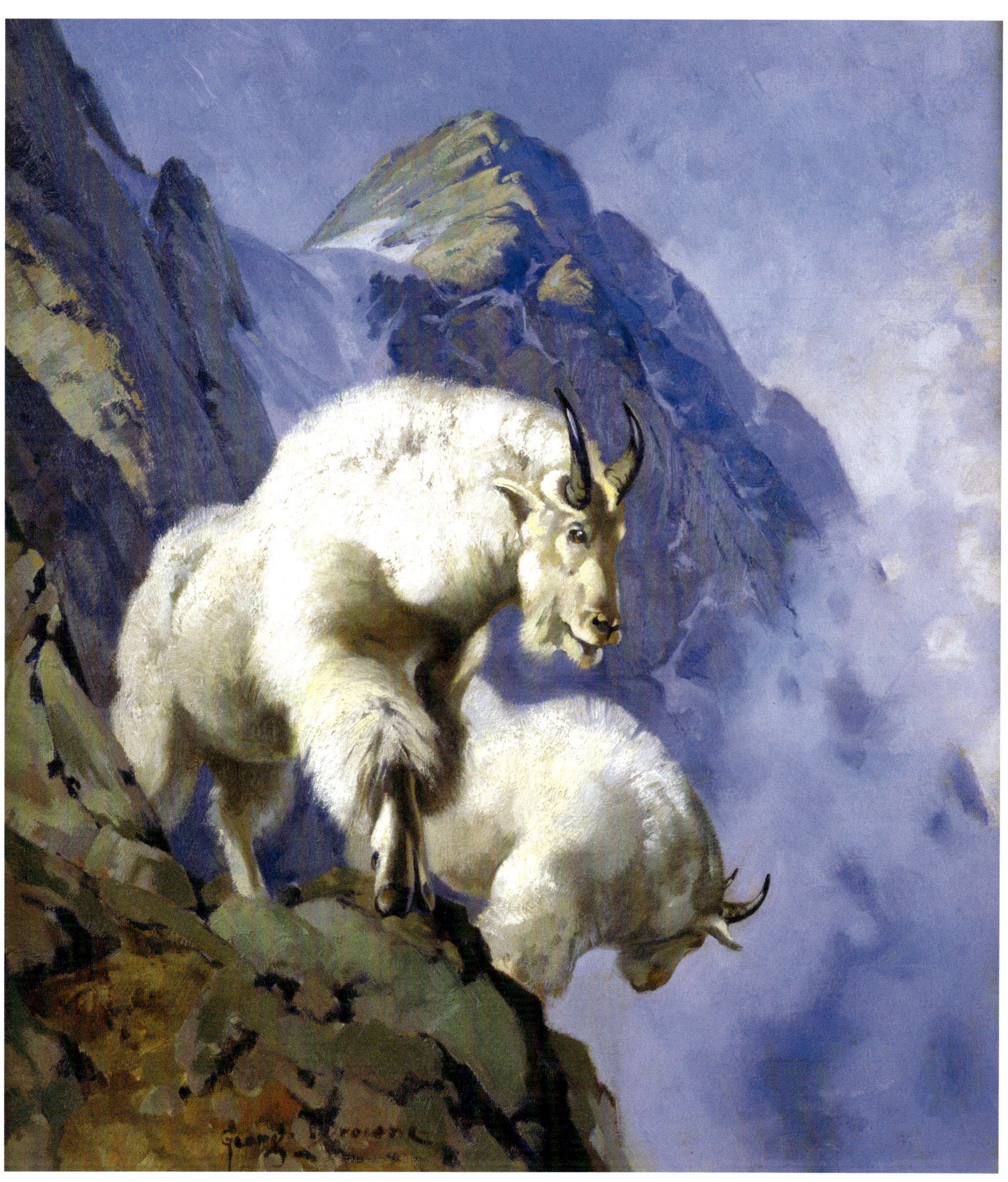

PLATE 53
George Browne
Goats 1942
oil on canvas, 20 x 18 in.
J.N. Bartfield and Thomas Nygard Galleries

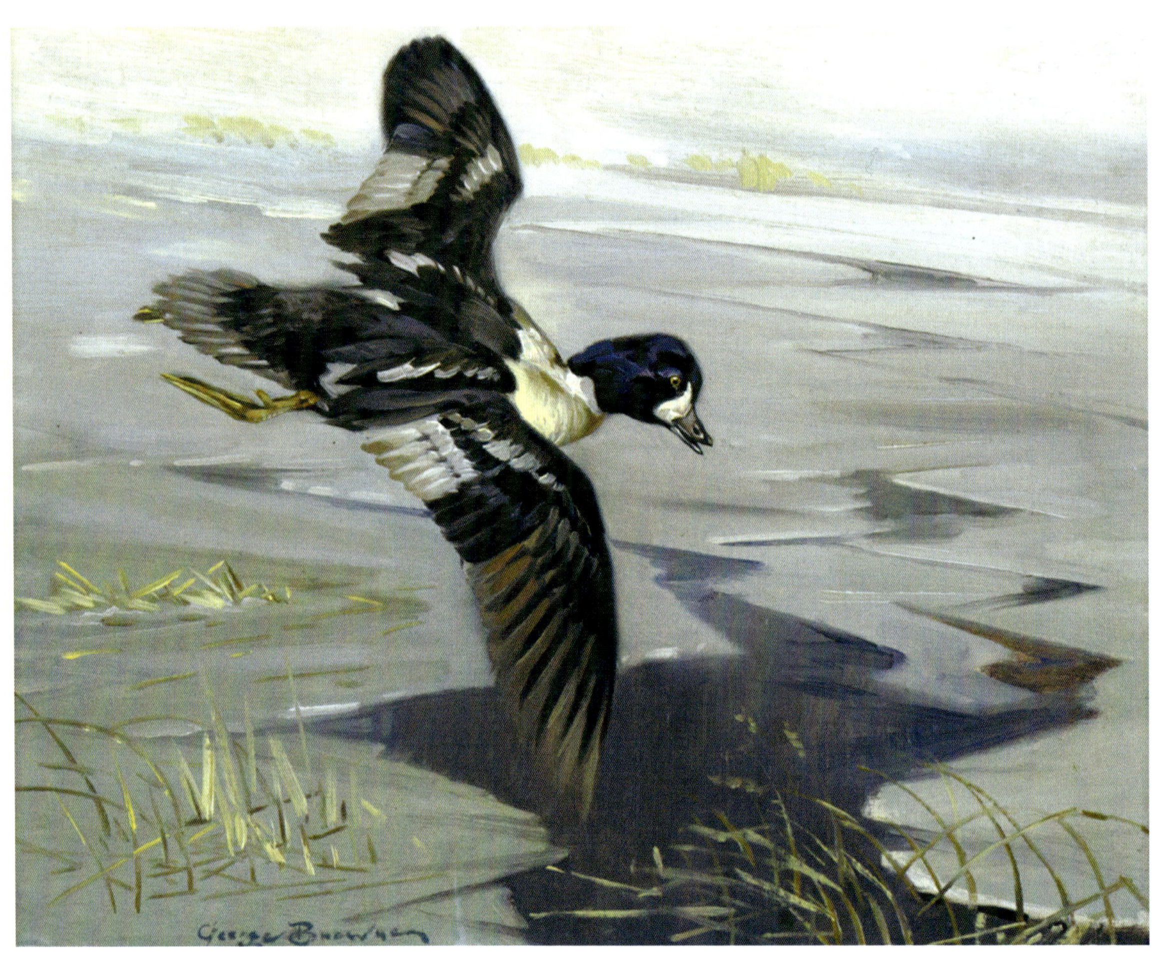

Plate 54
George Browne
Goldeneye
Date unknown
oil on board, 15¾ x 19¾ in.
J.N. Bartfield and Thomas Nygard Galleries

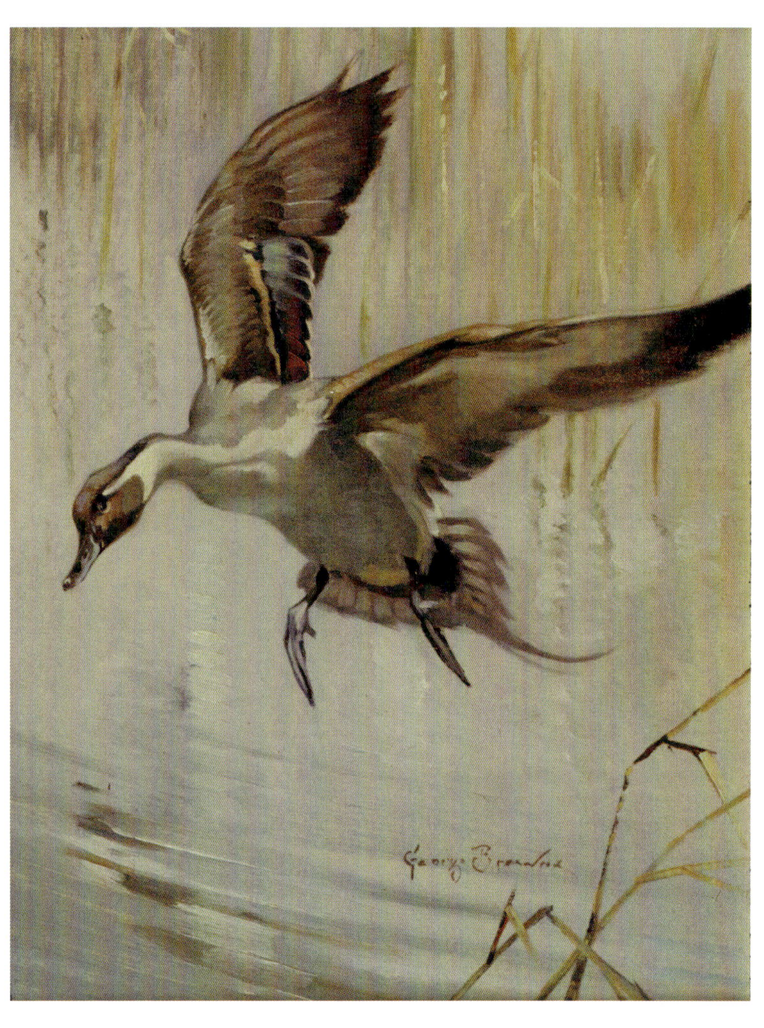

Plate 55
George Browne
Pintails
Date unknown
oil on board, 15½ x 12 in.
J.N. Bartfield and Thomas Nygard Galleries

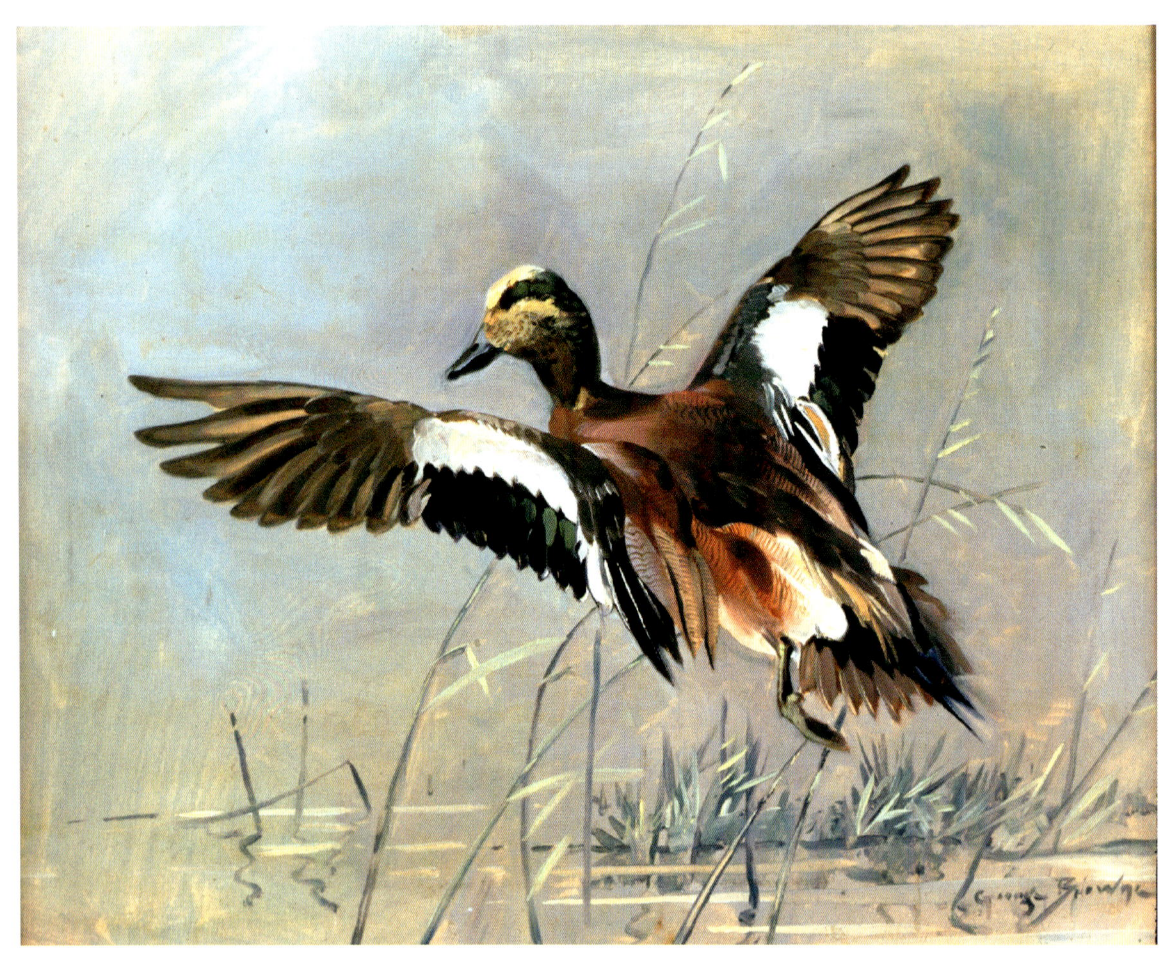

PLATE 56
George Browne
Widgeon
Date unknown
oil on board, 19⅝ x 15¾ in.
J.N. Bartfield and Thomas Nygard Galleries

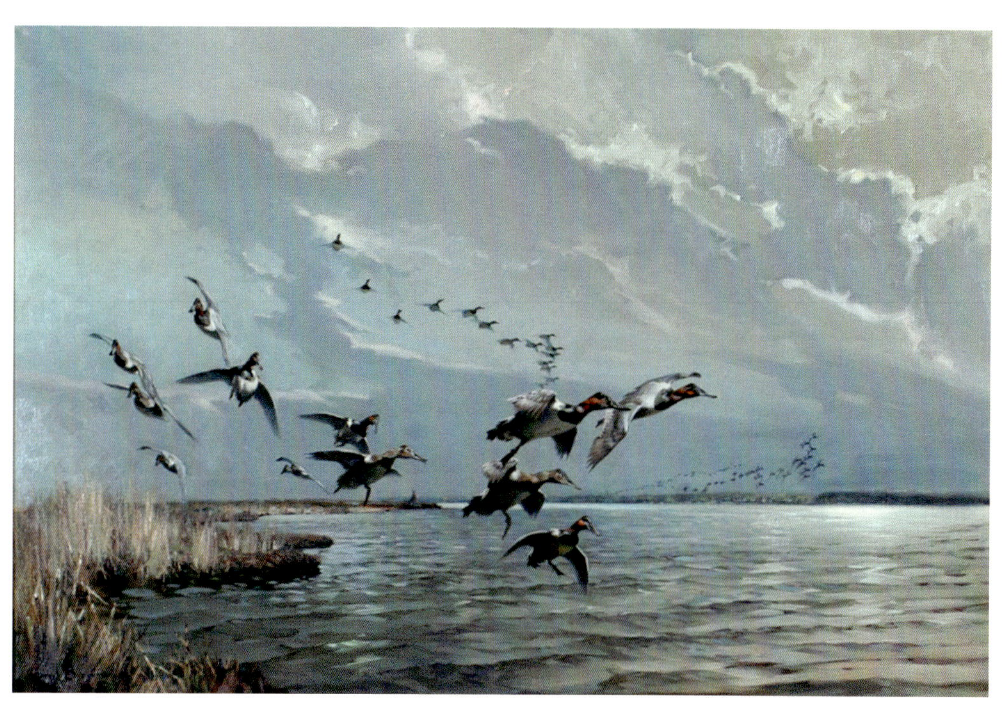

PLATE 57
George Browne
Canvasbacks on the Nanticoke River 1950
24 x 36 in.
Painted for K. Merrick Low

Appendix A

George Browne Log, 1934–1957: "Pictures Sold"
A list of 268 paintings and sketches, with year painted, title, size, and price.

Note: It is very difficult, if not impossible, to correlate a particular painting to a log entry. Titles often changed between logs, and the logs may not list all paintings. Also, the titles of the paintings were often changed by galleries prior to sale and sometimes by the painting's owner as well.

Pictures Sold

Date	No.	Name	Size	Price
1934/2	1.	Life Drawing	20x24	5 –
" /6	2.	Wood Duck.	12x16	25 –
" /6	3.	Tarpon	12x16	15 –
" /6	4.	Landscape	12x16	20 –
" /6	5.	Trout	12x16	20 –
" /8	6.	Landscape.	12x16	25 –
1938/1.	7.	Tarpon	12x16	15 –
" /1	8.	Salmon	12x16	15. –
" /3	9.	Trout	10x14	10 –
" /3	10.	Striped Bass	12x16	5 –
" /4	11	Black Bass	12x16	5 –
" /4	12	Striped Bass	12x16	10 –
" /5	13	Trout.	12x16	10 –
" /5	14	Landscape	12x16	10 –
" /6	15	Landscape	12x16	10 –
" /6	16	Landscape	12x16	10 –
" /7	17	Landscape	12x16	10 –
1939/1	18	Landscape	12x16	10 –
" /1	19	Landscape	9x11	10 –
" /3	20	Landscape	12x16	10 –
" /3	21	Letterhead	10x14	10 –
" /4	22	Horsehead	20x24	20 –
" /8	23	Horsehead	20x24	20 –
1940/1	24	Landscape	12x16	10 –
" /2	25	Bluebill	16x20	25 –
" /2	26	Magpies	50x70	75 –
" /2	27	Ram head	16x20	25 –
" /4	28	Dog head	15x10	15 –
" /4	29	Landscape	12x16	10 –
" /5	30	Restore	20x30	10 –
1941/2	31	G.W. Teal	12x16	25 –
" /2	32	Rainbow Trout.	12x16	25 –
/4	33	Salmon	12x16	25 –
/10	34	Backgrounds	—	350 –
/11	35	Landscape	12x16	10 –
/12	36	Landscape	12x16	10 –
1942/1	37	Chipmonk	12x16	10 –
" /1	38	Skunks	16x20	25 –
" /2	39	Rattlesnake	12x16	10 –
" /3	40	Chip Monk.	12x16	10 –
" /3	41	Doves	12x16	10 –
" /3	42	Porkypine	12x16	10 –
" /3	43	Owls	12x16	10 –
" /4	44	Goats Cliffs	16x20	50 –
" /4	45	Sheep on Mt.	16x20	50 –
" /4	46	Trout	16x20	50 –
" /5	47	Ruffed Grouse	16x20	50 –
" /6	48	Horse drawing	16x20	25 –
1943	49	Background	—	50 –
/8	50	Background	—	100 –
/3	51	Background	—	200 –
1945	52	Lesser Can Goose	10x14	25 –
"	53	Bighorn Ram.	12x16	50 –
"	54	Trout.	16x20	50 –
"	55	Lesser Goose	16x20	45 –
"	56	Buffelhead.	10x14	25 –
"	57	Widgeon Dr.	12x16	25 –
1946	58	Canvasback	20x30	100 –
"	59	Pheasant	12x16	9. –
"	60	Scaup.	10x14	10. –
"	61	Pintail	10x14	9. –
1947	62	Red head	25x30	450 –
"	63	Ruffed Grouse	20x24	175 –
"	64	Ch. Grouse	25x30	350 –
"	65	Trout	16x20	150 –
"	66	Pintails, Salt Marsh	25x30	325 –
"	67	Mt. Hackett.	18x24	312 –
"	68	" Evans.	12x16	95 –
"	69	" Corbley.	12x16	95 –
"	70	" Corbley.	12x16	95 –
"	71	" Pearsons	16x20	95 –
"	72	" Dennott	12x16	75 –
"	73	" Dellott	12x16	75 –
1948	74	Cans @ Sun Rise	25x30	325 –
"	75	Raft Red head.	25x30	175 –
"	76	"Band" horse.	16x20	150 –
"	77	Cal. Sprig (Hens.)	25x30	300 –
"	78	Mallard. (Hens.)	25x30	250 –
"	79	Wild Harvest.	30x40	750 –
1949	80	Cock Sprig (Grit)	16x20	82 –
"	81	Cock Teal. (Grit)	16x20	82 –
"	82	Windward Shore Can.	20x24	300 –
"	83	Following Shore Bu.	20x24	250 –
"	84	Jack Snipe	12x16	100 –
"	85	Baldpait	12x16	100 –
"	86	Grouse Study	10x14	75 –
"	87	G.W. Teal Wind	12x16	100 –
"	88	Ringneck Dr.	10x14	90 –
"	89	Afternoon Flight Spr.	25x30	460 –
"	90	Honkers.	25x30	450 –
"	91	Grouse in Snow.	12x16	100 –
"	92	"Freckles"	16x20	100 –
"	93	Mallards.	12x16	75 –
"	94	Following Cloudy Mal	25x30	262 –
"	95	After Squall L. Geese	30x40	175 –
"	96	Spring on North Lake	30x40	1100 –
" x	97	Flushed Sharptail	25x30	325 –
"	98	Startled Mallard	25x30	405 –
"	99	Barrows Golden eye	20x30	350 –
1950	100	Cans Estuary	30x40	800 –

Date	No	Name	Size	Price
1950 cont	101	G.W. Teal Cold Wea.	25x30	450 -
"	102	Straggler Buffle.	12x16	100 -
"	103	Bluebill Dr. (Bo)	16x20	175 -
"	104	Cedar point	18x24	320 -
"	105	Grouse Spring Sno.	12x16	100 -
"	106	Grouse in Woods	16x20	200 -
"	107	Grouse	10x14	75 -
"	608	Sent Forest Grouse	16x20	250 -
"	109	Monticoke Cans.	24x36	400 -
"	110	Mudge Cans	24x36	400 -
"	111	Keystone Valley.	20x36	330 -
1951	112	Winter Bay. Cans.	30x40	900 -
"	113	Cans @ Sunset	12x16	150 -
"	114	Winter Morn. Gr.	25x30	550 -
"	115	Buffle head (Stoa)	16x20	100 -
"	116	F.H. Re. to Water Mal.	24x36	500 -
"	117	Mallards in Stubble	30x40	700 -
"	118	Woodland Mal. Phil.	25x30	550 -
"	119	Stone Wall Gr.	16x20	300 -
"	120	Scaup, Squall	20x30	450 -
"	121	Burbour Gr.	16x20	200 -
"	122	Blacks Low	16x20	424.
"	123	Can. Hunt. Ryan.	24x36	400 -
"	124	Mal & Pintail Pri. St.	24x36	500 -
"	125	Decend Spring.	16x20	200 -
"	126	Mal Dropping	9x14	75 -
"	127	" Pitching	9x14	25 -
"	128	Ring Neck Ph.	12x16	150 -
"	129	Beating Out Ph.	12x16	150
"	130	Wood Land Mal.	25x30	500
"	131	Cock Ph.	12x16	150 -
1952	132	Pintail & Mal (A)	20x30	150 -
"	133	Robins	25x30	400 -
"	134	Napa Spring	16x20	200 -
"	135	Nanta Cans (Bull)	18x24	250 -
"	136	Brook in Wint. Gr.	20x24	400 -
"	137	Cans on the Pass.	24x36	600 -
"	138	Valley Quail	12x16	150 -
"	139	Hedge Pheasant	18x24	350 -
"	140	Pair Pheasant.	12x16	150 -
"	141	Alarmed Ph.	25x30	550 -
"	142	Birch W.C.	16x20	275 -
"	143	Brant	10x14	25 -
"	144	Spring. (Dibb.)	16x20	200 -
"	145	Brant Bol (Dibb)	16x20	200 -
1953	146	Scaup Hunt Low	16x20	250 -
"	147	Hunt. Cans. Fiske.	24x36	500 -
"	148	Cans @ Cove Ryan	24x36	500 -
"	149	Grouse Hem. Bull	36x29	525 -
"	150	Pembina Mal.	18x24	400 -

Date	No	Name	Size	Price
1953 cont.	151	Winter PM Gr.	25x30	550 -
"	152	Early Snows Gr.	25x30	450 -
"	153	Grouse @ Dusk.	16x20	300 -
"	154	Burbour Cans.	20x30	500 -
"	155	Dusk on Chesapeake	24x36	600 -
"	156	Farm Marsh Mal	24x36	500 -
"	157	Thicket Covey Qu.	20x24	400 -
"	158	Stubble Shoot	10x14	100 -
1954	159	Dec. Sun Scaup	16x20	300 -
"	160	Autumn Hill Gr.	24x36	600 -
"	161	Autumn Color WC.	24x20	400 -
"	162	Shore Ice Cans.	20x30	450 -
"	163	Evening Flt. Teal G.W.	25x30	460 -
"	164	Frost Stubble Gr.	25x30	550 -
"	165	Ebbing Tide Cans.	20x30	400 -
"	166	Swing Cove Blacks	16x20	157 -
"	167	Norfolk Buck.	20x30	425 -
"	168	Sandbridge Widgeon	20x30	425 -
"	169	Mallards Stubbling	20x24	225 -
"	170	Pine Barrens, Blacks	18x24	274 -
"	171	Forest dweller Gr.	12x16	300 -
"	172	Edge Cover Ph.	12x16	300 -
"	173	Circling Mallard.	24x36	475 -
"	174	Grouse, Thornapple	20x24	400 -
"	175	Sharptails in Stubble	20x24	300 -
"	176	"New Snow" Gr.	24x20	400 -
"	177	"Out of Weeds. Pheasant.	12x16	185 -
"	178	"Gliding in Geese"	20x16	250 -
"	178	"Foothills in November"	20x25	350 -
"	179	" Harvie Nol. Sharpt.	12x16.	150
"	180	"Verginia Farm Geese	25x30.	550 -
"	181	Fresh Snow GR.	12x16	150 -
1955	182	Brook Trout W.C.	12x28	200 -
"	183	Sun Set Moon Rise	16x20	300 -
"	184	Covey in Pine	20x24	400 -
"	185	River Bottoms Mal	24x30	550 -
"	186	Harvie #2 Pheasant	12x16	150 -
"	187	Harvie #3. Grouse	12x16	150 -
"	188	Willow Oak Quail	20x30	450 -
"	189	Pair Pheasant	20x24	400 -
"	190	Clearing Sky Redhead	24x30	150 -
"	191	Canada Geese Portrait	30x36	500 -
"	192	Harvie #4 Sprucegr.	12x16	150 -
"	193	Harvie #5 Hun.	12x16	150 -
"	194	Harvie #6 B.Grad	12x16	150 -
"	195	Atten, Quail Col.	12x16	200 -
"	196	Youngburg Spring	1520	200 -
"	197	"Close In" Cans	24x36	550 -
"	198	"Yellow Birch Gr.	24x20	400 -
"	199	"Single @ Sun Set Hun.	16x20	200 -

Date	No	Name	Size	Price	
cont 1955	200	DRUMMIES REST GR.	20×24	375	—
	201	WINDRIVER RANGE	24×36	600	—
	202	SURF FOLLOWERS.	20×30	450	—
	203	FOOTHILL GATEWAY	12×16	100	—
	204	EARLY FLIGHT SPRIG	20×30	450	—
	205	FOOTHILL MAL.	24×36	600	—
	206	KANANKIS VALLEY	20×26	400	—
	207	PAIR PHEASANT.	15×20	300	—
1956	208	GREENWINGS	20×24	250	—
	209	Timber Mallard	15×20	300	—
	210	MAPLE GROUSE	20×30	450	—
	211	Hill Top Covey Qa.	20×30	450	—
	212	Pintail & Decoys	20×30	450	—
	213	Autumn Pintail	24×36	600	—
	214	Outer Bay Cans.	20×30	450	—
	215	PINE SHADOWS QUAIL	24×30	350	—
	216	OLD RED RUFF GR.	20×30	450	—
	217	"BEECH HILL" GR.	15×20	300	—
	218	CANVASBACK 30/40	30×40	850	—
	219	Pine Land Covey qa	20×30	450	—
	220	Covey rise Qa.	20×24	500	—
	221	Out of North Ge.	24×36	600	—
	222	Weed patch Ph.	25×30	500	—
	223	Dec. Blacks	14×28	450	—
	224	Apt. Geese	14×28	450	—
	225	Black oval	11×14	200	—
	226	Mal oval	11×14	200	—
	227	Widg. oval	11×14	200	—
	228	Pint tail oval	11×14	200	—
	229	Brook Trout FKB.	11×14	70	—
	230	Black H Well.	24×36	650	—
	231	Hemlock land	25×30	156	—
	232	Calif qa. Hen	20×30	500	—
	233	Mallard CANAR	16×22	300	—
	234	Heater Mal. CanAd	18×24	300	—
	235	ON ATHABASKA Chick.	20×30	500	—
	236	"Pine Land" Quail	24×36	650	—
	237	Pot hole Mal.	18×26	400	—
	238	Soshe Geese	12×18	200	—
	239	Pine Land qa.	24×36	650	—
	240	Round T. Mal.	24×36	700	—
1957	241	Webb Whitetail	24×32	600	—
	242	Two Away W.C.	18×25	400	—
	243	Winter Cross gr.	24×36	650	—
	244	Along River W.D.	25×36	350	—
	245	North Shore Can	20×30	500	—
	246	Vt. Partridge gr.	24×36	650	—
	247	Even Qa. FKB.	18×26	450	—
	248	Autumn St gr.	18×24	400	—
	249	ALPine Past. SH.	20×24	400	—

No		Name	Size	Price
250	-	Setter and W.C.	15×20	260
251	-	Pair Pheasant	15×20	240
252	-	Mule Deer.	20×26	450
253	-	Landscape	12×16	150
254	-	Landscape	12×16	150
255	-	Landscape	12×16	200
256	-	Mule Deer.	20×30	550
257	-	Mallard Swift	15×20	300
258	-	Pheasant	24×36	650
259	-	Quail	18×26	450
260	-	Quail	24×36	650
261	-	Grouse	24×36	650
262	-	Grouse	24×36	700
263	-	Mal.	15×20	300
264	-	White Tail	22×32	650
265	-	Canvasback	24×36	700
266	-	Woodcock	18×26	450
267	-	Quail	24×36	400
268		Canvasback	15×20	300

Appendix B

George Browne Log, 1947–1952
Details of the daily development of paintings to completion.

Canvas 16X20
"Flights End"
Pintail.
June 22 Cutouts ink layin
June 23 Oil layin
July 24 First 2 ducks.
July 25 [illegible]
July 27 Sky
July 28 Landscape
Finished
6 days
Sold

Canvas 20X30
"The Early Flight" Pintail
June 24 Cutouts Pencil layin
June 26th Ink layin
June 27th Oil layin Ducks, landscape
July 16th 2nd duck
July 17th 3rd Duck landscape
July 18th 1st duck Sky
July 19th 2nd duck
July 20th 1st duck Sky
July 21st 2nd duck landscape
July 22nd landscape
Sold
Completed
10 days. 365
31.50 per day
300
9450.00

Canvas 24X36
"Afternoon on a Prairie Slough."
June 27. Ink layin Completed
June 28 Oil lay in Completed
July 2nd. 1st 2nd and third duck.
July 3rd 3rd Duck
July 4th 5th, 6th and 7th
July 5th 8th & 9th
July 6th 9th duck
July 7th 8th duck
July 8th 4 and 7th duck
9th Sky
July 10th Landscape (Background)
July 11th landscape
July 12th landscape Marsh foreground
July 14 landscape [illegible]
Completed. 14 days
Sold

Canvas 10X14
"Mallards Drifting in"
July 29th Completed
1 day
Sold

Canvas 10X14.
"Pitching in"
July 30th Completed
1 day
Sold

1949 Canvas 20X24
A Flock of Widgeon

Canvas 18X24
"Breaking Off"
Dec. 7th Inked in Ducks.
Dec. 10th Oil layin of landscape
" 18th Pencil corrections
16 Oil layin birds.

Canvas. 12×16 in.
[illegible]
August 1. Oil Layin
August 2. Completed
2 Days.
Sold

Canvas. 18X24
Ring Neck Pheasant.
1951
Aug 4th. Cutouts
Aug 8th Land Scape layin
1952 June 24th First Bird.
June 25th [illegible] landscape
June 26th [illegible] landscape.
Completed 5 days.

Canvas 18·24
[illegible]
Aug 6th Oil layin
Aug 7th 1st bird
Aug 8th Completed
3 days.
Completed

Canvas 16X20
Goose Illustration.
Sept. 12. Cutouts
Sept. 13 Ink
Sept 13 landscape layin
Sept 14 [illegible]
[illegible] Geese
[illegible] Geese
[illegible] landscape Geese
Sept 18 Figure
Sept 19 Background geese, ducks
Sept 20 Geese completed
Sept 21 Figure
Sept 22 Landscape foreground
Sept 28 Figure landscape
Complete 13 days.
Destroyed

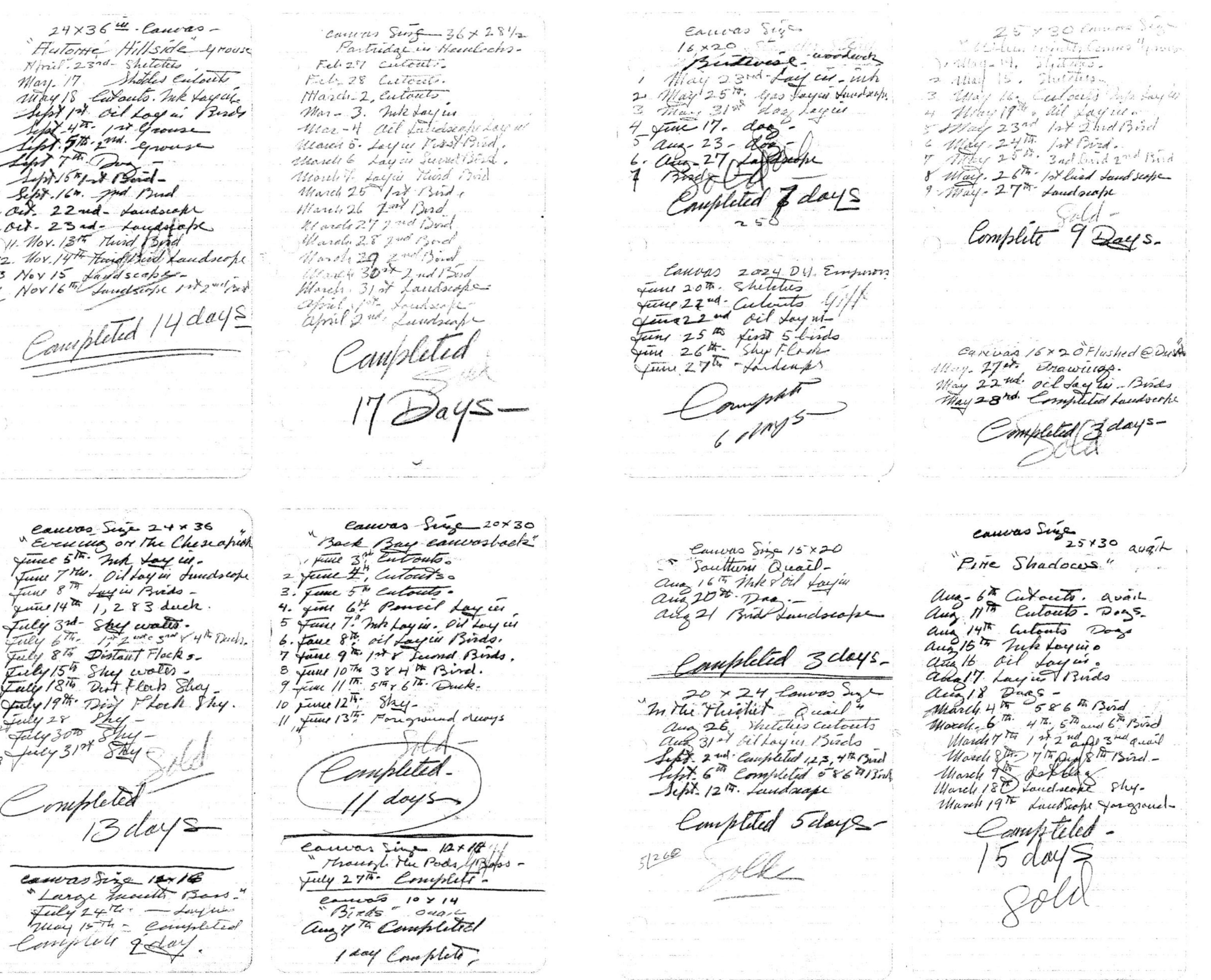

24X36" Canvas -
"Autumn Hillside" grouse
April 23rd Sketches
1 May 17 Sketches Cutouts
2 May 18 Cutouts. Ink Lay in
3 Sept 1st Oil Lay in Birds
4 Sept 4th 1st Grouse
5 Sept 5th 2nd Grouse
6 Sept 7th Dog
7 Sept 15th 1st Bird
8 Sept 16th 2nd Bird
9 Oct 22nd Landscape
10 Oct 23rd Landscape
11 Nov 13th Third Bird
12 Nov 14th Third Bird Landscape
13 Nov 15 Landscape
14 Nov 16th Landscape 1st 2nd 3rd
15
Completed 14 days

Canvas Size 36 x 28½
Partridge in Hemlocks
Feb 27 Cutouts
Feb 28 Cutouts
March 2 Cutouts
Mar 3 Ink Lay in
Mar 4 Oil Landscape Lay in
March 5 Lay in First Bird
March 6 Lay in Second Bird
March 7 Lay in Third Bird
March 25 1st Bird
March 26 2nd Bird
March 27 2nd Bird
March 28 2nd Bird
March 29 2nd Bird
March 30th 2nd Bird
March 31st Landscape
April 1st Landscape
April 2nd Landscape
Completed
Sold
17 Days

Canvas Size
16x20
Birdseye - woodcock
1 May 23rd Lay in - ink
2 May 25th Lay in Landscape
3 May 31st Dog Lay in
4 June 17 dog
5 Aug 23 dog
6 Aug 27 Landscape
7 Birds
Completed 7 days
250

Canvas 20x24 D.U. Emperors
June 20th Sketches
June 22nd Cutouts
June 22nd Oil Lay in
June 25th first 5 birds
June 26th Sky Flocks
June 27th Landscape
Gift
Completed
6 days

25 x 30 Canvas Size
May 14 Sketches
2 May 15 Sketches
3 May 16 Cutouts Ink Lay in
4 May 19th Oil Lay in
5 May 23rd 1st 2nd Bird
6 May 24th 1st Bird
7 May 25th 3rd Bird 2nd Bird
8 May 26th 1st Bird Landscape
9 May 27th Landscape
Sold
Complete 9 Days

Canvas 16x20 Flushed @ Dusk
May 21st Drawings
May 22nd Oil Lay in - Birds
May 28th Completed Landscape
Completed 3 days
Sold

Canvas Size 24 x 36
"Evening on the Chesapeake"
June 5th Ink Lay in
2 June 7th Oil Lay in Landscape
3 June 8th Lay in Birds
4 June 14th 1, 2 & 3 duck
5 July 3rd Sky water
6 July 6th 1st 2nd 3rd & 4th Ducks
7 July 8th Distant Flocks
8 July 15th Sky water
9 July 18th Dist Flock Sky
10 July 19th Dist Flock Sky
11 July 28 Sky
12 July 30th Sky
13 July 31st Sky
Sold
Completed
13 days

Canvas Size 12x16
"Large mouth Bass."
July 24th - Lay in
May 15th - Completed
Completed 2 day.

Canvas Size 20x30
"Back Bay canvasback"
1 June 3rd Cutouts
2 June 4th Cutouts
3 June 5th Cutouts
4 June 6th Pencil Lay in
5 June 7th Ink Lay in. Oil Lay in
6 June 8th oil Lay in Birds
7 June 9th 1st & Second Birds
8 June 10th 3 & 4th Bird
9 June 11th 5th & 6th Duck
10 June 12th Sky
11 June 13th Foreground decoys
Sold
Completed
11 days

Canvas Size 12x18
"Through the Pods" Bass
July 27th Complete
Canvas 10 x 14
"Birds" quail
Aug 7th Completed
1 day Complete

Canvas Size 15x20
"Southern Quail"
Aug 16th Ink & Oil Lay in
Aug 20th Dog
Aug 21 Bird Landscape
Completed 3 days

20 x 24 Canvas Size
"In the Thicket Quail"
Aug 26 Sketches cutouts
Aug 31st Oil Lay in Birds
Sept 2nd Completed 1,2,3,4th Bird
Sept 6th Completed 5 & 6th Birds
Sept 12th Landscape
Completed 5 days
Sold

Canvas Size 25x30 quail
"Pine Shadows"
Aug 6th Cutouts. quail
Aug 11th Cutouts. Dogs
Aug 14th Cutouts Dogs
Aug 15th Ink Lay in
Aug 16 Oil Lay in
Aug 17 Lay in Birds
Aug 18 Dogs
March 4th 5 & 6th Bird
March 6th 4th 5th and 6th Bird
March 7th 1st 2nd and 3rd quail
March 8th 7th and 8th Bird
March 9th [illegible]
March 18th Landscape Sky
March 19th Landscape foreground
Completed
15 days
Sold

Appendix C

George Browne Log, 1937–1957

A list of paintings completed yearly, with date, title, time to complete, price, where exhibited, purchaser and size.

1937.

Date	No.	Name	Time	Price	Exhibition	Locations	Purchaser	Date Sold	Size	Remarks
Oct 3rd	1.	Drawing (Charcoal)	2	5	Studio		B Shuman.	1937	20x24	
Nov 6th	2.	Wood ducks (Water Color)	4	25	Studio		EM Nichols.	1937	10x14	
Nov 30th	3.	Tarpon (Water Color)	4	15	Studio		H. Nichols.	1937	12x16	
Dec 2nd	4	Moutain Landscape	1	20	Studio		Mrs. Garvin.	1937	10x14	
Dec 2nd	5	Trout (Water Color)	2	20	Studio		Mrs Garvin,	1937	10x14	
Dec 16th	6.	Landscape	1	25	Studio		S. Ryne.	1937	25x30	
		Total		$110						
		1938								
Jan 3rd	1	Tarpon (Water Color)	4	15	Studio		H. Nichols	1938	12x16	
Jan 3rd	2	Salmon (Water Color)	4	15	Studio		H. Nichols	1938	12x16	
Jan 30th	3	Trout (Water Color)	4	10	Studio		M. Oaks-	1938	9x11	
Mar 3rd	4	Striped Bass (Water Color)	5	5	Studio		J. Painter.	1938	10x16	
Mar 4th	5	Black Bass (Water Color)	6	10	Studio		A. Ally.	1938	9x11	
Mar 5th	6	Striped Bass (Water Color)	4	5	Studio		J Painter.	1938	10x16	
Mar 10	7	Trout	3	10	Studio		Mr Boyd.	1938	10x14	
Aug 12th	8	Landscape	1	10	Studio		Mr. Benson.	1939	9x11.	
Aug 2nd	9	Landscape	1	10	Studio		Mr. Benson	1939	9x11	
Sept. 12	10	Landscape	1	10	Studio		Friend of Mrs Benson	1939	9x11	
Sept. 12	11	Landscape	1	10	Studio		Friend of Mr. Benson	1939	9x11	
		Total		$110						
		1939.								
Feb. 1st	1	Landscape	1	10	Studio		a Ad Ally.	1939	9x11	
Feb 29	2.	Landscape	1	10	Studio		Mr. Crane.	1939	9x11	
April 4	3	Letter head (Pen & Ink)	6	10	Studio		J Livermore.	1939	10x14	
May 12	4.	Horse head. (Charcoal)	2	20	Studio		Mrs. Greene.	1939	20x24	
June 30	5	Horses head. (Charcoal)	2.	20	Studio		A. Milton.	1939	20x24	
July 14	6	Landscape	1	10	Studio		Mr Forbes.	1939	9x11	
		Total		$80						
		1940								
Jan 10	1	Landscape	1	10	Studio		Mr. Forbes.	1940	9x11	
Feb. 15	2	Blue Bill	5	25	Studio		B. Starbuck.	1940	16x20	
Feb 20	3	Magpies	8	75	Studio		W. Bliss	1940	50x60	Screen in oil & wood.
Feb. 30	4	Ram Head	10	25	Studio		ES Spaulding	1940	16x20	
April 29	5	Dog Head - Charcoal	3	15	Studio		J. Painter	1940	16x20	
Mar. 10	6	Landscape	1	10	Studio		Mr. Forbes	1940	9x11	
Aug 12	6	Restore picture	2	10	Studio		S Eells.	1940		Repaint old Picture.
		Total		$170						
		1941								
Jan 12	1	Green Wing Teal	2	25	Chicago		P Stressen-Reuter Inc.	1941	16x20	Calender 1942
Jan 12	2	Rainbow Trout	5	25	Chicago		P Stressen-Reuter Inc.	1941	16x20	
Feb 2	3	Salmon	3	25	New York		American Museum (J. Clark)			Model in wood & oil
June 9		assisted in Three backgrounds	90	350	New York		American Museum (B. Brown)		25x60	average size
June 9	4	Ovis Poli Ram.	7	475	New York		J.d. Clark	1941	12x16	
June 15	5	Landscape	1	10	Studio		Mr. Forbes	1941	9x11	
June 15	6	Landscape	1	10	Studio		Mr. Forbes-	1941	9x11	
		Total		$445						

Date	No.	Name	Time	Price	Exhibition	Locations	Purchaser	Date Sold	Size	Remarks
		1942								
May 12	1	Chip Monk	3.	20	Studio		E S Spaulding.	1942	9 x 11	Illustration
May 15	2.	Skunks.	5.	25	Studio		E S Spaulding.	1942	12x16	Illustration
May 30	3.	Rattle snakes (Drawing)	2	10	Studio		E S Spaulding.	1942	12x16	Illustration
April 10	4	Chip Monk (drawing)	2	10	Studio		E S Spaulding.	1942	12x16	Illustration
April 30	5	Doves (drawing)	3	10	Studio		E S. Spaulding.	1942	12x16	Illustration
April 30	6	Porkypine (drawing)	3	10	Studio		E S Spaulding	1942	12x16	Illustration
June 8	7	Owls (Drawing)	2	10	Studio		E S Spaulding	1942	12x16	Illustration
Aug 3	8	Goats on Cliffs	10	50	Studio		C.M. DeMott.	1942	16x20	
Aug 5	9	Rainbow Trout	12	50	Studio		M. Stressen-Reuter	Dec. 1943	12x16	
Dec 20	10	Ruffed Grouse	10	50	Studio		Mrs. T. Blodgett.	1942	16x20	
Dec 30	11	Charcoal Horse Head. Total	4.	20 $270	Studio		J. Painter.	1942	20x24	
		1943								
Jan 1		assistant at Army N.H. Total		350 $350	New York		B. Browne	1942	30x60 ft.	average size.
		1944								
Aug 6.	1	Snow Geese & Lesser Canada	2	gift	Army.		Mr Moran	1944	10x14	
July	2nd	Ohio Lake.	1		Army				10x14	Sketch
July	3	Pheasant Landscape	1		Army				10x14	Sketch
Sept	4	Afternoon Light	1		Army				10x14	Sketch
Sept. 5	6	Corn Field	1		Army				10x14	Sketch
Oct 12	7.	Mud Flats Ohio River	1		Army				10x14	Sketch.
		1945								
Jan 15	1	Pintails over Marsh	3	gift	Army.		Mr. King	1945	10x14	
Feb 3	2	Horses on Butte	2	gift	Army		Mr. Moran.	1945	10x14	
Jan 5	3	Lesser Canada Geese	3.	25	Army.		Stewart Campbell	1945	12x16	
Mar.	4	Sea Rescue Scene	2	gift	Army		Stanwall - Fletcher 1945		18x24	Sketch
April 1	5	Sea Rescue Mural	14	gift	Army.		H.A.F. Bldg. 125 D.P. Ohio		20x60	Ex.
April 15	6	Big horn Ram.	3	50	Army.		Stewart Campbell	1945	16x20	
May 1	7	Cut Throat Trout.	6	50	Chicago		Stressen-Reuter	Dec. 1945	16x20	1946 Calendar.
	8	Lesser Canada Goose	2	45	Harlow Art gallery	N.Y.	?	1945	18x24	Purchaser unknown
	9	Buffle Head Duck.	2	25	Harlow Art gallery	N.Y.	?	1945	12x16	Purchaser unknown.
	10	Widgeon Drake	2	25	Harlow Art gallery	N.Y.	?	1945	16x20	Purchaser Unknown.
	11	Blue Bill Drake Total	2	$220	Harlow & Graves	N.Y. S.F.	Exhibition G.C.G.	1950	16x20	Cousin Elizabeth 175
		1946								
Mar 6	1	Canvas back Drake	8	100	Studio		C.M. DeMott	1947	18x24	
Mar 25	2	Calif. Ringnecks (Pheasant)	6	gift	Studio		N.T. Luxton	1947	12x16	
Dec 15	3.	Sketch for Blue Bill	2	10	Studio		A. Stine	1946	16x20	
Dec.	4	Bighorn Sheep $75 Total		$110	Studio		C. M. DeMott	1946	16x20	
		1947								
Nov 7	1	Canvasback Study	3.		Studio				25x30	Sketch
Nov 10	2	Red Head Drake.	4	$450	Grand Central Galleries	N.Y.	Grand Central.		25x30	Sold from G.C.G. Aug. 11th 1949
Nov 25	3	Ruffed Grouse	2	$	Grand Central Galleries	N.Y.			16x20	
Nov 28	4	Grouse Landscape	1						12x16	Sketch
Dec. 15	5	"Ol. Grouse"	16	$350 300	Grand Central Studio	N.Y. SF	N.B. Livermore 1949. 1947 Henderson of Pelam N.Y.		25x30	Result. Picture Returned on Paid Transferred to Boston. Mass
Dec. 30	6.	"Ebb Tide" Blue bill Shooting	15	$	Grand Central Annual	N.Y. SF			20x30	Exhibition Graves Gallery.
Aug.	7	Cut Throat Trout.	12	$150	Grand Central	N.Y.	Mr. Henderson of Pelam N.Y.	1947	18x24	
Jan 4	8	Pintails on a Salt Marsh	15	$325	Grand Central	N.Y.	Mr. Henderson of Pelam. N.Y.		25x30	

1947 Cont. →

1947 Cont.

Date	No	Name	Time	Price	Exhibition	Location	Purchaser	Date Sold	Size	Remarks
	9	1 North P.K. from Mt McGonical	1		New York.	RKO			12 x 16	
	10	2 Mather & Brooks from Mt McG.	1		New York.	RKO			12 x 16	
	11	3 Gun Sight from Mt McG.	1		New York.	RKO			12 x 16	
	12	4 Cash Creek Sheep hills.	1		New York	RKO			12 x 16	
	13	5 Bason Head of Cash Creek.	1		New York	RKO			12 x 16	
	14	6 Mt Brooks.	1		New York	RKO			12 x 16	
	15	7 Triperiniid Glacier	1		New York	RKO			12 x 16	
	16	8 Slopes of Tatum	1		New York.	RKO			12 x 16	
	17	9 Tatum & North P.K.	1		New York	RKO			12 x 16	
	18	10 North & South P.K. Camp. II	1		New York	RKO			12 x 16	
	19	11 Pioneer Rdg. from Camp II	1		New York	RKO			12 x 16	
	20	12 Great Serace – Camp. III	1		New York	RKO			12 x 16	
	21	13 Browne Tower from Camp III	1		New York	RKO			12 x 16	
	22	14 N.E. Rdg. & Harper Glacier Camp III	1		New York	RKO			12 x 16	
	23	15 North Shoulder – Storm Camp IV	1		New York	RKO			12 x 16	
	24	16 Mt Carpea Camp IV	1		New York	RKO			12 x 16	
	25	17 Head of Muldrow Camp IV	1		New York	RKO			12 x 16	
	26	18 Looking out from Camp V	1		New York	RKO			12 x 16	
	27	19 Head of Moose Creek.	1		New York	RKO			12 x 16	
	28	20 McK. from Wonder Lake	1		New York	RKO			12 x 16	
	29	21 McK. from Wonder. 10000 ft Clds.	1		New York	RKO			12 x 16	
	30	22 McK from Mt. Eilson	1		New York	RKO			12 x 16	
	31	N & S. P.K. from 7600 ft. Camp. II	8	$ 312	Studio	Seebe	W. Sackett	1948	18 x 24	
	32	NE Central Rdg. from Camp IV	3.	$ 95	Studio	Seebe	S1 Evans	1948	12 x 16	
	33	McKinly from Wonder Lake	3.	$ 95	Studio	Seebe	Cornbley.	1947	16 x 20	
Aug 15	34	McKinley from Mt Eilson	3	$ 95	Studio	Seebe.	Cornbley	1947	16 x 20	
Aug 30	35	McKinley from Kantishna	3	$ 95	Studio	Seebe	Pearson	1948	16 x 20	
Sept. 1	36	N & S P.K. from Camp. II	3.	$ 75	Studio	Seebe	DeMott	1948	12 x 16	
Sept 20	37	Landscape Mallard	1						12 x 16	Sketch
Sept 21	38	Moose Study Head	1						10 x 14	
Sept. 30	39	Moose Study full	1						10 x 14	
Oct 1st.	40	Moose Study Hd.	1						10 x 14	
Oct 2	41	Moose Study Hd.	1						16 x 20	
Oct. 10	42	Horse Study	1						12 x 16	for "Bard" A. Hammond
Oct. 11	43	Elk Study Head.	1						12 x 16	
Oct 12	44	Elk Study Head.	1						12 x 16	
Oct 15	45	McKinley from Wonder Lake	s3	75	Studio	Seebe	DeMott	1948	12 x 16	
Nov. 25	46	"Jumping Mallards"	s18	fee	Grand Central Galleries	N.Y.	Lay member Grand Central	1949	25 x 30	3rd and last Donation.
Dec. 10	47	Quail Study	1						12 x 16	
Dec. 11	48	Quail Study	1						12 x 16	
Dec 12	49	Quail Study	1						16 x 20	
Dec 29	50	Blue Bill (Hen)	1	100			E. ~~M. Stead~~ Bowland		16 x 20	10/15/5[illegible]
Dec. 30	51	Pintail Hen.	1						16 x 20	
		Total		1642						
		1948								
Jan 2	1	Bufflehead Drake	s1	100	Graves Gallery G e G	S.F. N.Y	Stow		16 x 20	↖ 11/9/53
Jan 4th	2	Blue bill Drake	1		Graves Gallery G e G	S.F. N.Y			25 20	
Jan 8	3	Pintail Drake	1						25 x 30	
Jan 15	4	Paradice Marsh Sun Rise	1						16 x 20	
Jan 21	5	"Cans at Sun Rise"	s18	325	Grand Central	N.Y.	Henderson of Pelham N.Y.	1948	25 x 30	Exchanged for "Oct grouse" 1948 cont. →

Painted from March 25th to June 30th.

1948 Cont.

Date	No.	Name	Time	Price	Exhibition	Location	Purchaser Date Sold	Size	Remarks -
Jan 26	6.	Ponds at Santa Vanicia	1					16x20	
Jan 31	7.	Coast Range Quail background	1					12x16	
Feb 14	8.	Spring Leaving The Marsh	S 18	Fee	Grand Central	N.Y.	Lay Member G.C. Galleries 1948	25x30	1st donation
Feb. 28	9.	Rafting Red Head.	S 81	170	Grand Central	N.Y.	? July 7, 1948	25x30	Sold to Hart Collection Aug. 8 1948
March 13	10	"The Band." (Horse)	S 161	180	Studio	Seeke.	A. Hammond. 1948	16x20	
June 2	11	Green Wing Drake & Hen.	S 2	250	Graves. G.C.G. Vose	SF Mass.		20x24	Landscape added. 1/12/56
June 4	12	Ruffed Grouse	1					16x20	
June 12	13	Lighting Canada Geese	1					12x16.	
June 14	14	Storm on a Wheat Field	1					12x16.	
June	15	Storm on a Wheat Field	1					12x16	
Aug 1	16	California Spring	S 18	500	Studio	Rose.	G. Henshaw. 1948	25x30	
Aug 2	17	McKinley Rams From Osler	2					20x24	
Aug 20	18	Western Goose Shooting	16		Grand Central ~~Graves~~	NY & ~~SF~~		20x24	distroyed
Sept 10	18	Ruffed Grouse Shooting	S 18	150	Graves Grand Central	N.Y. SF	J. Phillips (IBM) Ex. G.C.G.	20x24	
Oct 17	28	Hen Red Head - Study	1					16x20	
Oct 19	29	Jack Snipe Study	S 1		Graves.	S.F.		12x16	
Oct 20	22	Hen Widgeon Study	1					16x20	
Oct 22	23	Drake Mallard - Study	S 2	250	Studio	Ross	E.B. Henshaw	25x30	Frame Extra Nov 30, 1949.
Oct 30	24	Hen Mallard Study	1					16x20	
Oct 31	25	Shore Ice	1					12x16	
Nov 2	26	Sunlight on The Marsh.	1					12x16	
Nov. 6	26	Canada Goose portrait	S 2	500	Grand Central Vose.	N.Y. Mas.	G.C.G.	30x36	5/1/55
Nov 15	28	Study for "Oasis" (Teal)	S 1					15x15	
Dec. 4	28	"Wild Harvest" (Geese)	27	750	Grand Central	N.Y.	Seony Vacuum Oil Co. 1949	30x40	1950 Calendar.
Dec. 30	30	"New Oasis" for G.W. Teal.	S 15		Grand Central	N.Y.	Lay Member G.C. Gallery 1949	25x30	2nd Donation for Membership.
		Total.	-	~~1040~~					

1949.

Date	No.	Name	Time	Price	Exhibition	Location	Purchaser Date Sold	Size	Remarks -
Jan 4	1	Green Wing Drake -	1	gift	Studio		E. Browne	12x16	Sketch for J. Griffith's Order
Jan 5	2	Pintail Drake	1	gift	Studio.		E. Browne	12x16	Sketch for J. Griffith's Order
Jan 6	3	Drake Spring alighting	S 2	$ 82	Studio	Seeke.	J. Griffith 1949	20x24	8 1949
Jan 9	4	Green Wing Drake.	S 3	$ 82	Studio Vose. Can Art.	Seeke	J. Griffith 1949	20x24	1949
Jan 12	5	"Study for Windward Shore"	1					12x16	
Jan 12	6	Study for "Windward Shore"	1					12x16.	
Jan 17	7	Study for Flight W. Marsh.	1					12x16	
Jan 22	8	Study for Winter afternoon	1					12x16	
Jan 28	9	Flight to windward Shore	S 8	$ 300	Grand Central	N.Y.	?	20x24	Sold from G.C.G. Aug 11th 1949.
Feb. 4.	10	Following The Shore Study.	1					12x16	
Feb. 6.	11	"Following The Shore"	S 10	$ 250	Grand Central	N.Y.	Exhibition G.C.G. 1950	20x24.	Sold Bettie Dorais
Feb. 9th	12	Study for Morning Mist	1					12x16.	
Feb. 28	13	"Jack Snipe in the Spring Time"	S 6	$ 100	Grand Central	N.Y.	Exhibition G.C.G. 1950	12x16	
Mar. 10.	14	Bald pait "Dropping in"	S	$ 100	Grand Central	N.Y.	Sold Through G.C. Galleries	12x16	Dec 28 1949.
Mar 16	15	A pair of "Green Wings"	4				distroyed	12x16	Distroyed
Mar 21	16	Study for "Prairie Pintail"	1					16x20	
Mar 24	17	Study for N.H. Blacks.	1	gift.	Studio	Seeke	E. Browne	10x14.	
Mar. 31	18	Hen Grouse in Feb. Snow	S 2	$ x85			Exhibition G.C.G. 1950	10x14	1950
April 10	19	Green Wings before The Wind	S 4	$ 100	Grand Central	N.Y.	Exhibition G.C.G. 1950	12x16	1950
April 11	20	Spring Slough (April)	1					12x16	
April 14	21	Fresh Snow.	1					12x16	
April 15	22	Melting Ice	1					12x16	
April 17	23	Buffle Head Sketches	1					16x20	

1949 Cont →

1949 Cont.

Date	No.	Name	Time	Price	Exhibition	Location	Purchaser	Size	Remarks
April 18	24	Reeds drifted on ice. (Study)	1					12×16	
April 21	25	Barrows Goldeneye Drake	S1	100	graves. Y.C.G. Studio	SF	M. Stow.	16×20	Sale by Evelyn-
April 22	26	Bufflehead Drake	1					10×14	
April 23	27	Bufflehead Drake	1					9×11	
April 25	28	Ringneck duck Drake	S1	$90	graves YCG	NY SF	Exhibition YCG 1950-52	18×24	Converted to 12×16.
April 29	29	Barrows Goldeneye Hen.	3		graves	SF		12×16	Reduced to 10×14.
May 7	30	"Afternoon Flight" (Pintail	317	$ 450	graves YCG.	NY SF	Exhibition YCG 1950	25×30	Not for Sale. W.H Ranson. 1950.
May 11	31	Canada Goose Study.	S2	$ 450	graves YCG	NY SF	YCG 1950	25×30	Hurlins Terminal 1950
May 14	32	A pair of Bluewing Teal	S2		YCG. Vose	Mass. NY		16×20	
May 22	33	Windy afternoon	1					12×16	
May 23	34	Deadhorse Slough (East.	1					12×16	
May 24	35	Study for "Freckles" #1	1					10×14	
May 24	36	Study for "Freckles" #2	1					12×16	
May 25	37	Study for "Freckles" #3	1					12×16	
May 29	38	Study for "Freckles" #4	1					16×20	
June 25	39.	Study Grouse in Feb. Snow	S/6	$ 100	graves YCG	NY SF	Exhibition YCG 1950.	12×16	1950
June 29	40.	"Freckles" (Dog Portrait)	S7	$ 100	Studio	Seebe	R. Brewster	16×20	June 30 1949
July 1	41	Study for Lesser Geese #1	1	$				12×16	
July 3	42	Study for Mallards #1	1	$ 75	graves YCG	SF	Exhibition YCG 1950	12×16	Reduced to 10×14- 1950
July 4	43	Study for Lesser Geese #2	2					16×20	
July 7	44	Study for Mallards #2	1					12×16	
July 17	45	Stormy Afternoon, Mallards	S8					12×16	
July 28	46	Following the Slough. Mallards	S17	$ 267	graves YCG Vose.	Mass. NY SF	Exhibition YCG 1950	25×30	Purchased Hunters Show YCG
Aug 21	47	"After the Squak" (Lesser geese)	$33	$ 175	Studio YCG	NY	~~Destroyed~~ YCG 1949	30×40	contribution
Sept 3	48	Study for "Golden Eye Flight."	1					12×16.	
Sept 19	49	"Spring on a Northern Lake" geese	S14	250	graves YCG Vose YCG.	Mass. NY SF	R.R. West Virginia Pulp & Paper Co-	30×40.	Not for Sale
Oct. 8	50	Flushing Sharptail.	S2	325	graves YCG Can Art.	NY SF	Mr. Hindle.	25×30.	Can. Art. 1/54
Oct. 12	51	Bluewings Coming in	S7	destroyed	YCG	NY		20×24.	
Oct. 15	52	Hungarian Partridge at Sun Set.	S2	200	YCG	NY	CAN ART Dr. Buchanan-	16×20.	6/24/55
Oct. 23	53.	Sharptails in the Morning Sun.	S3	$ 300	Vose YCG Can Art	Mass. NY	Can. Art.	20×24.	6/[illegible]
Oct. 31st	54	Startled Mallards.	S4.	$ 405	graves YCG	NY SF	Exhibition YCG 1950	25×30.	Not for Sale, Sold Collection. Dec. 26.
Nov. 30	55	Sketch for "Cans Sliding in"	1					18×24.	
Dec. 1	56	Sketch for "Cans Sliding in"	1					12×16.	
Dec 14	57	Barrows Goldeneye Flight	S15	$ 350	YCG	NY	Exhibition YCG. 1950 Nov-	20×30	
1950									
Jan 3	1.	"Along the River Bottoms" (Wood Duck)	S4	350	YCG Vose C.Art.	NY	Can Art	25×30.	Jan 30th 1957
Jan 15	2	Coming into the Estuary (Cans)	S25	$ 800	YCG.	NY	Texaco Oil Co. (YCG)	30×40.	June 9th 1950
Mar. 28	3	Green Wings in Cold Weather	S7	$ 450	YCG.	NY	Mr. Lee Phillips	25×30.	May 13th 1950
April 4	4	The "Straggler" Buffle Drake.	S3	$ 100	Studio	Conn.	Daniel Hinde	12×16.	April 18th 1950.
April 13	5	Cedar Point, New Hampshire	S8	$ 320	Studio	Conn	Mrs. Walter H Wilcox	16×20.	April 17th, 1950.
April 16	6	Ruffed Grouse in Spring Snow	S3	$ 100	YCG.	N.Y.	? YCG	12×16.	April 28th 1950
May	7	Drake Sprig Alighting	S5	Gift.	Studio	SF	James Griffith.	20×24	May 1950 (-Gift)
June	8	Land Scape Sketch for Low Picture	1					18×24	
June	9	Land scape Sketch for Low Picture.	1					12×15	
June	10	Sketch of Maryland River	1					10×14	
June	11	Sketch for Scaring the Bay.	1					16×20	
July	12	Three Ruffed Grouse	28				Vose Galleries	10×14	
Aug.	13	Ruffed Grouse in the Woods.	23	$ 200	Studio Seebe		Vose Galleries	16×20	Sold. Dec. 6th 1950
Aug	14	Study for Rock Grouse	2	$ 75	Studio Seebe		H.C. Bowles	10×14.	Sold. Aug 18th 1951
[illegible]	15	[illegible] in the Forest Grouse	S3	$ 250	Studio Seebe		Vose Galleries Mr. Ryan.	16×20.	Sold Nov. 6th 1950

1950 (Cont.)

Date	No.	Name	Time	Price	Exhibited	Location	Purchaser	Size	Remarks
Aug.	16.	Canvasback on the Nanticoke River	21s	400	Studio Seebe		E Herrick Low	24"x36"	Commission
Sept.	17.	Black duck Scurrying the Cove	13s	158	Studio Seebe			16x20	
Oct.	18.	Keystone Valley. Sketch	1.		Studio Seebe			16x20	
Oct	19	Evening Slough Sketch	1.		Studio Seebe			12x16	
Nov.	20	Canvasback at Mubuko	17s	400	Studio Seebe		Leonard S Mudge	24x36	Commission
Dec.	21	"Keystone Valley"	11s	330	Studio Seebe		Eric L. Harvie	20x26	Commission
Dec.	22	Total for 1950 14 Pictures	7 Sketches		Total 21 pictures				

Date	No.	1951. Name	Time	Price	Exhibited	Location	Purchaser	Size	Remarks
Jan	1.	"Winter out on The Bay"	21s	500 / 700	Studio Seebe YLY		"Westraco" Magazine (R.R.)	30x40.	Reproduction Rights Sold Later.
Jan	2.	"Flood Tide at Sunset," Canvasback.	6s	150	Studio Seebe YLY		Resale YLY.	15x20	Donation for Ducks Unlimited
Jan	3.	"A Winter's Morning" Grouse	9s	550	Studio Seebe C.Art	Vose Crossroads.	Sold May	25x30.	
Feb.	4.	"Flushed Grouse"	15s	150	Studio Seebe YLY			25x30.	4/18/53 Donation YLY.
Feb.	5	"A Flight Returning" Mal.	12s	500	Studio Seebe C.Art		Mr. Cheshire	24x36.	Universal development Co.
Mar.	6	Mallards, "Gleaning the Stubble"	16s	700	Studio Seebe YLY.			30x40.	
Mar.	7	Mallards, "In The River Bottoms"	9s	450	Studio Seebe YLY		Phillips, Oklahoma	25x30	Commissioned by YLY.
April	8	The Old Stone Wall, Ruffed Grouse	7s	300	Studio Seebe, Vose	Crossroads	Crossroads -	16x20	Sold Jan 1953
April	9	Broadbill, Ahead of the Squall"	17s	450	Studio Seebe, Vose,	Crossroads	Crossroads -	20x30	Sold Jan 10th 1953
April	10	"Busting Out" Ruffed Grouse"	18s	200	Studio Seebe		Fred. K. Barbour, (Commission)	16x20	Trade E.H. Low for D.U. Donation
May.	11	"Evening at Mubuko" Black duck.	8s	Gift	Studio Seebe			15x20	
May.	12	"Canvasback against The Nanticoke Shore	13s	400	Studio Seebe		Mr. O'Neill Ryan, Mt. Vernon	24x36	Commission - New York-
July	13	"Prairie Afternoon" Mallard & Pintail	14s	500	Studio Seebe C. Art		John Cross.	24x36	11/21/65
July	14	"The Early Flight" Pintail.	10s	450	Studio Seebe.		Can Art.	20x30	
July	15	"Decending Pintail"	6s	200	Studio Seebe Ross	Studio	T.H. Blodgett	16x20	
July	16	"Mallards Drifting in."	1s	75	Studio Seebe		H.C. Bowles	10x14.	
July	17	"Mallards Pitching in"	1s	25	Studio Seebe		D. Motter.	10x14.	
Aug.	18	"Ringnecks Thundering Out"	2s	150	Studio Seebe		Can. Art.	12x16.	
Aug.	19	"Beating from Cover"	3s	150	Studio Seebe		Can Art.	12x16.	
Sept	20	"The Woodland Pond" Mallards	17s	500	Studio Seebe	Crossroads N.Y.	Crossroads May -	25x30	April 1952
Sept	21	Illustration for "Hurrican Honkers"	13s	[illegible]	Studio Seebe			16x20	turned down
Dec.	22	Cock Ring Neck.	3s	150	Studio Ross.	Canadian Art	Canadian Art.	16x20	Jan 6th 1953.
Dec	23	Cinnamon Teal Drake	3		Studio Ross.			16x20	
Dec	24	"Bullnecks" (Canvasback)	11s.	Gift.	Studio Ross.		Sand Bridge Club.	24x30	
Dec.	25	"A pair of Mallard"	11s.	6475	Studio Ross. Can. Art.	Can Art.		24x36	(13 sold out of 24) 4/30/54

Date	No.	1952	Time		Exhibited	Location	Purchaser	Size	Remarks
Jan	1	"A Heavy Flight in the Morning	15s	150	Studio Ross	Calif.	C.H. Allen	20x30	Commission Calif. 52
Feb.	2	"After the Rain" Pintail	13s	400	Studio Ross	Howel	H.B.S. D.U.	20x30	Gift D.U. Gift 2/11/54
Mar.	3	"Robins in the Madrona"	13s	400	Studio Ross	Calif	E.Y. Dieniche April.	25x30	Commission California 52
March	4	"Clearing Skys on the Napa Delta	5s	200	Studio Ross	Howels.	H.B.S.	16x20	7/10/53
March	5	"Brant Above The Surf.	1s	25	Studio Ross	Calif	C.H. Allen	12x16	Sold April 3rd 1952
April	6	"Drifting in" Spring.	3s	200	Studio Ross	Calif.	Harrison Dibblee Jr	16x20	Commission April 52
April	7	"Brant on the Bolinas Medows	4s	200	Studio Ross	Calif.	Harrison Dibblee Jr	16x20	Commission April 52
April	8	"Working in" (Can) on the Nanticoke	8s	250	Studio Ross	Calif.	E. Herrick Low	18x24	Commission E.H. Low for Bull.
May	9	"By the Brook in Winter" Grouse	8s	400	Studio Ross	Crossroads N.Y.		20x24	Nov. 1952
May	10	"Over the Pass" Canvasback	14s	600	Studio Ross		James Griffith	24x36.	Sold in May 1952.
May	11	"Heading Out on an Ebb Tide" Canvasback	5s	400	Studio Ross	Howels	YLY	20x30.	YLY. 2/11/54
May	12	"Up and out" valley quail	3s	150	Studio Ross	Howels	HBS -	12x16	7/10/53
June	13	"Out of the Hedge Rows" Pheasant	5s	350	Studio Seebe	C. Art	Crossroads	18x24.	9/16/53
June	14	"A Pair of Pheasant	3s	150	Studio Seebe	C. Art	Sold Aug 1952	12x16	Aug 53

1952 Cont.

Date	No.	Name	Time	Price	Exhibited	Location	Purchaser	Size	Remarks	
July	15	"Autumn Afternoon" Mallard	11½	225	Studio Seebe, Can Art		Mr. Hindle	20x24		3/16/54
July	16	"Greenwings at Sun Set"	9½	450	Studio Seebe, Can Art		N. Lougheed	25x30		1/26/54
July	17	"Circling Back" Mallard	10½	repaint	Studio Seebe Crossroads		Repainted. 8 Sold.	24x36		
Aug	18	"Alarmed" Pheasant	13½	550	Studio Seebe Crossroads	424	Fire Stone Rubber Co.	25x30		Dec 53.
Aug	19	"Through the Birches" Woodcock	3½	275	Studio Seebe Crossroads			16x20		Jan. 8
Aug	20	"On the Drumming Log" grouse	3½	375	Studio Seebe	CRS	CRS	20x24		7/31/53
Sept	21	"Cornered" Ruffed Grouse	15	450	Studio Seebe Can Art		Vancover	25x30		Oct 52
Nov	22	"Out of the North" Geese	17	600	Studio Seebe Crossroads	Can Art		24x36	Can Art	5/2 56
Nov	23	"Frost in the River Bottoms" geese	10	550	Studio Seebe Crossroads		424	25x30	424	2/11/54
Dec	24	"Early Snows" grouse	9	450	Studio Rowayton Crossr	...		25x30		Dec. 29th
		1952 Total 24 oils.		4250					12 ... in 1952	4000.00
		1953								
Jan	1.	"Broadbill @ the Point Blind"	8	250	Studio Rowayton.		C Herrick Low	15x20	Commission E.H. Low.	1/27/53
Jan	2.	"Afflight from Fishing Bay."	12	500	Studio Rowayton.		Pat Cavanaugh from O'Niel Ryan.	24x36	Commission O. Ryan	1/15/53
Jan	3.	"Mist on the Water" Broadbill	3	4??	Studio Rowayton.		Dick Dominic #275.00	16x20	Don. Ducks Unlimited	
March	4.	"Bighorn"	9	400	Studio Rowayton.	Can Art.		20x24		5/11/57
Mar.	5.	"Cans @ the Cove"	15	500	Studio Rowayton.		Charles Fiske.	24x36	Commission C. Fiske	4/15/53
April	6.	"Partridge and Hemlocks"	17.	525	Studio Rowayton.		E. Myron Bull	36x29	Commission M. Bull	3/10/53
April	7.	"Flairing Blacks" MAL	4.	300	Studio Rowayton.	Can Art.		18x24		9/14/56
April	8.	"Cross Shot" grouse.	4.		Studio Rowayton.	424.		10x14.		
April	9.	"Flight from the Pembina"	17	400	Studio Rowayton.		Samuel B. Webb.	18x24	Commission S.B. Webb.	8/15/53
May	10	"Moving to Cover" Grouse	9	550	Studio Rowayton.	Crossroads.		25x30		9/16/53
May	11.	"Flushed at Dusk" grouse	3.	300	Studio Rowayton.	Crossroad	J. F. Byers.	16x20		9/16/53.
June	12.	"Back bay Canvasback."	11	500	Studio Rowayton		Frederick H. Barbour.	20x30.	Commission F.H. Barbour.	
June	13	"Alaskan Emperors" geese.	6	???.5	Studio Rowayton		Certificate.	20x24.	Donation Ducks Unlimited	
July	14	"Lighting in" Blackduck.	12		Studio Rowayton	Crossroads		20x30		
July	15	"Dusk on the Chesapeake" Canvas.	10	600	Studio Rowayton.	Crossroad.		24x36		
July	16	"Large Mouth Bass"	2		Studio Rowayton	424		12x16		
July	17	"Farmland Marsh" Mallard.	13	500	Studio Rowayton	Crossroad	Sea Island Ga. CRS.	24x36		10/20/53
Aug.	18	"In the Feed Patch" Quail.	1		Studio Rowayton	424.		10x14.		
Aug.	19	"The Corn Patch" Quail.	4		Studio Rowayton	424.		15x20		
Aug.	20	"In the Thick of it" Woodcock.	6	240	Studio Rowayton	Crossroads		16x20		5/16/57
Sept.	21	"In the Thicket" Quail.	5	400	Studio Rowayton	Crossroads	C. Mellon. C.R.S	20x24		10/25/53
Sept.	22	"Northern Stubble Shooting" Mallard	2.	100	Studio Rowayton	Can Art.	Hindle Can. Art.	10x14.		1/5/54.
Oct.	23	"December Sun Shine" Scaup.	4.	300	Studio Rowayton	Terrill	Crossroads.	16x20		1/10/54
Oct.	24	"Snap Shot" grouse	4.		Studio Rowayton			12x16		1/10/54
Nov.	25	"Autumn Hillside" grouse	14	600	Studio, Rowayton.		H. Webb. C.R.S.	24x36		1/23/54
Dec.	26	"Autumn Cover" Woodcock.	11	400	Studio, Rowayton.	Terrill	Mrs. Hutton C.R.S	30x22		1/23/54
Dec.	27	"Along the Shore Ice" Cans	14	450	Studio, Rowayton		John R.H. Rehm	20x30	Rehm Commission.	12/31/53
		1954								
Jan.	1.	"Autumn Whitetail"	10	425	Studio Rowayton		Barbour Memorial.	20x30	Norfolk Library	3/3/54
Feb.	2.	"Baldpait @ Sauls Bridge"	8	425	Studio Rowayton		Barbour Memorial.	20x30	Norfolk Library.	3/3/54
Feb.	3.	"Evening in the Pine Barrens" Black	9	274	Studio Rowayton		E. Herrick Low.	18x24	Commissioned Low.	4/18/54
Mar	4.	"Pine Shadows" Quail.	14	350	Studio Rowayton.	424	Grand National Foundation	25x30		3/3/56
Mar.	5.	"Forest Dweller", grouse	7	300	Studio Rowayton		John Rehm	12x16	Rehm, Commission.	4/24/54
Mar	6.	"Edge Cover" Pheasent.	5	300	Studio Rowayton		John Rehm.	12x16	Rehm. Commission	4/24/54
April	7	"Grouse, white Pine & Thorn apple"	10	400	Studio Rowayton		John Hammett	20x24	Hammett Commission	5/10/54
April	8	"Cock Pheasant Flushing"	4	175	Studio Rowayton	Can. Art.		12x16		8/20/54

1954 Cont.

Date	No.	Name	Time	Sold	Price	Exhibited		Purchase	Size	Remarks	Date Sold
April	9	"Two Out" Pheasant	5	✓	240	Rowayton Studio	YCY		15×20		5/16/57
May	10	"Red Head @ Sand bridge"	10	✓	150	Rowayton Studio	YCY	Founders Show	25×30		4/10/55
July	11	"Flighting in" Canada Geese	2	✓	250	Seebe Studio	Can Art Gal		16×20		8/20/54
July	12	"Verginia Farm" Geese	11	✓	550	Seebe Studio	CRS ✓	Manville	25×30	Commission Canada Geese	Com 12/15/5
July	13	"New Snow" Grouse	10	✓	400	Seebe Studio	CRS ✓	C.R.S.	20×24	Catalogue	6/20/55
Aug	14	"Dead Timber" Mallard	10	✓	650	Seebe Studio	CRS	C.R.S.	24×30	Catalogue	1/20/55
Aug	15	"Flight of Mystery" Woodcock	7	✓	300	Seebe Studio	CRS	C.R.S.	15×20	Catalogue	1/20/55
Aug	16	"Among the Pines" Quail	10	✓	400	Seebe Studio	CRS ✓	C.R.S	20×24	Catalogue	1/20/55
Sept	17	"Winter Roost" Grouse	3	✓	150	Seebe Studio	Can Art Gal	Harvey	12×16	~~Commission~~	12/25/54
Sept	18	"Open Water" Mallards	7	✓	350	Seebe Studio	Can Art	Mr Fish	20×25		11/23/54
Sept	19	"Winter Morning" Grouse	6	✓	400	Seebe Studio		Jock Smith	24×20	Commission	9/4/54
Nov	20	"Covey in the Willow Oak" Quail	11	✓	450	Seebe Studio		CRS	20×30		"
Nov	21	"Sharptail Grouse" #1	4	✓	150	Seebe Studio		Eric L. Harvie	12×16	Commission	12/13/54
Nov	22	"Ruffed Grouse" #2	4	✓	150	Seebe Studio		Eric L. Harvie	12×16	Commission	1/18/55
Dec	23	"Ringneck Pheasant" #3	4	✓	150	Ross Studio		Eric L. Harvie	12×28	Commission	1/18/55
Dec	24	"Brook Trout"	5	✓	200	Ross Studio		F.R. Barbour	12×28	Commission	12/4/55

1955

Date	No.	Name	Time	Sold	Price	Exhibited		Purchase	Size	Remarks	Date Sold
Jan	1	"Timber Mallard"	6	✓	300	Ross Studio	CRS	Crossroads H.H. Webb	16×20	Commission	
Feb	2	"Above the Oaks" Pheasant	6	✓	400	Ross Studio	C.R.S.	Harry H. Webb. CRS	20×24	Commission	3/16/55
Feb	3	"Twilight" Pheasant	8	✓	500	Ross Studio	YCY	Can Art (Brown)	25×30		5/2/56
Feb	4	"From the Outer Bay" Cans.	6	✓	450	Ross Studio	~~YCY~~	Crossroads	20×30		2/1/56
Feb	5	"Harvie #4. Spruce Grouse"	3	✓	150	Ross Studio		Eric L. Harvie	12×16	Commission	4/22/55
Mar	6	"Close In" Cans.	14	✓	550	Ross Studio		O'Neil Ryan Jr.	24×36	Commission	6/20/55
Mar	7	"Canvasback"	19	✓	533	Ross Studio	YCY		30×40		3/15/56
April	8	"Harvie #5 Hungarian Partridge"	4	✓	150	Ross Studio		Eric L. Harvie	12×16	Commission	5/9/5
April	9	"Harvie #6 Blue Grouse"	3	✓	150	Ross Studio		Eric L. Harvie	12×16	Commission	5/9/55
April	10	"Mapa Delta" Sprig	3	✓	200	Ross Studio		Youngburg	15×20	Commission	6/3/55
April	11	"Blackberry Roost" V. Quail	5	✓	200	Ross Studio		Allen. C.H.	12×16	Commission	5/24/5
May	12	"Above the Decoys" Sprig	10	✓	450	Ross Studio		Crossroads	20×30		2/1/56
May	13	"Bolinas Mesa"	10	ı		Ross Studio			20×30		
June	14	"Chuckar" "Harvie #7"	4	✓	105	Seebe Studio		Harvie	12×16	Commission	8/20/5
July	15	"Wind River Range"	8	✓	600	Seebe Studio		Holcombe	24×36	Commission	8/28/5
July	16	"Prairie Chicken" Harvie #8	4	✓	105	Seebe Studio		Harvie	12×16	Commission	8/20/5
July	17	"Autumn Afternoon" Sprig	10	✓	600	Seebe Studio	CRS	D.U. Crossroads	24×36		2/1/56
July	18	"Ptarmigan" Harvie #9	4	✓		Seebe Studio		Harvie	12×16	Commission	8/20/5
Aug	19	"Hilltop Covey" Quail	12	✓	450	Seebe Studio	CRS	Crossroads	20×30		2/1/5
Aug	20	"Beneath the Maples" Grouse	12	✓	450	Seebe Studio	CRS	Crossroads	20×30		2/1/56
Sept	21	"The Surf Riders" Brant	8	✓	450	Seebe Studio		Allen	20×30	Commission	9/20/53
Sept	22	"Foothill Gateway" Allen	1	✓	100	Seebe Studio		Allen	12×16	Commission	10/3/53
Oct	23	"The Getaway" Pheasant	7	✓	300	Seebe Studio		Brewester	16×20	Commission	12/31/5
Nov	24	"Kananaskis Valley"	7	✓	400	Seebe Studio			20×26	Commission	1/56
Nov	25	Alberta Mallard	8	✓	600	Seebe Studio	Can. Art.	McCarthy	24×36	Commission	12/5/5
Dec	26	"Old Red Ruff" Grouse	4	✓	450	Norfolk Studio	Crossroads	F.K. Barbour	20×30		3/13/5
Dec	27	"Among the Hardwoods" Gr.	4	✓	300	Norfolk Studio	Crossroads	— (Shown in Banks)	15×20		4/26/5

1956

DATE	NO.	NAME	TIME	SOLD	PRICE	PAINTED	EXHIBITED	PURCHASER	SIZE	REMARKS	DATE SOLD
FEB	1.	COVEY RISE #1. QUAIL	9	✓	500	STUDIO NORFOLK.	LUMBUS GA.	CASON CALLAWAY	20×24	COMMISSION.	3/30/56
FEB.	2.	COVEY RISE #2. QUAIL	12	✓	450	STUDIO NORFOLK.	LUMBUS GA.	LEGRAND ELEBASH	20×30		3/29/56
FEB.	3.	"ROOSTING COVER" VALLEY QUAIL	10	✓	500	STUDIO NORFOLK	STILLPOND	Henslowe.	20×30	commission	6/17/56
MAR.	4	"BUDDING RED RUFF." GR.	8	✓	450	STUDIO NORFOLK	STILLPOND	F.A.H. REAM	20×26	COMMISSION	6/16/56
MAR.	5	"MALLARD LANDSCAPE"	1	✓	150	Studio NORFOLK	STILLPOND	Henslowe	25×30	COMMISSION.	6/17/56
APRIL	6	"DECEMBER BLACKS"	9	✓	450	Studio NORFOLK	STILLPOND	Meldrum	14×28	COMMISSION	6/6/56
APRIL	7	"THE MARSH @ DUSK", BLACKS	12	✓	650	Studio NORFOLK	STILLPOND	Webb. A.	24×36	COMMISSION	6/14/56
MAY.	8	"PASSING GEESE!"	10	✓	450	Studio NORFOLK	STILLPOND.	Meldrum	14×28	COMMISSION.	6/6/56
MAY.	9	MALLARD OVAL.	4	✓	200	Studio NORFOLK	STILLPOND.	Meldrum.	11×14	COMMISSION	6/1/56
MAY.	10	BLACK DUCK OVAL.	3.	✓	200	Studio NORFOLK	STILLPOND.	Meldrum.	11×14	COMMISSION.	6/1/56
MAY	11	PINTAIL OVAL.	3.	✓	200	Studio NORFOLK	STILLPOND.	Meldrum.	11×14	COMMISSION.	6/1/56
MAY	12	BALDPATE OVAL.	2	✓	200	Studio NORFOLK	STILLPOND	Meldrum.	11×14	COMMISSION.	6/1/56
MAY	13	BROOK TROUT OVAL	1	✓	70	Studio NORFOLK	STILLPOND	F.K.B.	11×14		5/25/56
JUNE	14	POT HOLE MALLARD.	6	✓	400	Studio NORFOLK	STILLPOND - CRS.	Jordan	18×26		11/14/56
JULY	15	WINTER CROSSING GROUSE	9.	✓	650	Studio SEEBE	CRS	(catalogue)	24×36		1/15/57
July	16	"TWO AWAY" Woodcock	9.	✓	400	Studio SEEBE	CRS	(catalogue)	18×25		1/15/57
July.	17	"FLOODED LAND" MAL.	7.	✓	300	Studio SEEBE	Turner.	B. MacKid.	15×22		3/22/56
Aug.	18.	"VERMONT PARTRIDGE"	10.	✓	650	Studio Seebe	CRS		24×36	COMMISSION	7/20/57
Aug.	19	"QUAIL" in the Pine lands.	14	✓	650	Studio Seebe	CRS	(Catalogue)	24×36		
Sept.	20	"ON THE NORTH SHORE" CANS.	8	✓	500	Studio SEEBE	CRS	(catalogue)	20×30		2/3/57
Sept.	21	"NORTHERN HARVEST" SHARPTAIL	10	✓	500	Studio Seebe		D. S. HARVIE	20×30	COMMISSION	11/13/56
Sept.	22	"CALIF PINTAIL"	7	✓	500	Studio Seebe	CRS.		20×30	COMMISSION.	3/27/57
Nov.	23	"ROUND T SPRING" MAL.	10	✓	700	Studio Seebe	CAN A	K. RONISH	24×36	COMMISSION.	12/27/56
Nov.	24	"On the South SASKATCHEWAN Ge"	3	✓	200	Studio Seebe	CAN A.		12×18		12/4/56
Dec.	25	"Whitetails in the Snow"	11	✓	600	Studio Norfolk	CRS.	KATE WEBB	24×32	COMMISSION	12/20/13/57
			188								

DATE	NO	NAME	TIME	SOLD	PRICE	Still PAINTED.	EXHIBITED	PURCHASER	SIZE	REMARKS	DATE
Jan	1.	UNDER THE RIM ROCK DEER	11	✓	450	Studio Norfolk	C.R.S.	Mellon.	20×26	~~Commission~~	5/16/57
Jan	2.	N.F. Uplands grouse	8	✓	400	Studio Norfolk	C.R.S.		18×24		4/15/57
Jan	3.	Vermont uplands grouse	13	✓	650	Studio Norfolk			24×36	COMMISSION	2/28/57
Feb.	4.	THROUGH THE OAKS - quail	13	✓	650	Studio Norfolk	CRS		24×36		7/20/57
Feb.	5.	November Swamps Mallard	6	✓	300	Studio Norfolk		Mrs. Wm Smith	15×20	-	6/22/57
Feb.	6.	Evening quail	6	✓	450	Studio Norfolk		F.K. BARBOUR	18×26		3/21/57
APRIL	7.	Evening quail	9	✓	450	Norfolk		Helen Jordan	18×26	commission	7/13/57
april	8.	Breaking out Pheasant	8	✓	650	Norfolk	CAN ART		24×36		6/24/57
april	9.	Oregon Mule Deer (Armour)	10	✓	550	Norfolk	CRS	Philip Armour	20×30	commission CR	6/20/57
May.	10	Landscape (McKinley)	1	✓	150	Norfolk		W. Read.	12×16	COMMISSION	5/18/57
May.	11	Black Duck "Drifting in"	9	✓	400	Norfolk	CRS.		18×24		9/23/57
May.	12	Landscape McKinley	2	✓	150	Norfolk		W.B. Reid	12×16	Commission	5/29/57
May.	13	Landscape McKinley	1	✓	200	Norfolk		(Replacement)	12×16	Bid Ref.	6/1/57
June.	14	"Evening Arrival" Mallard	7	✓	450	Norfolk			18×26		6/1/57
June.	15	"River Mist" Pintail	10	✓	350	Norfolk			20×30		2/25/58
June	16	"Moon Rise" Mallard	5	✓	300	Norfolk.	Can Art.		15×20		9/20/57
July	17	"Channel Entrance" cans.	11	✓	700	Norfolk	CRS		24×36		10/15/57
July	18	"Breaking off" cans.	4	✓	300	Norfolk	CRS		15×20		12/30/57
July	19	"The Strike" Rainbow trout	4			Norfolk			15×20	Commission	
Aug	20	"Rocking in the Poplars" W.C.	8	✓	450	Norfolk	CRS	Frederick Barbour	18×26		11/1/57
Aug	21	"HIGH Country Deer	8	✓	650	Norfolk	CRS		22×32		9/25/57

1957 CONT.

MO.	NO.	NAME	TIME	SOLD	PRICE	PAINTED	EXHIBITED	PURCHASER	SIZE	REMARKS	DATE SO.
Aug.	22	"Ready to Roost" Grouse	8	✓	700	Norfolk	CRS	Brenda Beale —	24x36	on Time	9/15/57
Sept.	23	"Under the Pines" Quail	10	✓	700	Norfolk	CRS	Buckley —	24x36		11/15/57
Sept.	24	"Topping the Alders" Wd.	6	✓	450	Norfolk			12 x 16		1/24/55
Sept.	25	"Grouse and apple tree"	10	✓	700	Norfolk		Mellon	24 x 36		1/26/55
Sept.	26	"Mallards & green heads"	3	gift.	—	Norfolk		C. Welch	14 x 20	Sold trip —	9/15/58
Nov.	27	"Dropping In" Woodcock"	7	✓	450	Norfolk	CRS.	Waters	18 x 26	commission,	12/30/57
Dec.	28	"White tail Buck and Doe."	9	✓	650	Norfolk	CRS.	Manville	22 x 32	commission.	4/26/58
Dec.	29	"Canada Geese"	9	✓	500	Norfolk	CRS.		18 x 26		4/28/58
Jan.	1.	McMullens Pond	20			Norfolk			30 x 40	Commission	
Jan.	2.	"Down from the High Country" Mule Deer	6			Norfolk			14 x 20		
Feb.	3.	"Desert Travelers" Pronghorn	10			Norfolk	CRS.		22 x 32	Commission	

Appendix D

Belmore Browne Log, 1922–1954: "Completed Paintings"

A list of paintings completed and numbered by year, with title, size, purchaser, seller, where exhibited and disposition.

Revised Price List. 1957

9 X 11 = $ 50.00
10 X 14 = 85.00
12 X 16 = 100.00
16 X 20 = 175.00
18 X 24 = 250.00
25 X 30 = 350.00
30 X 40 = 500.00
36 X 40 = 600.00
36 X 48 = 800.00

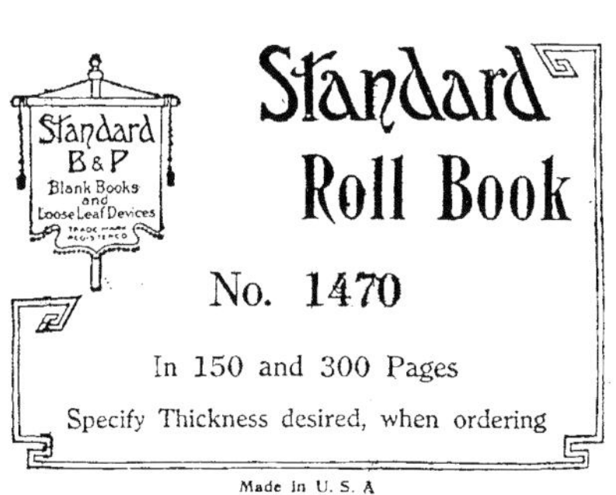

Belmore Browne.

List of Pictures beginning with the year 1922. At Banff, Alberta, Canada. Giving dates of completion, sales, exhibitions etc.

Price List

36 X 48 = $1000.00
36 X 40 = 800.00
30 X 40 = 750.00
25 X 30 = 500.00
18 X 24 = 300.00
16 X 20 = 250.00
12 X 16 = 175.00
10 X 14 = 125.00
9 X 11 = 100.00

Dii

Page 4. List of Pictures Completed in 1925.

31. Oct. Evening Aspens. 12x16 Gift. John Spaulding.

No.	Titles	Size	Sales	Bought by	Sold by	Exhibited at	Repainted	Disposed of	Reproduced	Museum	Remarks
1.	~~"Lake Louise: Early Spring"~~	~~36x48~~				Ontario Society. N.A.P.A. Art. Am.F.A. Rotary.		Destroyed.			
2.	"Moraine Lake"	30x40	Sold. 1926	Mrs Cooke	McClees.	Sealed to Marion Bechtel 1955					
3.	"Spray River Early Spring"	30x40	Gift.			N.A. McClees.		Given to Rental Rec'd.			
4.	"Aspen Grove: October"	30x40	Sold		Courvoisier	McClees. Casson. St.B.					
5.	"Spring: Canadian Rockies"	30x40	Sold. 1926	J.G. McIlvain	McClees	N.A. [illegible] Venice Biennial			C.P.Ry. Am. Mag. of Art.		
6.	"Falling Leaves"	25x30	Sold. 1932	Dr. A.F. Heimlich	Studio	McClees '26 Casson '27 O'Brien '29	1932.				
7.	"Mt. Temple from the Pipestone R."	25x30	Sold 1938		Pollinger Gallery.	do do do	1937.		Copy to C.P.Ry.		
8.	"On the Assiniboine Trail"	25x30	Sold '30		O'Brien.					Permanent Collection Rochester.	
9	"Lake Louise: Before the Ice Breaks"	25x30	Sold. 1927	Mrs. Strong	Macbeth	do do do / Casson O'Brien McClees					
10.	"Mt. Rundle from the Bow Valley"	22x32	Sold 1931		O'Brien	St.B. '29 Springville Utah	1928.				
11.	"Forest Ranger"	18x24	Sold 1929		Macbeth.	do O'Brien McClees	1927		Macbeth Catalogue.		
12.	"Summer Pasture" (Flint Park)	18x24	Sold. 1926	Mr. Woodside	McClees.	do do do					
13.	"Falls on Cascade River"	18x24				McClees, Casson, O'Brien					
14.	"Distant Snowstorm"	18x24	~~Sold 1935~~	~~John M. Forbes~~	~~Studio~~	do do do					Exchanged for 25x30 Assiniboine
15.	"A Log Jamb"	16x20	Sold. 1926		McClees.	do					
16.	"Mount Assiniboine"	16x20	Sold. 1927		O'Brien	do do do					
17.	"Ranger's Cabin"	16x20	Sold. 1926		McClees	do					
18.	"The First Snow"	16x20	Sold. 1926	Walter Janney	McClees	do			Alpine Club.		
19.	"Unnamed Lake" (Goodsir Plateau)	16x20	Sold. 1926	C.P.Ry.		do do					
20.	"Wenkchemna Pass"	16x20									
21.	"Sky Scrapers"	18x24	Sold. 1928	W.L. Lazit.	Macbeth.	C.P.Ry. Office N.Y. Casson. Newman's '35. S.F. '37				Ross-	
*22.	"Lake Louise before the Ice Breaks"	10x14	Sold 1937	Mrs. Jennings	Studio.	McClees. McB. O.B. Bushnell '36					
23.	"Mount Assiniboine"	9x11				do do do					
24.	"The Blue Abyss"	10x14				do do do	1929				
25.	"Head of Healy Creek"	9x11	Sold 1925	Mrs. Hartshorn							
26.	"The Valley of the Cascade"	9x11	Sold. 1926		Casson.						
~~27~~	~~"Mt. Assiniboine"~~	~~12x16~~				do St.B. do do Jan.	Do	Destroyed.			
28.	"The End of Winter Lake Louise"	18x24	Sold 1933			Macbeth Bushnell 3/8/32	1927	Given to the Starbucks.			
29.	"Wind in the Pines"	18x24	Gift			St.B. '27 '29					
30.	"A Valley in the Rockies: Autumn"	18x24				St.B. 29. Dec. Macbeth 31	1929 – 1931				Sambach Paris from Jennings Canyon.

Page 7. List of Pictures commenced in 1928

No.	Titles	Sizes	Sales	Purchaser	Sold by	Exhibited at	Repainted	Disposed of	Reproduced	Remarks
1.	"Spray Valley March."	9x11								Repainted 36x48-1933
2.	"Mt. Rundle: Evening"	10x14	Sold '28	Col. J. A. Grant. Elbridge						
3.	"Ice-Bordered Pool: Spray R."	12x16	Sold '28	John Washington						
4.	"The Winding River"	25x30	Sold '30		O'Brien.	St.B.'29. Springville.				Honour Award Springville Utah. O'Brien '29
5.	"Snow Covered ~~Willows~~ Cliffs"	9x11								
6.	"Under the Cliffs of Rundle"	36x40	[illegible]			Portland Art Asso. O'Brien '30 St.B.'29. C.P. Hotel. Banff '29	'33 '35 '29 Wash. State Fair. '33			~~Repainted '29~~ Circuit.
7.	"Valley of the Kicking Horse" Early	16x20				St.B.'29. Casson. '30			Nov 31	Budworth. Oct 31 Returned to St.B.
8.	"Cathedral Mountain: Spring.	12x16				St.B.'29 Casson '30			Nov 31	Budworth Oct. '31 Returned to St.B.
9.	~~"Cathedral Mountain: Evening"~~	~~12x16~~						Destroyed '33		
10.	"The Late Spring" (Cascade Mt.)	10x14	Sold '29	Mrs. Geo. Clement.	St.B. Art League	St.B.'29				
11.	"Clouds on Castle Mountain"	9x11				St.B.'29.				
12.	"The Slopes of Mt. Rundle"	12x16	Gift			St.B.'29. Casson '30		Al Lenzo Italiana.	Nov 31	Budworth Oct. 31 Returned to St.B
~~13.~~	~~"Lake Shore: Evening" (Hector L.)~~	~~10x14~~						Destroyed.		
14.	"Hector Lake" "Storm Clouds"	9x11				St.B.'29 Casson '30			Nov. 31	Budworth Oct. 31 Returned to St.B.
15.	"Windy Point" (Hector L.)	16x20				St.B.'29 Feb.				
16.	"Mountain Lake" do. do.	30x40	Sold '30	Geo. W. Pettier		St.B.'29. Dec.	'29. '30			
17.	"Below the Cliffs of Hector"	25x30	Sold '28	Dr. Thompson.						
18.	"Study of the 40-mile Peaks"	10x14	Gift.	Given to J. W. Elbridge						
19.	"The Silver Thread" (Mosquito Creek)	12x16	Sold. '30		O'Brien	St.B.'29 Springville. O'Brien '29.				O'Brien '29
20.	"Sun on the Water" (Mt. Hector)	12x16	Sold '35	Patty Ryan	Studio.	Wash. State Fair '33 St.B.'29 O'Brien '30-'33				
21.	"The White Cloud"	16x20				Purie R. Calgary. St.B.'29. Springville.	1951.	Name Changed to "Mt. Rundle. Banff"		O'Brien '29.
~~22.~~	~~"Mt. Hector: Evening"~~	~~9x11~~				St.B.'29		Destroyed		
23.	"~~Below Storm Mountain~~ (~~Lake~~)"	~~30x40~~				St.B.'29		Destroyed.		
24.	~~"Lifting Clouds" (Bow L.)~~	~~12x16~~				St.B.'29	'30	Destroyed		
25.	"Bow Glacier"	12x16	Gift.			St.B.'29		Gift to Jim Simpson.		
~~26.~~	~~"The Wilds of the Saskatchewan"~~	~~12x16~~						Destroyed.		
27.	"The Distant Glacier" (Bow Pass)	12x16	Sold '30		O'Brien.	St.B.'29 O'Brien '30				
28.	"Aspens Under Rundle	12x16	Sold '34			Salmagundi Auction '34 St.B.29 Casson '30			Nov. 31	Budworth Oct. 31 Returned to St.B
29.	"Bear Creek Valley"	9x11	Sold '29		St.B. Art League	St.B.'29				

57

PAGE 37. PICTURES COMMENCED IN 1953

	TITLES	SIZE	SALES PURCHASER	SOLD BY	EXHIBITED	REPRINTED	REPRODUCED	REMARKS
1.	IN THE HEART OF THE RANGE.	30X40	"				Sketch	White Sheep
2.	" " " " "	18X24						" "
3.	When the Snow Melts.	25X30						Vermilion R.
4.	Grass Slopes · Spring.	16X20						" "
5.	Numa Valley. "	12X16						" "
6.	The Trail Blazers.	25X30						Sketch for Large Picture
7.	Tom Simeons Coyose	16X20						Study
8.	The Single Horse	16X20						"
9.	Moraine L. Evening.	16X20						
10.	Valley of the 10 Peaks.	25X30	Acct D Atty mint.					
11.	Approach to Moraine L.	18X24						
12.	Valley of The Ten Peaks.	16X20						
13.	Mt. Washington	20X30						order.
14.	" "	20X30					From Boot Study	Bear Group.
15.	" "	12X16					From Spur.	Boston Museum of
16	" "	12X16					" Wild Cat.	Science
17	" "	12X16					" " "	Figures added
18	" "	12X16					" Tuckerman's Ravine	
19.	~~Sarty~~	~~12X16~~					"	"
20	The "Gray" Teton	12X16						
19.	Alaska Brown Bear.	Cage.						
21.	Ipswich Beach Group	Cage.						

The Sketches are included in Final background Completed 1954. Listed next page. Sketch for 30X40

2 { Boston Museum of Science
{ Boston Museum of Science — Francis Lucky Game Room.

Appendix E

Known paintings by George Browne not reproduced in this book

Glenbow Museum (Calgary, Alberta, Canada):		
1. "Keystone Valley, Alberta"	oil on canvas	50.8 x 66.4 cm
2. "Sharptail Grouse"	oil on canvas board	31.8 x 41.3 cm
3. "Fresh Snow"	oil on canvas board	30.5 x 40.6 cm
4. "Ruffed Grouse"	oil on canvas board	30.5 x 40.6 cm
5. "Ring-necked Pheasants"	oil on canvas board	31.8 x 41.3 cm
6. "Spruce Grouse"	oil on canvas	30.5 x 40.6 cm
7. "Hungarian Partridge"	oil on canvas	30.5 x 40.6 cm
8. "Blue Grouse"	oil on canvas	30.5 x 40.6 cm
9. "Prairie Chicken"	oil on canvas	30.5 x 40.6 cm
10. "White-tail Ptarmigan"	oil on canvas	30.5 x 40.6 cm
11. "Chukar Partridge"	oil on canvas	30.5 x 40.6 cm
12. "Spring Budding"	oil on canvas	50.8 x 66 cm

National Museum of Wildlife Art (Jackson Hole, WY)		
1. "Man and Grouse"	oil on board	10 x 14 in.
2. "Mallard and Hen Ducks"	oil on board	12 x 16 in.
3. "Greenwing Teal Ducks and Hen"	oil on board	12 x 16 in.
4. "Eight Geese Coming In"	oil on board	11½ x 15½ in.
5. "Two Snipe"	oil on board	13¾ x 9⅞ in.
6. "Landscape"	oil on board	12 x 16 in.
7. "Fall Landscape"	oil on canvas	9 x 11 in.
8. "Mule Deer at Top of Hill"	oil on board	9 x 10 in.
9. "Bass At Fly"	oil on board	12 x 16 in.
10. "Hunter Rising to Six Geese"	oil on board	12 5 16 in.
11. "Doe"	oil on board	9 x 13 in.
12. "Bull Elk"	oil on board	12 x 16 in.
13. "Mountain Goat"	oil on board	9¾ x 13¾ in.
14. "Quiet Canyon"	oil on canvas	20 x 30 in.

California State Museum Resource Center/Nan and Roy Jones Archives		
1. "The Brant of Duxbury"	oil on canvas	16 x 20 in.
2. "Robins in the Toyon Bush"	oil on canvas	15 x 18 in.
3. "Brant Near Duxbury Reef"	oil on canvas	18 x 26 in.
4. "Ducks"	oil on canvas	16 x 20 in.
5. "Bolinas Lagoon from Pine Gulch Creek"	oil on canvas	16 x 20 in.
6. "Georgia Quail"	oil on canvas	
7. "Grouse and Maples"		
8. "Oregon Male Deer"		
9. "Keystone Valley, Alberta"	oil on canvas	20 x 16 in.

List of Color Plates

Appendix B, page viii
Appendix C, page vi, #6, 3/51

PLATE 22 (PAGE 80)
George Browne
Pintails At Sunrise date unknown
Oil on canvas, 25 × 30 in.
Drummond Gallery

PLATE 23 (PAGE 81)
George Browne
Pintails date unknown
Oil on canvas, 16 × 20 in.
Bell Museum of Natural History/American Museum of Wildlife Art Collection

PLATE 24 (PAGE 82)
George Browne
Newfoundland Point
Date unknown
Oil on canvas, 24 × 36 in.
Ward Museum of Wildfowl Art/ Permanent Loan Private Collection

PLATE 25 (PAGE 83)
George Browne
Black Ducks 1928
Oil on canvas, 16 × 20 in.
Drummond Gallery

PLATE 26 (PAGE 84)
George Browne
Blue Bills date unknown
Oil on canvas, 16 × 20 in.
Drummond Gallery

PLATE 27 (PAGE 85)
George Browne
Broadbills Before the Squall 1956
Oil on canvas, 19½ × 29 in.
Private Collection
Appendix B, page viii
Appendix C, page vi, #9, 4/1956
Crossroads of Sport catalogue 1952–1953

PLATE 28 (PAGE 86)
George Browne
Baldpate Widgeon date unknown
Oil on canvas
Robert Fraser Sporting and Southern Art

PLATE 29 (PAGE 87)
George Browne
The Farm Marsh date unknown
Oil on canvas, 24 × 36 in.
Sportsman's Edge Ltd.
Crossroads of Sport catalogue 1982

PLATE 30 (PAGE 88)
George Browne
Winter On The Bay 1942
Oil on canvas, 30 × 40 in.
Private Collection

PLATE 31 (PAGE 89)
George Browne
Canvasbacks Swinging the Channel 1950
Oil on canvas, 24 × 36 in.
Private Collection
Appendix A, page ii, #109, 1950 (Nanticote Cans)
Appendix B, page xii (A Heavy Flight On The Nanticote)
Appendix C, page vi, #16, 8/1950 (Canvasbacks On The Nanticote River)

PLATE 32 (PAGE 90)
George Browne
Cove Blind At Mubulo–Canvasbacks
Date unknown
Oil on canvas board, 22½ × 34½ in.
Bell Museum of Natural History/American Museum of Wildlife Art Collection

PLATE 33 (PAGE 91)
George Browne
Cutthroat Trout (unsigned) 1945
Oil on canvas, 12 × 16 in.
Private Collection
Appendix C, page ii, #7, 1945

PLATE 34 (PAGE 92)
George Browne
Rainbow Trout 1941
Oil on canvas, 12 × 16 in.
Robert Fraser Sporting and Southern Art
Appendix A, page i, #32, 1941
Appendix C, page i, #2, 1941

PLATE 35 (PAGE 93)
George Browne
Bobwhite date unknown
Oil on canvas
Robert Fraser Sporting and Southern Art

PLATE 36 (PAGE 94)
George Browne
Roosting Cover 1956
Oil on canvas, 20 × 30 in.
Len Braarud Fine Art
Appendix A, page iii, #232, 1956 (California Quail)
Appendix B, page xvii (Valley Quail)
Appendix C, page ix, #3, 1956

PLATE 37 (PAGE 95)
George Browne
Winter's Morning (Ruffed Grouse)
Date unknown
Oil on canvas, 24 × 30 in.
Sportsman's Edge Ltd.

PLATE 38 (PAGE 96)
George Browne
Woodcock 1957
Oil on canvas, 18 × 26 in.
Robert Fraser Sporting and Southern Art
Appendix A, page iii, #266, 1957

PLATE 39 (PAGE 97)
George Browne
Whitetail Deer date unknown
Oil on canvas
Robert Fraser Sporting and Southern Art

PLATE 40 (PAGE 98)
George Browne
Mule Deer 1956
Oil on canvas, 20 × 30 in.
Robert Fraser Sporting and Southern Art
Appendix A, page iii, #256, 1956

Appendix B, page xx
Appendix C, page ix, #9, 1956

Plate 41 (page 99)
George Browne
At The Crossing 1957
Oil on canvas, 22 × 32 in.
J.N. Bartfield Galleries
Appendix A, page iii, #264, 1957
Appendix B, page xx (Whitetail Deer And Doe)
Appendix C, page ix, #21, 1957 (High Country Deer)

Plate 42 (page 100)
George Browne
Bull Moose 1947
Oil on canvas, 16 × 20 in.
J N. Bartfield Galleries
Appendix C, page iii, 10/1/47

Plate 43 (page 101)
George Browne
Mt. McKinley from the Kontishna 1947
Oil on canvas, 16 × 20 in.
Robert Fraser Sporting and Southern Art/Len Braarud Fine Art
Appendix A, page i, #67, 1947
Appendix B, page i
Appendix C, page iii, #30, 1947

Plate 44 (page 102)
George Browne
Mule Deer 1956
Oil on canvas, 22 × 32 in.
Collection of Hugh Robinson
Appendix B, page xx, 1956
Last painting by George—unfinished

Plate 45 (page 103)
George Browne
Alan Ranch, Seebee Alberta 1956
Oil on canvas, 12 × 16 in.
Thomas Nygard and J. N. Bartfield Galleries

Plate 46 (page 104)
George Browne
California Quail 1955
Oil on canvas, 12 × 16 in.
Thomas Nygard and J. N. Bartfield Galleries
Appendix A, page ii, #195, 1955
Appendix B, page xvi
Appendix C, page viii, #17, 1955

Plate 47 (page 105)
George Browne
Mallard Going Out 1948
Oil on canvas, 25 × 30 in.
Thomas Nygard and J. N. Bartfield Galleries
Appendix A, page i, #78, 1948 (Mallard)
Appendix B, page ii
Appendix C, page iv, #23, 1948 (Drake Mallard Study)

Plate 48 (page 106)
George Browne
Pheasants Rising 1952
Oil on canvas, 20 × 30 in.
Private collection
Appendix B, page xi (Alerted, Pheasant)
Appendix C, page vii, #18, 1952 (Alarmed)

Plate 49 (page 107)
George Browne
Prairie Longhorns 1958
Oil on canvas, 22 × 32 in.
Thomas Nygard and J.N. Bartfield Galleries
Appendix B, page xx
Appendix C, page x, #3, 1958 (Desert Travelers)

Plate 50 (page 108)
George Browne
Swinging The Cove 1954
Oil on canvas board, 16 × 20 in.
Steven B. O'Brien, Jr. Fine Arts
Appendix A, page ii, #166, 1954 (Swinging The Cove Blacks)

Plate 51 (page 109)
George Browne
Teal date unknown
Oil on canvas, 14 × 12 in.
Thomas Nygard and J.N. Bartfield Galleries

Plate 52 (page 110)
George Browne
Blue Mountain date unknown
Oil on board, 12 × 16 in.
J.N. Bartfield and Thomas Nygard Galleries

Plate 53 (page 111)
George Browne
Goats 1942
Oil on canvas, 20 × 18 in.
J.N. Bartfield and Thomas Nygard Galleries
Appendix A, page i, #44, 1942 (Goats cliffs)
Appendix C, page ii, #8, 1942 (Goats on Cliffs)

Plate 54 (page 112)
George Browne
Goldeneye, date unknown
Oil on board, 15¾ × 19¾ in.
J.N. Bartfield and Thomas Nygard Galleries

Plate 55 (page 113)
George Browne
Pintails date unknown
Oil on board, 15½ × 12 in.
J.N. Bartfield and Thomas Nygard Galleries

Plate 56 (page 114)
George Browne
Widgeon date unknown
Oil on board, 19⅝ × 15¾ in.
J.N. Bartfield and Thomas Nygard Galleries

Plate 57 (page 115)
George Browne
Canvasbacks on the Nanticoke River 1950
24 × 36 in.
Painted for K. Merrick Low
Appendix A, page ii, #109, 1950
Appendix B, page vi, 1950
Appendix C, page vi, #16, 8/1950

List of Figures

PAGES 58, 59
Cutouts George made for painting layouts
George Browne estate, courtesy of Hugh Robinson

PAGE 61
Sketch by George—*Mallards*
George Browne estate, courtesy of Hugh Robinson

PAGE 62 (LEFT)
Sketch by George—*Woodcock*
George Browne estate, courtesy of Hugh Robinson

PAGE 62 (RIGHT)
Sketch by George—*Grouse*
George Browne estate, courtesy of Hugh Robinson

PAGE 63
Sketch by George—*Pheasant*
George Browne estate, courtesy of Hugh Robinson

PAGE 64
Sketch by George—*Big Horn Sheep*
George Browne estate, courtesy of Hugh Robinson

PAGE 65
Sketch by George—*Antelope*
George Browne estate, courtesy of Hugh Robinson

PAGE 66
Sketch by George—*Whitetail Buck*
George Browne estate, courtesy of Hugh Robinson

PAGE 68
Sketches by George—grouse as seen when shot
George Browne estate, courtesy of Hugh Robinson

About the Authors

JOHN ORDEMAN, who has a degree in art history from Williams College and graduate degrees in English and school administration from Columbia University and Johns Hopkins, spent forty years as a school master, twenty-eight of them as the headmaster of several independent schools. He now lives in retirement on the Eastern Shore of Virginia.

For the past two decades, Ordeman's principal avocation has been writing on American sporting artists. He is the author of *Frank W. Benson: Master of the Sporting Print; To Keep a Tryst with the Dawn: An Appreciation of Roland Clark*; *William J. Schaldach: Artist/Author/Sportsman*; *Frank W. Benson's Etchings, Drypoints and Lithographs* and *The Aquatints, Drypoints and Etchings of the Derrydale Press*, and he edited the catalogue and served as curator for the 1996 exhibition, *Frank W. Benson: His Sporting Art*, at the Ward Museum in Salisbury, Maryland.

MICHAEL SCHREIBER has B.S. and M.D. degrees from Tulane University. He has been in the private practice of Dermatology for 41 years and was a Clinical Associate Professor and Senior Clinical Lecturer in the Department of Medicine at the University of Arizona School of Medicine. He has been involved in epidemiologic cancer research since 1971 at the University of Arizona Cancer Center. He was a member of the Advisory Council and served on the Board of Trustees at the Arizona Sonora Desert Museum from 1987 to 1991. He has published thirty-one articles in peer reviewed medical journals and has written chapters in medical books. For the past fifty years he has collected art, predominately wildlife and sporting art.